BRING ME THE HEAD
OF SERGIO GARCIA!

Tom Cox's writing has appeared in the *Sunday Times,*
Daily Telegraph, Observer, Mail on Sunday, Guardian and
Golf International magazine. He is the author of three
other books: *Nice Jumper,* which was shortlisted for the
2002 National Sporting Club Best Newcomer Award,
Educating Peter and *The Lost Tribes of Pop,* a collection of
his columns for the *Observer,* and is a founding member
of The Society of Secret Golfers (www.secretgolf.co.uk).
He was born in 1975 and lives with his wife in Norfolk.
For more information on Tom, visit www.tom-cox.com.

By the same author

Nice Jumper
Educating Peter
The Lost Tribes of Pop

Tom Cox

BRING ME THE HEAD OF SERGIO GARCIA!

YELLOW JERSEY PRESS
LONDON

Published by Yellow Jersey 2007

2 4 6 8 10 9 7 5 3

Copyright © Tom Cox 2007

First published in Great Britain in 2007 by
Yellow Jersey
Random House, 20 Vauxhall Bridge Road,
London SW1V 2SA

www.randomhouse.co.uk

Addresses for companies within
The Random House Group Limited can be found at:
www.randomhouse.co.uk/offices.htm

The Random House Group Limited Reg. No. 954009

A CIP catalogue record for this book
is available from the British Library

ISBN 9780224078603

The Random House Group Limited makes every effort to ensure that the
papers used in its books are made from trees that have been legally sourced
from well-managed and credibly certified forests. Our paper procurement
policy can be found at: www.randomhouse.co.uk/paper.htm

Typeset in Scala Regular by Palimpsest Book Production Limited,
Grangemouth, Stirlingshire

Printed and bound in Great Britain by
Clays Ltd, St Ives plc

In Memory of Jeremy Feakes

Prologue

It has often been pointed out, both by people who do and don't play my favourite sport, that there is nothing about me that screams 'Golfer!' I don't look like I should play golf, I don't speak like I should play golf, and I don't dress like I should play golf. But that's just the superficial stuff – what you might call 'presentation'. If you really want to see how illogical my love of the game is, you need to experience the way I handle a day at the golf course.

It's not as if I don't begin the day with the best of intentions. I have a reliable body clock, so I'll rise early, giving myself ample time for the drive to the course and half an hour's warm-up. Having clumsily lugged my golf bag through the house, chipping paintwork, I'll set off for my local club, only to realise, after about three miles, that I've left my pitching wedge in the front room. Fifteen minutes later, after a swift journey back to retrieve a club that, in all honesty, I would probably have done better without, I'll arrive in the clubhouse car park. Here, I will change into golf shoes still damp, mud-caked and full of bunker sand from my last full round, eight days previously, and be told off for not using the locker room by a man in his sixties with hair on all the wrong parts of his face and knitwear that hurts my eyes. Because of my flustered state, it will only be an hour or two later that I come up with a pithy riposte to Colonel Stuffy Sweater ('Apparently the locker room has shaving facilities too – you might want to use them on your nose').

With my tee time drawing ever nearer, I'll hurry across to the club professional's shop, where I'll stock up on balls, tees and water, and – in order to mark my scorecard – a pencil, which I'll lose somewhere in the region of the third tee (I will find this three weeks later, along with six of its brethren, in a forgotten pocket of my bag, only for all seven to have mysteriously disappeared by the time of my next round). I'll then remember that the pro shop – which, though never less than up to the second in golf equipment, in financial terms is only just reaching March 1997 – doesn't 'do' debit card transactions of under £20 and that I never did get to that cashpoint on the way here, as I'd hoped. Deliverance from panic will arrive in the form of £16.51 credit behind the counter, my winnings in a sweep I hadn't realised I'd entered, in a competition from the dim and distant past.* At which point I'll head out to the first tee, to meet my playing partners for the day.

---

* The same competition whose prizegiving I had failed to attend due to 'other commitments' – a rerun of *Buffy the Vampire Slayer*, probably – and whose third place prize of some hideous cut glass I had been accidentally on purpose forgetting to collect from the club secretary's office for the past fourteen months.

It is unlikely that, in any other walk of life, my path would cross those of Ron or Roy. A sweet soul at his core, Ron will have the nervous laugh of a man trying to make light of a funeral for a non-blood relative, a keen interest in bird life, and a slight limp. Later, as I watch his swing, I will be reminded of the spider that I accidentally drowned whilst running a bath earlier that morning. Roy, on the other hand, will be an all-out mercenary – a quick-walking, quick-talking, born competitor: the kind of guy who shoots 82 off a four-teen handicap and doesn't just call it a 68, but *believes* it's a 68. During my first creaky backswing of the day, he will jangle some change in his pocket and, as my scuzzy, insomniac's six-iron shot limps toward the front apron of the green, I will see fire in his eyes.

I tell myself that I don't want to be the kind of golfer who only plays with people of his own ability and age group. I tell myself that I like the way golf allows me to mix with people that I would never otherwise meet. I tell myself that this is why I phone up at the last minute to get a place in my club's monthly medals, and find myself playing with people like Ron and Roy. But these are lies. The real reasons I take my place at the last minute are: a) I am a freelance journalist, and thus chron-ically incapable of planning ahead, and b) I'm worried that, if I put my name on the competition entry board in advance, I will tempt fate, and it will rain. Despite knowing all this in my heart of hearts, I convince myself that by playing with Roy and Ron I am doing something goodly karmic and wholesome, and it is only as I reach the eleventh tee that I begin to ask myself questions like 'What the piss am I doing here?' and 'Didn't I learn anything from last month's Cyril Harris Greensome Stableford Shield?'

At seven over par with just seven holes remaining, it might seem, to all intents and purposes, that there is little left to play for, but it will be around now that a steely inner resolve kicks in. Who knows what will flick my switch? Maybe it will be losing my last Titleist and resorting to playing with that antediluvian ball – the one with an inner core seemingly made of pure Norfolk flint – that has been lurking at the bottom of my bag since the last Conservative government. Maybe it will be Ron's habit of shouting 'Great shot!' at me every time one of my drives goes more than 130 yards. Maybe it will just be that, after almost three hours of trudging through wet grass looking for balls, crouching under foliage getting a faceful of pine tree backwash, having my flared cords eyed suspiciously ('I know there is a by-law prohibiting these somewhere – I just can't think where,' say Roy's raised eyebrows), losing my headcovers, and watching more late-middle-aged fury than you'd find in an episode of *The Sopranos*, I decide that, since it's not productive to get mad, I'd better get even (par).

Whatever the case, over the next few holes I will play something close to the top-quality amateur golf of which I know I am capable. As my drives sail three hundred yards down the fairway, my short-iron shots spin in a way suggestive of hidden air brakes, and the occasional medium-length putt begins to find its target, nothing will stand in my way: not the esoteric, free-with-a-1984-issue-of-*Golf-World* rubber gadgets that Ron keeps getting out of his bag, not Roy almost playing my ball by mistake for the sixth time, not the fact that my favourite eight-iron is still somewhere near the thirteenth tee. I know from experience that when you're on a roll like this it's best not to consult your scorecard, and mobile phones are banned on the course, so as the three of us stand on the eighteenth fairway, waiting while a man in plus fours sizes up a putt from eleven different angles ('This for a 95'), I quickly tot up my scrawled pencil marks, then listen to a voicemail from an editor who wants to know if I can turn around a 1300-word think piece on 'Why Golf is Trendy' for five p.m. that day. The inevitable double bogey that follows is not quite enough to fully dampen my spirits.

'Yes, I *enjoyed* that,' Ron and Roy will say as they shake my hand on the eighteenth green and I thank them for the game. They will say it as if genuinely surprised, as if they really didn't expect to enjoy it, but in truth, everyone I play club golf with always says, 'Yes, I *enjoyed* that' – I'm never quite sure whether that's just what you say these days at the end of a round, or that's just what you say these days at the end of a round with a hirsute ungolfy author in his early thirties with a mucky pitching wedge.

'I thought I had you on the back nine,' says Roy, who in his head has been pitted against me in some kind of Clash of the Titans. Because I have been marking Ron's card – and because Roy scares me slightly, and I have been keeping to the opposite side of the fairway from him whenever possible – I have no idea what Roy has scored. It could be 79, it could be 112. 'I can see you gloating there,' he continues. 'That's me, though – I was born unlucky. You'll realise that as you get to know me better, Tim. You'd realise it even more if you saw my ex-wife!'

I know that in the next few seconds I am going to be asked into the clubhouse for a drink. It's a tough call: I'm aware that, as time goes on, I'm getting a bit of a reputation at my home club for 'skipping off' after rounds. Also, I like having a chat with Jacqui, the no-nonsense Scouse barwoman. On the other hand, if I wanted to eat stale egg sandwiches and listen to sexist banter whilst staring at portraits of self-important men with prominent chins, I'd have joined the local Rotarians. Then there is Roy, who, since finding out I write for newspapers for a living, seems keen to talk to me about 'a potential piece of investigative journalism' regarding some garden tools that were recently stolen from his allotment. Offering my excuses – that call from my editor comes in handy – I hurry to my car, not bothering to change my golf shoes. I feel that I must run from this place, and everything that it has put me through: the tedious banter, the fluffed chip shots, the lost balls, the taunting bit in the middle where, very briefly, I became Tiger Mickelson III Jr.

I may look calm, but inside I'm churning. As I deftly manipulate the clutch and accelerator in soft spikes, leaving clods of earth in the footwell, I begin to evaluate the day's performance. I wonder why I bother with this game, which is still largely played by blinkered people with no dress sense and senses of humour that would have been booed off a stage in Blackpool in 1967 for being 'stuck in the dark ages', this game which mocks me with flashes of a better life but ultimately always results in an experience comprised of at least 70 per cent abject woe. I think about all the other, more productive, ways I could have spent the last five hours. And then I really start in on myself. Why didn't I take a penalty drop from behind that tree on the seventh, instead of attempting to curve a seven-iron eighty yards in the air, left-to-right, Seve-style, to a green two hundred yards away? When will I learn that I cannot play well without warming up amply beforehand? I can't shake the feeling, after a bad or indifferent round of golf, that something heavy has fallen on top of my life, crushing the air out of it.

It is at this point that the final stage of my post-round analysis, Release, arrives, and I remember that I am an adult, established in a profession I love, and not sixteen, playing the Midland amateur circuit, desperately trying to prove that I have what it takes to be the next Nick Faldo or Ian Woosnam. This is crazy! It's only golf! Nobody is *making* me play! I could even give up if I wanted! After all, I did it once, didn't I?

It's only about twenty minutes before I feel a desperate, nagging need to hit another ball.

I suppose if an outsider was witnessing all this they might mistake it for a mild form of madness. Why bother with something that puts you through this much pain and disappointment? It's at times like this that I think of a favourite P.G. Wodehouse story of mine, 'The Clicking of Cuthbert', where a disgruntled young player storms into the clubhouse with virtual steam coming out of his ears, and asks a wise old member of the club, 'Is golf any *use*? . . . Can you name me a single case where devotion to this pestilential pastime has done a man any practical good?' I've asked myself the same questions a million times. Golf has always got me where it hurts, infuriated me and repelled me, but it has always beckoned me back seductively, too, and I know that the masochism is part of the appeal. I managed to stay away for eight years at one point – Wodehouse's hothead only manages what appears to be about half an hour, before being talked round – and I don't know how I did it. Sometimes I think it was a mistake to come back – a failing of character. Wasn't I perfectly happy, living without the wretchedness of missed three-foot putts, final-hole double bogeys and obnoxious blokes called Roy? Living without bad sweaters and unimaginative 'I'd like to thank the greenstaff for the condition of the course' victory speeches? Perhaps. But the truth was, golf and I had a score to settle, and it was probably always just a matter of time before we renewed our acquaintance. Probably better that we did it while I was still (just about) supple enough to make a full-length backswing and yet to descend into the kind of argyle-wearing middle-age dementia that makes your major life priorities whose table you end up on at Saturday's dinner dance and getting a reserved parking spot that says 'Greens Committee Chairman'.

And, when golf and I got back together, it was always going to be a struggle. Some people – me, mostly – were inevitably going to ask, 'Is this really any *use*?' There was also the likelihood that, before I'd had a chance to work out the answer, I would get a little carried away.

But isn't that the nature of unfinished business? That it's always going to be tough?

Otherwise, you probably would have finished it earlier, wouldn't you?

DRIVING RANGE

'The only way to find out a man's true character is to play golf with him.' – P.G. Wodehouse

'Golf is an antechamber to death.' – John Peel

Sometimes I think none of this would have happened if I hadn't met Jerry. At other times I think it was all down to the most perfect eight-iron of my life, struck one idyllic summer evening on the Norfolk–Suffolk border. At other times I just blame it all on Sergio Garcia.

Sergio Garcia is a Spanish man with strong wrists, a hyperactive manner and dubious shaving habits. He is also periodically my favourite golfer, but it would perhaps be better for my health if he wasn't. When, after a long lay-off, I began to get an urge to play golf again, Garcia had just exploded onto the pro scene, and he was largely responsible for reigniting my interest in the game. Often, I think he is the most exciting player who ever lived. Equally often, for the very same reasons, I think I hate him. Over the last few years he has played with my emotions like no other pro. There is not another modern European player who seems more capable of winning multiple major championships, yet nobody has so frequently got in the running, only to make a cow's arse of things. You never know what you're going to get with Garcia from one round to the next. He could reel off five birdies in a row and hit an impossible shot from behind a tree and go charging off up the fairway in pursuit of it like a hyperactive child. Alternatively, he could make a double bogey, then take his shoe off for no apparent reason and throw it in a bunker. When Garcia gets angry, he does so in a wholly original manner; in the early noughties, he even invented his own golfing affliction, when he suddenly became unable to stop waggling the club whilst addressing the ball. I like that kind of irrational behaviour in my golfers. That's another reason I am drawn to Garcia: he reminds me of me.

It's probably important that I qualify that statement. In many ways, I am nothing like Garcia. I do not have a penchant for lurid, buttock-gripping man-made fibres that make me look like the Studio 54 answer to Bananaman. And, while I do have some Spanish in my blood, from my mum's side of the family, my Latin temperament is more likely to come out when I'm being kept in a call waiting queue than when I've just missed a downhill six-footer for par.

More importantly, I am nowhere near as good as Sergio Garcia at golf. But, when it comes to a general tee-to-green mission statement of 'Crap One Day, Dead Good the next', Sergio and I have a lot in common. The difference, perhaps, is that one can almost believe Sergio's erraticism is a deliberate gesture in the name of entertainment – a stand against conveyor-belt robo-pros, and those big-chinned men who sit in the commentary booth muttering about there being 'no pictures on the scorecard'* – whereas, with me, it seems a little more like a disease.

Of course, you'll find lots of golfers who will tell you that this is the nature of the game: one day you've got it, one day you haven't. It's just that, for me, the essence of each of those days happens to be exaggerated. I'm not talking about the bigger picture here: we've covered that. Chaotic my wider golfing life might be, but there is at least a predictability to the chaos. What I'm referring to here is the meat of the equation – the striking of the ball itself – and the frustration that comes from not knowing whether your seven-iron will fly 130 yards or 170 yards, of not knowing whether you will hit your driver like Greg Norman or Norman Wisdom. It is the same frustration that makes you feel, sometimes, as if you are living a golfing lie. But just occasionally, it can make you feel like God.

As luck would have it, these 'God' days tend to occur most frequently when I'm on my own – those late-summer evenings when the birds are singing, there isn't a Ron or a Roy in sight, and, for once, the imaginary game between the two scuffed, regenerated lake balls that you bought from the pro shop (i.e. 'Mickelson' and 'Garcia') doesn't seem quite as much of an exercise in childish fantasy. But, every so often, they have occurred when I've been with Jerry.

I wouldn't exactly call Jerry a close friend, but in the months leading up to May 2005 I had come to look upon him as a benevolent golfing presence. Maybe if

---

* Yes! But there are pictures on the TV screen, and isn't it important that we make them interesting?

the two of us bumped into one another at the local super-market we would have said a quick hello and been on our way, but within the confines of our golf club, we were allies: if not crusaders against the tucked-shirt masses, then kindred outsiders looking in, perplexed, at the fishbowl that contained the Sunday fourball elite. Since my return to golf, I'd noticed that a lot more men like Jerry played the game: fiercely competitive, football-loving, straightforward blokes in their late thirties whose love of golf had nothing to do with cheaply engraved cut glass or reserved parking spots or blazer badges. To Jerry, golf was like any other sport, only better, and he had decided that waiting until the age of thirty-three to start wasn't going to stand in his way of being bloody good at it.

Jerry said it was depressing, being him, and playing with me. There he was, hitting the practice ground four times a week, chipping slowly away at his fifteen handi-cap, while this scruffy, fly-by-night, once-a-fortnight chancer pulled into the car park three minutes before his tee time and proceeded to nonchalantly accumulate birdies. What Jerry didn't know was that he was my lucky charm. Somehow, with him at my side, the Tom that I flattered myself was the 'real Tom' would come effort-lessly to the fore, easing into his drives like an only slightly more ungainly Fred Couples.

Being a competitive sort, with a manner as austere as his grade-one haircut, Jerry would very rarely comment on my good play, but I could tell that he was monitoring me. If I told him about a monumental drive I'd hit the previous week, he would mysteriously have heard about it on the club grapevine. 'Yeah. 320 yards. Nine-iron into the green. I know,' he'd say. Seemingly unimpressed, he'd quickly deflect the conversation back to his attempts to cure his violently hooking long irons. But one day, in May 2005, his equilibrium cracked.

On the long par-four fourteenth, a new 'freewheel through the ball' swing thought helped send my drive hurtling into a realm that it was assumed only John 'Smasher' Briggs, the club's ex-assistant pro, could reach. I charged off the tee in overexcitable, somewhat disbelieving pursuit, but Jerry stopped behind me.

He was leaning on the tee marker, and he had a tiny crooked smile playing about the corner of his mouth. 'So, have you ever really thought about it?'

'Thought of what?' I asked.

'Turning pro. Making a go of it. Living the life.'

'I did once, but it's sort of too late now. Anyway, I'm not good enough.'

'But you only play once or twice every two weeks, and you play like this. What if you came up to the course more? Do you realise how many people would love to hit the ball that well? I tell you, Tom, I've been to The Open twice now, and I've seen those guys hit it, and I've seen you hit it. It makes the same *sound*.'

'But that's only part of it, isn't it, the sound? What about the putting, and the chipping?'

'I'm telling you, mate, big hairy balls to the putting. Arse to the chipping. You'll sort that. I reckon there's a handsome living out there for you. I know what I'd be doing, if it was me. I wouldn't be fucking around here, writing for the *Eastern Daily Press*.'

'But I don't write for the *Eastern Dai* . . .'

'Potaytoe, potahtoe. Who wants to be pissing around

slaving over a typewriter for a living, or one of them laptop thingies or whatever it is you use, when they could be hanging out with Tiger Woods? I'm telling you, mate, now's the time. You're still young. If you've been given something great in life, you should do something with it, that's what I always say.'

Plenty of people had told me, since my golfing reincarnation, that I 'should be on Tour'. I knew that was sheer misguided flattery, and I knew about the huge gap between a four-handicap amateur like me and even the worst touring pro. Coming from someone like Jerry, however, the enthusiasm seemed to mean so much more. Clearly he wasn't the kind of bloke who gave away compliments lightly. But what really affected me was his indignation. To him, my lack of interest in my golfing talent seemed scandalous, an insult to those who struggled along, barely getting the ball 200 yards off the tee. Maybe it was because I was on the verge of my thirtieth birthday, but in the weeks that followed I found myself marinating in his comments.

Everyone tells you that reaching thirty is a big deal, but nothing can prepare you for the event itself. I used to think that twenty-seven sounded old, and that after that landmark ages would all be much of a muchness, but thirty is an eloquent slap in the face. Suddenly, a considerable portion of the endless unfurling 'future' that you've been talking about for much of your twenties has already passed. I had been determined not to let it bother me. I'd even grown my first full beard especially for the occasion. After all, what was there to worry about? I was happily married, I had friends I could count on (even if most of them thought I was a bit weird for playing golf), I had a writing job that I loved, and I had a mortgage on a house that, two years after I had bought it, could still make me go 'Wow!' Still, when the big day itself hits, it's impossible for even the happiest person not to do a bit of evaluating, ask themselves a 'What if?' or two. And, for me, the big 'What if?' was always golf.

Seventeen is an awfully young age to make any major decision about your life. But that was how old I'd been when I'd walked off a golf course as a budding pro golfer for what I believed, with all my broken heart, would be the last time. The scene of my exit has stuck with me – probably more like a memory of a memory now, but no less clear for that. The place: a forest in Staffordshire. The tournament: The Beau Desert Stag. My ball: abandoned (by hand and not, for once, by club) in some heather 400 yards behind me. My hands: sticky and callused. The smell: hot pine needles. My hat hair: not much of a hairstyle in the first place but now, if anything, looking more like two separate non-hairstyles. My golfing dreams: gone up in smoke. It had been one of those occasions when you can almost hear the click as your life changes direction. That night I would attend a rock concert – not a very cool rock concert, or even a very great one, but one loud and energetic and different enough to suggest that there might be another life out there for me that didn't involve spiked shoes and winner's speeches. In the days following, golf would never seem quite as important. Soon, as I stopped playing altogether, it would seem like an aberration at best, a dirty secret at worst. I remembered it like a brief schizoid episode: something that had nothing to do with the real me.

But now here I was – a fully-grown man, and still

9

only a half-grown golfer. I definitely felt like the real me, yet I also couldn't help feeling, just as I had at seventeen, that the secret to life itself was held in that lightning second when the body waits for the club and everything arrives at the ball in perfect sync. I'd initially told myself that my golfing rebirth was to do with getting fit and researching my golf memoir, *Nice Jumper*. And that is all it had been . . . for about a month or two. But in 2003, my first full year back playing, I had won my club's Scratch Cup. Increasingly, I would arrive home from the course and explain to my bewildered wife, Edie, in the manner of a man outlining plans for his family's financial future, that I thought all I really needed was to curtail my backswing by five inches and we'd be just about there. Maybe I was not playing golf with quite the obsessive fervour with which I'd played it as a teenager, but it would not have have taken a genius to see that this was about more than fresh air and a bit of gentle, competitive fun, and that something long-submerged was pressing to the surface. In short, I had begun to ask myself a little question.

Who really knows who they are at seventeen? Had I really given golf a proper go back then? It wasn't as if I'd started playing as soon as I'd learned to walk, like many kids I'd known back on the Nottinghamshire golf scene. I'd actually come to the game quite late, and left it quite early. I'd been pretty good for those four and half years, too, hadn't I? Within a couple of years, I'd become Club Champion at my home course, Cripsley Edge, the winner of a dozen junior competitions and one of the very best young golfers in Nottinghamshire, if not quite in the Midlands. But by the time I'd reached my seventeenth birthday, it had become abundantly clear that I wasn't good enough: that two handicap of mine just wasn't getting any lower, and, as I struggled to combine late nights in a minimum-wage job with early mornings on the tee, I could see the interest dying in the eyes of the men in the bile-coloured suits who patrolled the fairways looking for young talent. I'd only ever been a half golden boy in the first place, but now I was an ex-half golden boy. I was also one with some appalling GCSE results and two very anxious parents.

That period had felt like a mini-lifetime while it was happening, but what was four and a bit years, from a properly adult respective? It could take four and a bit years to unpack all your possessions after moving house, to fully settle into a new job, to untangle yourself from an unsuccessful relationship . . . to get round to mending a garden fence.

Could it be true? Had I been a bit rash on that hot day all those years ago in Staffordshire?

I'd seen older friends go through similar epiphanies. Upon reaching thirty, it had suddenly dawned on them that, *no*, at sixteen stone, with a mortgage and a steady job in the civil service, perhaps they *weren't* going to fulfil that dream of playing on the right wing for Nottingham Forest after all. My predicament, however, was slightly different. Footballers (goalkeepers and Teddy Sheringham excepted) may be washed up at thirty, but, as of May 2005, the average age of the top fifty players in golf's world rankings was 32.06. I actually had two full years until I was due to hit my peak! Granted, most 32.06-year-olds on the PGA Tour had spent their twenties hitting three hundred balls per day and playing high-level tournament golf forty weeks a year, rather than hanging around with rock musicians and drinking too much, but it was important not to quibble. There was a plentiful supply of hope here.

Also, hadn't my decision to leave my pro golf ambitions behind been based, at least in part, on the awful, outdated attitudes surrounding golf, rather than on the game itself? And did those attitudes still even exist? Admitting to a love of golf might have still been tantamount to admitting to being a member of the Bruce Forsyth Fan Club in 1992, but in 2005, who *didn't* like golf? Alice Cooper played, Lou Reed played, Catherine Zeta-Jones played, even that weird buttery-faced kid from *The Sixth Sense* played. When I was a teenager, I'd felt odd for not wanting to be Gary Lineker quite as much as most of my male classmates did, but now Lineker – just one of a seemingly endless supply of Premiership and ex-Premiership footballers who seemed to regret choosing studs over spikes – was shaping up to be the new face of BBC golf. As I'd been told repeatedly, golf was hip, and while the trousers worn by my Saturday Medal partners might fairly firmly refute that claim, I could see that plenty had changed for the better in my lost decade. Dress codes had been relaxed. Owing to the rise of pay'n'play and family-oriented hotel-spa courses, the back-scratching social infrastructure of private clubs was falling apart, and the result was a game played by people who were aware of the world beyond the eighteenth green – or so I hoped. Surely the professional level of a game like this – i.e. what you would assume is the most evolved level – would be a place where I could fit in?

Two weeks after I'd played with Jerry, and two days before my thirtieth birthday, I made a list called Pros and Cons of Becoming a Golf Pro, and showed it to Edie. It read as follows:

Cons:

1. Bad back (already here, could get worse).
2. Financial problems (how exactly does a person break into the male-escort industry?).
3. Would rather leap naked into a pit of vipers than travel anywhere by plane.
4. How many times exactly can someone have a conversation about 'shaft torque' before losing the will to live?
5. May need to dress in German businessman sports casual in order to 'blend in'.
6. Flashbacks to childhood trauma.
7. Less time to write (1000-page East Anglian answer to Stephen King's *The Stand* will probably have to be put on back burner).
8. Potential to descend into sport anecdote hell, leading to divorce and blackballing by non-golfing friends.
9. Will probably have to keep clubs clean.

Pros:

1. Fresh air and exercise.
2. Closure on lingering 'Did I take the right path?' questions.
3. No better non-sexual feeling in life than great golf shot.

4. Good excuse to finally buy that driving net for the back garden.
5. Get to do that thing where you pick your ball out of the hole and hold it up to the crowd and mouth 'Thank you'.
6. No more handicap silliness and competitions with needlessly complex scoring formats and names like The Ralph Badger Jubilee Greensome Stableford Salver.
7. Get to enter The Open (*The Open!!!!*)
8. No grumpy retired hotelier jingling pocket change on my backswing.
9. Might get to play with Sergio Garcia.

At 9–9, I needed a tie-breaker. In the end, I got two. The first came from Edie.

'I think you need to get it out of your system. And who knows – you might actually win something,' she said, which I thought was very magnanimous and supportive coming from someone who: a) didn't like golf, and b) had just had three episodes of *America's Next Top Model* wiped from her Sky Plus box by extended coverage of The FedEx St Jude Classic.

The real decider, however, came from my eight-iron.

The night I'd made my list, I'd been on the Internet and checked out the 2006 schedule for the Europro Tour – a relatively new, fast-growing professional golf circuit. Although it was not as famous as the PGA or European Tours, the Europro Tour seemed to contain its fair share of former big(ish) names and touted future stars within its ranks. I already had my eye on the Qualifying School event, ten months away, as a potential curtain-opener for my new career. I shut my laptop unusually decisively that night, like a man with a plan. Then, for a couple of days, I completely emptied my mind of all golfing thoughts. In forty-eight hours I would have left my twenties behind, and there were other, more pressing matters to think about – charcoal briquettes and six-packs, for example.

I suppose it's possible that, had things not happened the way they did that weekend, all this 'Should I have a go at being a pro?' might have drifted away, only to be remembered as a brief, fading-youth-related freak-out. Or maybe not. All I know is that the day following my party, after the final sleepover guests had staggered away, I had a visceral urge to hit some shots.

These are often the times that golf is most rewarding, I find: when it's an unplanned thing, something that crops up on the shuffle mechanism of life's iPod. There is no scorecard, no 'Is it going to rain?' anxiety. Quite simply, one balmy, hungover afternoon, you feel a bit of a second wind coming on, and you realise that there's no place you'd rather be than in a patch of bastardised countryside, feeling the satisfying swish of metal against rubber. It would have been hard to have been this impulsive with other sports. As I hopped straight onto the picturesque ninth tee with only a couple of friendly dog walkers to judge me, and compiled a string of three textbook pars, I was already thinking 'This is the life! This is me!' What came next was purely a bonus.

Over the years, I've holed many spectacular golf shots. I've had twos on par fours, threes on par fives, slam-dunked 180-yard iron shots, even brushed the hole with my tee shot on a couple of short par fours, but as I reached the tee of the par-three twelfth hole at Diss Golf Club in Suffolk that day, I was still yet to have a hole-in-one. Of course, as a good player, this wasn't supposed to concern me. Hole-in-ones, as anyone who *really* knows about golf will tell you, are a fluke – nothing to get too worked up about in the grand scheme of things. They are also a bit of a bind, in that the main long-term result of them is that the holer must buy everyone in the vicinity a round of drinks afterwards – a tradition that may do more to sum up the inherent masochism of golf than any other. 'Have you had a hole-in-one?' is a question for the non-golfer to ask the golfer, but not a subject for men who know their lob wedge from their gap wedge. Nevertheless, in aesthetic terms, this one was worth waiting for. Not only did the ball come crisply off the clubhead, then drift gently in on the breeze, it found its intended target without bouncing. 'Whumf!' Straight down the hole, like the most nimble, spatially aware rabbit you have ever almost clapped eyes on.

You expect some response after a shot like that. Applause, at the very least. Instead, the late-afternoon silence seemed even more deafening than usual. If a ball falls in a golf hole in the woods, and there's nobody around to hear it, does it still count? I looked around, slightly frantically, but the ailing electric trolleys of the two middle-aged women playing ahead of me had crept over the brow of the hill in the distance. Where, when I needed him, was the tracksuit-wearing man with the Rottweiler who had said 'Nice *shot!*' after seeing my sclaffed nine-iron land thirty feet from the flag on the previous hole? One part of me was thinking, 'So, is this *it?*' Another was admiring the purity, thinking, 'How can you not take this as a sign?' And then there was the final part, which was looking at the bigger picture, taking a 'glass is half full' view of the situation – or, more specifically, a 'glass won't ever get filled in the first place' approach – giving the other two parts a serious talking-to: this stays between the two of you, me, and our bar tab.

COURSE

'There was not an athlete I had spoken to from other sports – the roughest of them: football, hockey, basketball – who did not hold the professional golfer in complete awe, with thanksgiving that golf was not *their* profession. The idea of standing over a putt with thousands of dollars in the balance was enough to make them flap their fingers as if singed. Golf was the only major sport in which the tension remained throughout – where each shot was far enough apart in time for doubt to seep in and undermine one's confidence, so that there was no way of establishing an equanimity of mood. Other sports were not similar: the tension would mount, but as soon as the first whistle blew or the contact began, that was the end of it.'

– George Plimpton

One

You Wanna be Startin' Somethin'?

'I saw you hitting some shots out there the other day,' said the man behind the counter, handing me two little silver tokens for the ball-dispenser. 'You looked like you were bombing it. What do you play off?'

'Oh, I don't have a handicap. I'm a pro. Just turned, in fact,' I said.

I was lying, actually. It was the tail end of winter, 2006, and I had two weeks left until I officially lost my status as an amateur golfer – possibly forever, and almost certainly for at least two years – but I figured it couldn't hurt to take my new profession for a trial run. 'I'm a pro,' was something I was going to have to get used to saying over the coming months. Much as I'd been looking forward to speaking the words, though, I found that they tasted sticky and odd in my mouth. I wasn't completely convinced that the assistant pro at Hemingford Abbots Driving Range in Cambridgeshire wasn't going to unmask me, or at the very least call his co-worker over and play piggy-in-the-middle with my ailing, all-weather 'London Golf Show 2005' golf glove. As I did my best to look collected and pretend that an expression like 'bombing it' was a part of my everyday golfing vocabulary, I found myself studying him unusually closely. Was that the first sign of a smirk in the curve of his upper lip? Was he looking at my Gap jumper and thinking, 'Yeah, right. Like a serious player would be seen dead in *that*.'

'Congratulations!' he said. 'So, are you playing the circuit?'

'Yep. Going to give it a go. See what happens.'

'Where are you attached?'

'Oh, I'm kind of out on my own.'

There's a lot of guff talked about how hard it is to become a golf professional. People will tell you that, in order to play golf for a living, you have to learn byzantine things about the inner mass of the head of a three-wood, that you have to spend a large chunk of your life in retail limbo, selling tee-pegs and mending the shafts of the clubs that irate ten-handicappers have broken over their knee in the previous month's Clive Wilkins Salver or Ron Davies Bowl. They'll tell you that you need to be playing to a handicap of four, at worst, and that if you are seriously thinking about playing the game for a living, you'd be wise not to consider doing so until you're at least six digits better than that. But this is untrue. Becoming a pro is really a lot easier than you might imagine.

When 80 per cent of golf professionals say 'I'm a pro,' what they mean is that they have joined the PGA, aka the Professional Golfer's Association, professional golf's governing body. To do this, they have to gain their card by serving a three-year apprenticeship working for a qualified teaching professional in a pro shop, learning about equipment and the fundamentals of the swing, sometimes – if their boss is a lenient, unselfish type – squeezing in five or six holes before nightfall, and taking a training course and exams at the PGA headquarters at the Belfry, near Birmingham. But mostly just spending an awful lot of time giving advice to old men about clubs they don't really need. At the end of this period – at which point they must have a handicap of four or better – the budding PGA pro may, if he has not had it beaten out of him, still nurture a dream of making a living from his playing skills, but, if this doesn't come to fruition, at least he has the fallback option of one day overseeing his own mini retail empire and driving a VW Golf with really big spoilers.

In days gone by, it was not uncommon for a feisty young 'un from the wrong side of the golfing tracks (e.g. Lee Trevino) to fight his way out of a low-paid assistant's job and onto one of the main tours, where he would rub up against his more affluent, conventionally primed peers with incendiary results. But thanks to an increasingly well-structured and carefully monitored amateur circuit, and the rise of American golf scholarships, such occurrences are now about as common as openly bisexual Ryder Cup players. When you look at the top hundred of golf's world rankings these days, you are by and large looking at a list of the former heroes of international amateur golf.

Have Luke Donald and Sergio Garcia ever soldered the head of a five-iron back onto its shaft, or been paid £18 for taking a septuagenarian member of the Ladies' Bridge Club up to the practice ground for half an hour in an attempt to help her get her three-wood shots flying above shoulder level? Of course they haven't. This is because, for them, the life of the PGA-qualified pro has never been a practical option. Instead, like most of their contemporaries, they have risen inexorably through the junior and amateur (and, in Donald's case, American college circuit) ranks. Then, one day, when continuing to play for pride alone would be futile, they have arrived at a professional tournament and said, 'I'm a pro. Should I perform to the best of my ability in this event, I would like to be paid some prize money. And while you're at it, could you get someone to ferry me to the driving range in one of those cool newfangled buggies over there?' It really is that simple. Sort of.

Since making my final decision to turn pro, last June, I had found the life surprisingly fuss-free. There had been no forms to fill in, no maths tests to take, no apprenticeships. The main significant difference really was that now, when I left the house for the golf club, I was able to tell Edie, 'I'm off to work!' According to the man I spoke to on the phone at the Royal & Ancient, which is the ruling authority of golf everywhere except the United States and Mexico, turning pro is defined as 'breaching amateur status by agreeing to accept prize money for playing'.* In other words, anyone can do it. The tricky part is the immediate aftermath. You might be able to *call* yourself a pro, but whether you will receive the tournament invites that allow you to attempt to function as one is another matter entirely. Moreover, as the man from the R&A told me, 'It could take anywhere between a year and two years for you to get your amateur status back.'

---

* I presumed that the £3.46 I'd won in the sweep for getting a two on the fifteenth hole at Diss last September didn't count.

No more Monthly Medals with Roy and Ron? I figured I could live with that. I could also quite happily live without the handicap system. What are handicaps anyway, if not a really good, legal way of cheating, for people who happen to be a bit rubbish? You don't see football teams going out onto the field, assessing another team's ability, and giving them 'free' goals, do you? (Well, not unless you're watching England, you don't.) As a pro, the playing field would be levelled – just me and my fellow competitors, battling against par.

All right, so I could see there were *some* downsides to no longer being an amateur golfer. I would have to turn down a place on the British team in the annual GB vs US golf writers' event, which would be a bit of a bind. When I went to play my monthly games at Richmond Golf Club in Surrey, with my best golfing friends Simon and Scott, I would be giving them gargantuan respective twelve- and twenty-three-shot head starts. And I wouldn't be regaining my Scratch Cup Championship from two years ago. But . . . I WAS TURNING PROFESSIONAL! That fact in itself was more than enough to compensate. The additional fact that I had contacted the Europro Tour and found out that I was eligible to officially turn pro at their Qualifying School event, at Stoke-by-Nayland Golf Club in Essex, seemed close to a miracle. If, as a seventeen-year-old, I'd known the pro system worked like this, might I currently have been mounting a campaign for my third successive Ryder Cup appearance?

Having made my decision, I was a little slow to investigate the nuts and bolts of the process itself. Instead, with the spectral voices of old junior organisers and coaches echoing in my head, I'd fixated on that magic number four, supposing that since this was the requisite handicap for a PGA pro, it would be the requisite one for a playing pro as well. My handicap had been going up steadily for a while now – in fact, its rise coincided almost perfectly with the first time I'd mooted the pro idea. I was now 5.1 – a whole 1.5 worse than my adult-period best – and climbing. One of the reasons I'd put off my enquiries with the Europro Tour and the R&A was that I was worried that, by not shooting down to four, as per my plan, I'd scuppered my chances. Now I knew differently, the relief was immense. When I thought about all the rounds and entry fees and Roys and Rons and nerve-jangling three-foot putts and horrible cut glass it would have taken to reduce my handicap even back down to its all-time low of two, I couldn't help sitting back and admiring the ease of all this: 'I think I am a golf professional, therefore I am a golf professional.' Perhaps more astonishingly, other golf professionals seemed to believe me.

Well, an assistant golf professional at an obscure driving range in Cambridgeshire seemed to believe me, anyway. Whether the playing pros on the Europro Tour would too . . . I'd find out soon enough.

From what I'd heard about the Europro Tour in my months of preparation for my new golfing life, it was at the bottom of the pecking order, as far as full-time pro golf circuits went. This became obvious merely from comparing its financial rewards with those of its competitors. On the PGA Tour, golf's untouchable premier circuit, based in America, the twentieth-placed player on the 2005 money list, Chad Campbell, won close to

$2.5 million. By contrast, the twentieth-placed player on the 2005 Europro Tour order of merit won just over £9000. When I mentioned my intention of playing the tour to my more knowledgeable golfing friends, many of them gave me the kind of look more readily associated with root-canal surgery than the dawn of a glamorous sporting career. 'Just don't expect to be signing any autographs,' warned a fellow golf scribe who had recently covered the Europro Tour's climactic, season-closing event. Nonetheless, perusing a list of Europro regulars, I was impressed. Mark Davies? Was that the same long-hitting Mark Davies whom I'd frequently watched on my visits to the PGA Championship at Wentworth in the late eighties and early nineties? The one who twice won the Austrian Open, and whose swing Seve Ballesteros once called 'the best in Europe'? It was. Could that really be the same Michael Welch who'd been coached by the father of 1988 US Masters Champion Sandy Lyle and who, when I'd watched him at the Brabazon Trophy in 1991, had been the subject of expectations not hugely dissimilar to those shouldered by the teenage Tiger Woods? It could. It was hard to suppress some butter-flies when I realised that this was the company I'd be keeping. Perhaps more exciting still was the fact that if you said 'Europro Tour' really quickly, it sounded a bit like 'European Tour'.

Judging by the entrance fees, the Europro Tour couldn't be *that* low-rent. To be permitted to enter one of its regular tournaments, I had to cough up the not incon-siderable sum of £275, for which I would get two rounds of golf – four, if I made the thirty-six-hole cut – and a free pitchfork, with which to repair the marks my ball made when it landed on the green. The Qualifying School itself, meanwhile, would cost £325. On top of that, I would have to consider the extra expense of my equipment, accommodation and travel. This presented a problem that I perhaps should have foreseen: I needed to take time off from writing in order to give my golf a proper chance, but the more writing I did, the less of a struggle I would have supporting my new golfing life. Either that, or I would have to get friendly with a couple of local oil barons with a passion for supporting maverick, late-blossoming sporting talent in its early thirties.

In January, I'd visited the opulent Essex mansion that doubled up as the headquarters of the Europro Tour and the home of the Tour's MD, Eddie Hearn, son of the legendary boxing promoter, Barry. I'd wanted to meet Hearn, partly because I'd heard that it was not unknown for him to personally sponsor some of the more promising players on his own tour; but despite my frequent references to my victory in the 1991 Kedleston Junior Open, he didn't seem to be taking the bait. I was clearly going to have to give the matter of sponsorship some serious thought. I also needed to consider my 2006 schedule. If I made it through Stage One of the Qualifying School, then finished in the top hundred or so out of 240 in the final stage, I would be an official member of the Tour, with dozens of events to choose from in the coming months. What, however, if I didn't? I wouldn't be eligible to play in smaller, non-Tour-affiliated, regional pro tournaments, as these were only for PGA-qualified club pros. Sure, there were other tours out there, but the Challenge Tour – the far-flung 'little brother' of the European Tour – was generally only for people who'd already done very well on, or bypassed, the Europro Tour. Entering the Qualifying School for the mighty European Tour itself, meanwhile, cost almost £2000, and required a letter of reference from a golfing official, testifying to one's ability. When I'd asked the man at the R&A if five-handicappers who'd turned pro were permitted to enter The Open, he said, 'Probably not.' And while I hadn't actually approached Augusta National for confirmation, I was guessing that an invite to The Masters was out. But there was no point trying to cross a bridge at which I had yet to arrive . . . particu larly if it happened to be erected over a shark-infested lateral water hazard, with no drop zone. For now, I was revelling in the sheer novelty of my new status as a professional sportsman, and the reactions it would provoke as I dropped it nonchalantly into conversations.

'You're going to be a golf pro? Wow. What did you have to do to be able to do that? I bet you're really good.'

'Will you give me a lesson some time? I *love* golf.'

'God, I am so jealous. I would love to do that. I bet it's the best job in the world!'

Somewhere deep in my brain, I was still conditioned to think that there was something embarrassingly bour-geois about being a golfer, but now, having fully embraced the golf world for the first time since my late teens, I was feeling the force of the mini-revolution that had occurred while I'd been away. This revolution wasn't about the golf-themed fashion show I'd seen earlier in the year, with models in plus fours strutting along a catwalk to the sound of gangsta rap, waving their extra-large umbrellas around. It wasn't about Sky Sports using popular indie rock hits to funk up their US Open coverage. Who cared if golf was 'cool'? The important thing was that in the early Tiger Woods years – the years when golf had been but a blip on my radar – it had gained cultural acceptance. As a result, before I had even struck my first pro shot, people in the most unlikely places seemed impressed with my career choice.

It was probably just as well, all things considered, that I had Steve Gould to help me keep my feet on the ground.

'Hand action's better,' said Steve. 'Cleaner. The problem is, you're still going through the ball like a complete puff.'

I'd met Steve the previous spring, after an on-form golfing friend had recommended his services. Over the years, he, his colleague Dave Wilkinson and their late, legendarily thorny guru, Lesley King (a man described by Steve as 'golf's answer to Brian Clough'), had built up an impressive list of pupils at their underground golf school, on a quiet, regal street just behind Harvey Nichols, in London's swanky Knightsbridge district. Amidst the signed photographic testimonies on the wall from Christopher Lee, Des Lynam, Hugh Grant, Bryan Ferry and Geri Halliwell, I definitely recognised a picture of a bloke I remembered finishing quite high up in the Portuguese Open a few years ago – for the time being, I just couldn't quite remember his name. To be fair, Steve and Dave had taught quite a few future golfing stars in their earlier days – it was rumoured, for example, that the swing philosophy that had brought Nick Faldo's old coach, David Leadbetter, to prominence in the eighties had its roots in Knightsbridge – but, having been left bruised by a couple of incidents of heartless abandonment, they now preferred to teach within the amateur ranks. That these amateur ranks also happened to look not unlike the guest list at an Elton John house-warming party had nothing to do with a policy of exclusivity; it was simply a measure of how adept celebrities are at keeping a good thing to themselves. Still, Knightsbridge Golf School couldn't stay a secret from the outside world forever, and my presence in itself suggested there'd been a wrong turn somewhere along the grapevine.

'We had [then Chelsea midfielder] Gianfranco Zola in here not long ago,' said Steve. 'He's a total hero of mine, but he had one of the worst swings I've ever seen. Took the club so far around his body that he smashed that mirror behind him – even worse than you, Tom. We put him right, though.'

Over the nine months I'd known him, I'd found that my mentor was far more interested in talking about the fortunes of Chelsea FC and the recent albums of Neil Young than golf, or the ever-increasing number of rich and famous people who played it. In fact, from what I could gather, Steve no longer bothered playing the game, in its conventional outdoor incarnation, at all ('Full of stuffy retired colonels, isn't it?'). That did not mean, however, that he wasn't on a mission to scientifically perfect its execution, here in his underground lab. If, indeed, you could apply the term 'lab' to a shabby former squash court equipped with an ageing video camera and recorder, four Astroturf mats and a couple of nets that looked as if they'd played host to the leisure pursuits of an overzealous panther cub.

'Ninety-five per cent of golfers suffer from the same faults,' Steve would explain repeatedly to me. 'We tend to teach people the same things here. It's like a conveyor belt. Why do you think people call us the swing factory? Tell him why they call us the swing factory, Dave.'

'Because we're like a conveyor belt, Steve,' Dave would say.

'That's right, Dave. Come over here and tell me what you think of Tom's backswing. Cleaned up nicely, hasn't it, Dave?'

'Ooh, yes, cleaned up nicely, Steve. Tom, is Steve bullying you? Don't let Steve bully you.'

'I'll bully him if I like, Dave. You like being bullied, anyway, don't you, Tom? That's what you need, isn't it? If you don't have me nagging on at you, you're never going to get any better, are you? Isn't that right, Dave?'

'No, that's right, Steve. Listen to your uncle Steve, Tom; he's always right, you know.'

'Thank you, Dave.'

I wasn't entirely sure if the 1980s-sitcom nature of Steve and Dave's relationship was a device intended to disorientate their pupils into submission, or simply the result of spending too many years in a small window-less room with one another, but they had quite a double act going. Apparently, the previous summer, the newly golf-crazed Ant and Dec had visited the school for a couple of lessons, but had never returned, and I couldn't help wondering if the Geordie entertainers had simply got spooked by meeting their comic match.

While Dave often chipped in with comments on my backswing – usually to the chagrin of whichever lord or soap star he was supposed to be teaching at the time

– it was Steve who wore the trousers in the partnership, and it was he who had taken me, quiet flatteringly, under his wing. Like all the best golf coaches, he managed to find just the right balance between crushing insults and grudging compliments, thus keeping me on my self-critical guard, yet not quite depressed enough to give up hope. When he talked about my swing being 'puffy', I wasn't quite sure whether he was talking about homosexuality or pastry, but I thought I knew what he was getting at. The Cox action had always been a loose, wristy beast, but now that I could see it before me on screen, contrasted with the smooth, wide actions of Ernie Els and Tiger Woods, it had become obvious that its flail and flick made it a critical anomaly. When Steve had complained that I was 'living in the past', I'd originally thought he was insulting my Led Zeppelin T-shirt, but I soon realised he was talking about something else. Nobody, according to him, swung the club like me any more.

'The main problem is that your swing's a relic,' he had explained. 'You're stuck in 1989. People thought that flicky stuff was all right then, but now everyone swings the club with width. It's all about keeping the arms away from the body these days. Of course, we've been telling people all this stuff for years.'

What Steve wanted me to do, he'd said, was simple: I had to forget about my scores, spend as little time on the course, and as much on the driving range, as possible. It was imperative that I broke my swing down to its individual components, pausing halfway up my backswing, then at its apex, then, later, stunting my follow-through a microsecond after impact – continually checking the angle of the club and shaft to the ground, regarding the whole process scientifically. It would take hard work, certainly, but one day, he assured me, I would step out onto the course and everything would click into place subconsciously. It made a lot of sense at Knightsbridge, with Steve and Dave's quickfire instructions ringing in my ears, but all too often, back in Norfolk, after a few disciplined shots I'd let temptation get to me, and I'd begin to bash away at the ball in a more random, care-free fashion. Now, here I was, at what should have been the moment of truth, and I was wondering where the last ten months had gone. Sure, I'd *intended* to hit the eight-hundred-balls-per-week minimum Steve had told me was required, but there had been a book to finish, a stack of extra journalism to take on in order to help fund the golf, and then it had been winter, the practice ground had been a bit muddy and, to be honest, I've never been that fond of those cold, thin iron shots where it feels as if iced electricity is pinging around the inside of your forearm. Without doubt, I'd probably hit more balls recently than at any point since I was a college-bunking sixteen-year-old. I also knew that I was hitting very slightly straighter and – rather worryingly – shorter than before. I was sure something about my swing had changed; I was similarly sure, though, that in Steve's programme I was probably just reaching the stage he'd intended me to reach around July last year.

Now, as Steve packed away the balls, I made a quick estimation: if I continued at this rate, I would complete my transformation into Fred Couples by August 2011.

'We'll put you right in no time, Tom. Won't we, Dave?' said Steve, producing a Polaroid and handing it to me.

I studied the photo: it was a freeze frame of my some-what cramped position at the exact point of impact with the ball. I looked *quite* like I was playing golf, but equally, I could easily have been mistaken for a man performing a complicated task with an extra-long electric screw-driver.

In the background, Des Lynam – who'd recorded the outgoing message on Steve and Dave's answering machine – took an enquiry from someone whose voice I thought I recognised from *EastEnders*.

'We'll put him right in no time, Steve,' repeated Dave. 'You've got to learn to trust your uncle Steve, Tom. Hasn't he, Steve?'

'That's right, Dave. Now, when are you going to come down here again? You know what you ought to do, Tom? Get a flat above here. Then we'll really sort you out. Ask Dave. He'll tell you, won't you, Dave?'

'That's right, Steve. Dead right.'

'Yep, all you need is a cool million or two, and you're there.'

'A million pounds will be nothing to you soon. You just wait. You've got to work on that hand action, though, and not be a naughty boy. Isn't that right, Da . . .'

Sensing that this could go on indefinitely, I made my excuses and emerged, blinking, into the bustle of lunchtime Knightsbridge. It was terrific to hear Steve and Dave's encouragement, but there was just one minor problem: I *had* no time. In just a week, I would be hitting my first shot as a pro. I'd promised Steve that I'd see him one more time before my debut, but I knew that in reality I probably wouldn't. It was time to get off the conveyor belt. It was dangerous to fill your head with technical talk on the course and, as unsure as I felt about the science of my swing, I knew it was important to turn my attention to the game itself now: the simple concept of getting the ball in the hole in as few strokes as possible. And who could tell how I would react when I was under the gun? Maybe I'd beat the odds, and my doubts would fly away on the wind?

'Haven't I proved myself before?' I reasoned, thinking back to my trial for membership at my first club, in Nottinghamshire, as a nervous thirteen year-old: the way, saddled with the pressure of not having a Lyle & Scott sweater to my name or a family member on the committee, I'd proceeded to dispatch fifty of the smoothest seven-iron shots imaginable straight down the practice fairway, to the wonder of the junior organiser. Pretty soon, I fell into a reverie: the compressed feel of ball on turf, the winning putt (always a carbon copy of Seve's in the 1984 Open, the slightly misdirected one that seems to find the target in response to the sheer force of his will), the acceptance speech. I think I am a golf professional, therefore I am a golf professional . . .

I'd walked almost all the way to Oxford Circus before I came out of the daydream, and as I did, I immediately became aware of a small, squeaky 'hee-hoo' noise, cutting through the rumble of frustrated traffic. Then, shortly afterwards, I also became aware of the two teenagers ten yards to my left who were making it, pointing at me, and moonwalking on the pavement.

As I touched my left hand and the synthetic, dried-out feel of all-weather fibre confirmed my worst fears, I had an instinct to be embarrassed. However, this was quickly overridden by the impressive realisation that I'd walked two and half miles through the busiest city in Britain at the busiest time of the day wearing a single white – well, sort of off-white now, to be honest – glove before anyone had thought to hurl any abuse at me and, when they finally had, they had not hurled it because I was a golfer, they had hurled it because they had mistaken me for a Michael Jackson fan. Was this acceptance? I think it was!

Suddenly suffused with a warm glow, I peeled off the offending item and examined it. That 'London Golf Show' logo was fading now, and the hole in the index finger was getting bigger. If beef jerky had been beige, it might have looked something like this. I'd heard that Bernhard Langer used three or four gloves per round, which, if you asked me, was just downright wasteful. I'd been using this one for eleven months, and it had served me well, but I was feeling expansive – carefree, even. Maybe, just maybe, if I played well next week, I'd treat myself to a replacement.

Two

The Sweet Smell of Success

If you speak to enough people within the sphere of professional golf, you'll soon realise that there's no hard and fast way to prepare for a tournament. Some players, like Vijay Singh, will blast balls on the range every hour that daylight allows. Others, like Colin Montgomerie, will keep their warm-up to a gentle minimum, perhaps keen to save their best shots for the course. Practice isn't about rules. Still, it can be said that most tournament professionals will do their utmost to put themselves into a calm state of mind before teeing up the first ball of the day. They will strive to get a decent amount of sleep. Then, when they play their practice round, they will make sure that they play it on the right course – preferably the one where the tournament in question is being held.

I'm not quite sure where I went wrong in the lead-up to my debut at the Europro Tour Qualifying School. Having left Knightsbridge, I'd surprised myself with a few days of knuckling down and reaching the levels of training regime discipline that I'd been promising, but not quite achieving, for most of the winter. My practice sessions became almost disturbingly efficient. On one visit to my local driving range I had hit two hundred eight-iron shots, using a 'one-two' counting routine that I'd picked up from Timothy Gallwey's celebrated book, *The Inner Game of Golf*,* and each had landed within the same ten-yard radius, roughly 160 yards from where I stood. With some encouragement from the newly golf-savvy Edie, I'd even begun to devote some time to fine-tuning my putting – a part of the game in which I'd last shown serious interest shortly after my fifteenth birthday. I'd topped off my preparatory routine with one final game as an amateur, at Richmond Golf Club with Simon and Scott, during which I'd driven to the fringe of the green on a 320-yard par four and Simon had pointed to me and shouted over to an onlooker on the adjacent practice ground, 'He's a pro, you know!' Later that evening we'd returned to Simon's Shepherd's Bush flat to watch the Players' Championship, golf's all-but-official 'fifth major', held at the TPC course at Sawgrass, with its picturesque, alligator-guarded holes and its habit of coaxing my favourite players – long-hitting, aggressive players – to the top of the leaderboard. There could have been no tournament I would rather have watched for inspiration.

'I can't believe that's going to be you in a couple of days,' Simon said as we watched Sergio Garcia – who,

---

* The idea being to blank out interfering thoughts and instil rhythm by counting 'One' on the backswing and 'Two' on the downswing . . . and to keep your voice low enough so the person in the adjacent bay doesn't hear you and mistake you for a simpleton.

once again, had been unfairly getting our hopes up – pull an elementary ninety-yard wedge shot into a green-side bunker. 'Lucky fucker.'

'Well, sort of,' I said. 'Except I'm not going to be Spanish. And I'm going to be in Essex, not Florida. Oh yeah, and my putting average is still seven worse than the average for the PGA Tour.'

'Are you nervous?' Scott asked.

I was surprised to find that the answer was 'not really'.

That night I drove back to Norfolk feeling positive, but somewhere between then and the next day – the last day before I signed away my amateur status – something odd happened to my body.

At first, I thought it was 'flu. I also wondered if it was exhaustion from the two thousand miles I'd driven in the previous fortnight. It could, I suppose, just have been nerves making a belated showing. Whatever the case, it was highly unusual. Performing the simplest of household tasks, I would find myself dropping things and walking into furniture. If I couldn't keep hold of my novelty 'Golf: Violating the Rules of Fashion for Three Hundred Years!' coffee mug, what hope did I have of keeping hold of my wedge during a difficult chip shot off a hanging lie?

I find that there are a surprising number of physical conditions that I can allow to get in the way of good golf, but tiredness is undoubtedly the most niggling. When I'm suffering from fatigue, I dwell morbidly from all angles on the destruction it wreaks on my swing. But in this instance I slapped myself about a bit. Did I think Retief Goosen went moaning to his peers that he needed a bit of shut-eye, after yet more golfing globetrotting?

Crikey! I was only going to Stoke-by-Nayland in Essex, not Dubai. And so what if the wind was blowing at 30-plus mph? This wasn't the Monthly Medal. That old 'sore throat' excuse wasn't going to cut it. In tomorrow's practice round, I was due to plot out the most important eighteen holes of my life. This was no competitive amateur circuit day out, where a player could take a chance and negotiate a course 'blind', with only the aid of a yardage map. I was a pro now, and pros did their homework. It was not uncommon to hear stories of the likes of Phil Mickelson arriving at a tournament venue a month before the action was set to begin, or indulging in eight-hour practice rounds in order to familiarise themselves with every contour of every green, every hidden hillock beneath every ostensibly irrelevant heather patch. I needed to weigh up my grassy adversary as Frank Lloyd Wright might have weighed up a proposed site for an architectural masterpiece. Or, at the very least, I needed to get an idea of which hole was which, in order to avoid a repeat of the time my friend Mousey and I got ourselves disqualfied for holing out on the wrong green in the 1990 Minchinhampton Junior Open.

After another night of fitful sleep, I hauled my wobbly bones out of bed, carried out my customary check of the pampas grass in my back garden in order to gauge wind strength (estimate: 38 mph), gave my clubs a quick going over with an old nailbrush, and set off on the ninety-minute drive to Essex, stopping for a warm-up – albeit one more in the tradition of Montgomerie than Singh – at a driving range in Suffolk. Having unpacked my clubs and chased my woolly hat across

Stoke-by-Nayland Golf Club car park, I then stifled the desire to drive back home, pull my bedcovers over my head and not remove them until the following morning. Instead, I headed for the pro shop. Here, a damp-haired, listless assistant pro, clearly unhappy to be distracted from his mid-afternoon Mars Bar, directed me towards the first tee. As I walked past the putting green, I scanned my surroundings in the vague hope of spotting some sign of touring pro life – a giant leaderboard, perhaps, or a passing Ian Woosnam, here to weigh up young talent, his mind already on wild-card picks for his debut as European Ryder Cup captain that autumn – but all I could see were a couple of pros in a practice net to my right, stroking one another's three-woods. At least, I assumed they were pros, since they had those fluorescent shirts and 'drenched hedgehog' hairstyles – wetter versions of the one David Beckham had in about 1999 – that all supertalented male golfers under twenty-five seem to have these days. Either that, or they were Carphone Warehouse employees who'd got lost on their way to a cycling meet.

It's not a bad golfing layout, the Constable Course at Stoke-by-Nayland, if alarmingly on the hilly side for East Anglia, and, in late March, a tad marshy underfoot. But, sadly, on practice day at the Europro Tour Qualifying School, I didn't have the pleasure of playing it. It was only when I reached the fifth green that it occurred to me that I was playing Stoke-by-Nayland's other, somewhat inferior, course, the Gainsborough. Maybe I might have realised this earlier, had I been in a less drowsy state of mind. Little signs may have alerted me to my mistake: the fact that several of the tee-markers seemed to have gone missing, the profusion of worm-casts growing out of the greens, or the regularity of the shouts of 'Fore!' emitted by the four overweight men in bobbled hats playing ahead of me.

Spotting two more pink-shirted, hedgehoggy heads on an elevated tee a couple of hundred yards away, I picked up my bag and ball and began to head in their direction. I'd walked about fifty yards towards what I now gathered was the eighth tee of the course I *should* have been playing – I still had no idea where the first tee was – when the heavens opened.

They opened in the kind of way I thought they only opened in disaster movies. What came out of them was a bit like rain but more serrated, and that in turn became something a bit like hail, but heavier (and still just as serrated). I forget at which point during this meteorological marvel it was that my bag fell off its metal stand and rolled down a mountainside, but I know that somewhere in the process of retrieving it from a puddle, peeling off my sodden new leather Titleist glove, rummaging about for its redoubtable all-weather predecessor and realising that neither it, nor any form of waterproofs, was present, it became clear that a practice round was no longer top of my list of Life Priorities. What was top of my list of Life Priorities was my car heater. As I trudged back to the clubhouse, still ignorant of the delights of the Constable Course, I felt that special kind of calmness that comes from the knowledge that nothing can possibly get any worse.

At 9.09 a.m. the following day, things got quite a lot worse.

It is well known that a professional golfer has no control over his tee time or grouping. A few years ago, Sergio Garcia made some sarcastic, harrumpty noises about Tiger Woods getting preferential treatment in this area, but an uproar soon followed, and Garcia was coerced into a public apology for daring to be so facetious.* But while the frequency with which crowd-pulling threeballs turn up at commercial, viewer-friendly times of the day in golf's four major championships can seem a tad suspicious, it's all a lottery at the lower level of the sport. As tee times went, the one of 8.38 that I'd been allocated by the Europro Tour officials seemed reasonably serviceable: not quite early enough to be stiff-limbed and unsociable, yet not late enough to be prey to the spike marks made by the shoes of the other hundred or so players in the field. Most importantly, perhaps, it would not allow me to spend half a day chewing my nails over that all-important opening shot.

The first encouraging thing I noticed, upon arriving at Stoke-by-Nayland at half past seven, was that the bad weather had passed, replaced by a light breeze and a low, hazy sun. The second was that it now looked like something approximating the venue for a proper golf tournament. Here, in the clubhouse foyer, was that leaderboard I'd been fantasising about. OK, maybe it wasn't quite as big or as colourful as the ones on TV, but I still had to catch my breath as I saw my name a few columns down, in the first row, alongside those of

* One wonders, sometimes, how the pro golf world would react if anyone said anything *genuinely* controversial, or if it would actually just have a collective embolism and cease to exist.

Michael Freake from Australia and Grant Willard from Farnham, Surrey. *One of my playing partners had come all the way from Australia to play in this?* Wow. For the first time, it hit me: there was no going back; this was it. Dazed, I announced my presence to a middle-aged man sitting at a desk in a bright red car-dealer's jacket with 'PGA' written on the back and signed in, bought two little ball tokens from the apple-cheeked blonde lady at the clubhouse reception desk, then made my way over to the practice ground. It was only when I arrived there that I realised I was clutching a small black-and-white course planner, full of scribbled lines, endless numbers and tiny esoteric symbols. I had no recollection of buying it from the man in the tournament office, nor of being charged the outrageous sum of £12 for the privilege (a full £9.50 more than the price I typically paid for the more colourful, aesthetically pleasing planners that are sold as standard in most pro shops).

The first tee shot of your first professional golf tournament is a nerve-racking experience, but I would argue that visiting the practice ground can be infinitely more so. Everyone knows you're supposed to be nervous on the first tee. If you send the ball scuttling along ahead of you in a worm-worrying manner, or curving off into a lake eighty yards from your intended target, the chances are that those witnessing the travesty will sympathise and chalk it off to nerves. But the practice ground is supposed to be the easy bit: nobody expects you to fluff a shot there, because it's the place where the pressure's off, where it's most easy to stay within your own blasé cocoon, unconcerned with exterior influences. It's been said that if every pro hit the ball the way they hit it on the range, they'd all be Tiger Woods, but that's not true. What they would really all be is golfing cyborgs, able to shape and flight the ball at will in any given situation. In other words, the range is a place where, if you mess up, you're going to be noticed.

Me? I kept my eyes to the floor and walked along the line of well-oiled swings and polo shirts and took my place as far to the right as possible, mindful of the range scene in *Tin Cup* where Kevin Costner sends a series of ninety-degree hosel shots – or shanks – whizzing past the noses of his more accomplished peers. Even if I hit my most violently left-veering shot, I wasn't going to trouble the players next to me. The right-hand side was more of a worry: I'd always been liable to the 'shank' – the most violent stroke in golf, the one where the ball is squeezed into the join between clubhead and shaft – and I've been particularly liable to it at times when the word 'shank' is skipping around my head like a dainty fork-tailed parasite. Times like now, in other words. However, I reasoned that as long as the area immediately in front of my eyes remained clear of human activity, I could avert a crisis.

I'm sure if I'd seen the small man with the jet black hair and the surprisingly ungolfy clothes approaching in good time, I would have made a deft manoeuvre around him, even further towards the trees in front of me, doing my best to mould my features into a 'Golly! I could do with some shade!' expression. As it was, he caught me off-guard, sneaking up and taking his position next to me as I was admiring one of my drives – my first really pure shot of the day – tracking a distant pylon.

I watched him set up, noting that he was the first pro I'd seen so far that morning who didn't seem to be wearing one of those big-buckled belts that said 'JL' on them. Playing for time, I began to pretend to clean some dried mud out of the grooves of my four-iron with a tee peg.*

He removed a club from his bag, and began to make a jerky, pushing motion with it. I suppose it might have looked a bit like swinging, in a certain light. Equally, though, if there had been a sooty chimney just above his right shoulder, he wouldn't have seemed out of place.

I watched, fascinated, as he proceeded to use the same action to dispatch four or five balls into the middle distance.

'Hi,' I said. 'What time are you off?'

'I'm sorry,' he said, with a French lilt. 'English, no. Erm.' He shrugged exaggeratedly and stuck out his bottom lip.

'Time. Teeing off? You?' I persevered, pointing at my wrist and thinking that maybe I should have paid a bit more attention in those secondary school French lessons – maybe even attended a few of them – but he just continued to shrug apologetically. He looked behind him and beckoned to a tall, chic-looking blonde woman in checked trousers holding a lead attached to a small, hairy dog. She made her way over, and I waited, expecting her

---

* A ridiculous activity, not just because cleaning the grooves of a club is usually intended to promote backspin and what I needed from my four-iron, at the present time, was topspin, but also because the grooves didn't actually contain any dirt.

to act as some kind of interpreter. Instead, the two of them began a conversation of their own. This went on for a couple of minutes, after which they looked at me – or maybe at my woolly hat – and smiled, then continued talking. I may have imagined it, but I thought I saw a sly grin playing around the lips of the Pomeranian, too.

When I'd looked forward to my first bit of behind-the-scenes pro golf banter, this hadn't been quite what I'd envisaged.

Now I had a dilemma. About twenty balls remained in my basket. Ideally, I would like to hit these. Also, it would appear a bit odd if I abruptly packed up and left. I didn't want my new friend and his entourage to feel that I had something against French golfers. Or hirsute dogs. Or blonde women who looked as if they'd stepped freshly out of a Chanel advert. Nonetheless, that 'shank' demon was still there.

The traditional pre-tournament warm-up routine of a pro begins with the shortest clubs in the bag – a few finesse shots with the wedges, for example – and gradually moves through the bag in order of power, before finally reaching the big-headed, long-flying metal clubs still confusingly referred to as 'woods'. But I'd been impatient, keen to move quickly onto the macho clubs, all of which have less of a curve at the join between head and shaft and are thus less easy to hit destructively to the right. Now I knew that, to feel properly prepared for my day, I really needed to test out my lob wedge and gap wedge. In other words, the two most shank-happy clubs in the bag.

As I addressed the ball and took a nervous waggle, the headlines flashed before my eyes.

THREE-TIME DORDOGNE INVITATIONAL CHAMP
  DECAPITATED!
'FORE!': SERGIO GARCIA COPYIST GOES ON
  RAMPAGE. WITNESSES SAY: 'WE COULD TELL
  HE DIDN'T BELONG HERE AS SOON AS WE SAW
  HIS PUFFY SWING.'
'I WAS ONLY DOING WHAT KEVIN COSTNER DID,'
  CLAIMS GOLFING SLAYER OF THREE!

I waggled once more. In my peripheral vision, my
neighbour took another jerky backswing. I looked at the
ball again, and had two simultaneous revelations.

1. I was a proper golf pro.
2. I was not the golf pro with the worst swing at the
   tournament.

Steadily, confidently, I swiped at the ball. I watched
as it hissed through the air, about twenty yards lower
than intended, then landed about thirty yards past the
flag at which I'd been aiming. As wedge shots went, it
was a freak of nature, a true runt of Satan. It was also
definitely, definitely not a shank. I was elated.

After that, my opening drive of the competition was
a mere trifle. Well, actually, that's not true: it was still
one of the hardest shots I've hit in my life. As drives
go, it was no oil painting – it only travelled about 220
yards and landed in some scruffy wet grass to the left
of the fairway, but it did the crucial thing, which was
get airborne. Ten minutes later, I was grazing the hole
with my attempt at a dream opening birdie three, then
tapping in for par from the kind of inconsequential

distance that Beaker from *The Muppets* wouldn't have got in a flap about.

Here's a tip. If you're ever feeling stressed whilst watching the first round of a golf tournament, and need to soak up some relaxing vibes, try standing next to the second tee. Providing, of course, that there have been no major disasters on the first hole, it is quite possibly the most mellow sporting environment in the universe. On the first hole, I and my playing partners, Grant and Michael, had been three bunched fists disguised as men, but now, having secured two pars and a birdie and passed beyond the physical and metaphorical thicket that separated the first green from the tee of the short par-four second hole, we all but let out a harmonious sigh. The three tee shots that followed – each of them gently tracking the right-to-left dogleg of the fairway – might have been hit by those cyborgs I was talking about, but only if said automatons had been smoking vast quantities of weed beforehand. If we bent down to pick up our tee pegs before we'd established the destination of our shots, it was not just the gesture of men with a piercing sun in their eyes, it was also the gesture of men with a Zen understanding that their balls would be in, or close to, the ideal part of the fairway, leaving only elementary shots to the green.

As we walked to our balls, I learned a little about Michael and Grant's backgrounds. Michael, who shared a coach with Colin Montgomerie, split his time between the UK and Australia and funded his tournament play by selling Astroturf putting greens. Grant, meanwhile, had just quit his job as an assistant pro in order to play full time, but seemed vague on the subject of funding.

They also learned a little about me – namely that the starter on the first tee had said, 'On the tee, representing England . . . Tom Cox!' not because I represented England in any official capacity, but because I didn't really represent anywhere else.

Having located my ball – a Titleist number two – in the fairway, ten yards behind those of Grant and Michael, I proceeded to flump a wedge shot fifty yards short of the green – and about five yards short of the accompanying divot – thus learning my first lesson as a pro golfer: Don't Get too Heavily Involved in a Conversation Just Before You Hit Your Shot.

My second, slightly more severe, lesson came about ten minutes later.

When the man with the silly deep voice tells you on the advert that Titleist is 'the number one ball in golf' he's not just being a man with a silly deep voice talking crap. There are other balls that crop up on the pro circuit – the odd Srixon, the occasional Nike, the lesser-spotted Maxfli – but the chances are, if you're watching three pros in action, you'll be seeing three pros playing with the same ball: either a Titleist Pro-V1 or the slightly lower-flying Titleist Pro-V1X. Back in my junior golfing days, a soft, high performance ball – which the Pro-Vs are intended to be – also meant a ball that, in the aftermath of a shot struck anything less than delectably, could very quickly take on the shape and texture of a Satsuma. It was an understatement to say that, in the intervening years, golf ball technology had come on. Despite the fact that they cost almost £4 each, I couldn't help being seduced by the Pro-Vs – their smooth enamel texture, the way they were somehow simultaneously soft and robust – and, if you ignored the time a couple of years ago when I'd won a pack of twelve Nikes in a local long-drive competition, I'd become a little bit of a purist about them.

One byproduct of the culture of everyone choosing the same ball is that it becomes all the more important to find a way of distinguishing yours from those of your playing partners.

Each Titleist is stamped with a single digit number, usually between one and four, to help with differentiation, but it is a cast-iron rule that, in addition to this, each player must mark his ball individually. Some pros will use their own stamp or, as was the case with the Titleists of Michael and Grant, clandestine squiggle. My plan had been to draw a small Cox's apple on mine, but since that would have proved time-consuming, and my shaking first-tee hands probably would have made it look more like a pear, I'd gone for the more reliable – and somewhat old-school – 'three green dot' formation in permanent marker pen: one above the Titleist logo, and one on either side of it.

The problem with permanent marker ink, of course, is that, like life, or good golf, its permanence is only an illusion. On a dew-sodden morning it can sometimes rub off as a ball makes its journey through fairway, rough and – quite possibly, in my case – shrubbery. And so it was that, as I marked my ball before putting for my par on the second hole, I noticed that it no longer had three dots on it, only two. Consumed by the task of stabbing my ten-foot par putt wide of the hole, I dismissed the matter from my mind. After all, it had happened before, plenty of times. If my Titleist shed more of its ink, then

I'd attend to the situation, but for now the important thing was that it was still distinguished from Grant's and Michael's. I didn't really think about the matter again until I reached my approach shot on the third hole, marked my ball and began to clean it.

I noted, once again, that the ball bore just two green dots.

I also now noted that these dots were in a slightly different place on the ball, about an eighth of a centimetre below where they'd originally resided.

Additionally, I noted that they were very slightly bigger than the ones I had made with my pen.

I called Grant and Michael over from the opposite side of the fairway, showed them the ball, and explained. Their faces turned grave: maybe not 'someone has died' grave, but certainly 'something has died' grave.

Is there another game with rules as multifarious and intricate as golf? It's doubtful. I find it remarkable that professional golfers' brains don't short-circuit from trying to keep all those carefully worded provisos and stipulations in there. Every so often on your golfing travels you'll meet some little bloke, possibly with a moustache and a bit of an issue about the fact that he's only five foot two, who doesn't appear to have a hell of a lot going on in the rest of his life, who'll claim to know it all; but one day, say when his ball lands in a soft drink bottle that also happens to be resting in a rabbit scrape, even his encyclopaedic disciplinary knowledge will fail him. Nobody can possibly know the correct course of action in every situation in a game played in as many different topographical habitats, with as many permutations, as golf. That said, when it comes to playing the wrong ball, most good players are pretty savvy – largely because playing the wrong ball is one of the most senseless and crushing of golfing mistakes. As Michael would generously say to me half an hour later, 'It happens to nearly all of us once, but it very rarely happens twice.'

I've never been one to hunker cackling under the duvet with a pen torch and a copy of that year's updated R&A Rules of Golf, but even I knew that playing a ball other than your own means a two-stroke penalty. But here's the real kicker: if you fail to identify and declare that alien ball on the hole where you first played it, the penalty is outright disqualification. No second serve. No 'Go back, have another go.' The end. Goodbye.

There was no doubt in my mind that the lethal switchover had happened on the second hole, not the third – I'd just been too dopey, or too neglectful, or too inexperienced, to realise it. Now, as Grant recalled that he'd seen another ball a couple of inches off the fairway on the second hole, not far from his ball and the one I'd thought was mine, it became clear that the crucial moment had occurred just before my second shot. Possibly because of nerves, possibly because I'd been yammering, I had neglected to clean my ball and check its identity before playing it, other than noting that it was a Titleist Pro-V1X, marked with a number two. But we'd hit three good shots off the tee into the sun, all of which had seemed to go straight. Then we'd arrived to find three balls in the fairway. Why would we have imagined – particularly when the adjacent holes were both a fair distance away – that any of those balls was not ours? More to the point, what were the odds – even in a Titleist-dominated world – that someone else had been playing a green-dotted Titleist with the exact same specification and number as mine, and left it in this particular fairway? And who was this wasteful, struggling pro who could afford to discard perfectly good £4 missiles in a tournament that cost £325 to enter and – if you ignored Qualifying School Stage Two – only carried a £1000 prize fund? I wanted to meet him. Maybe we could strike a deal: if he apologised nicely and kept me in Titleists for the rest of the season, I'd agree not to steal his driver and throw it into the lake next to the first tee.

There had, of course, been another option open to me when I'd noticed that I had the wrong ball: I could have kept quiet about it and played on. It is doubtful that Michael or Grant would have noticed, and I could always have changed the ball for a fresh one on the next hole. Quite a few non-golfers subsequently asked me why I didn't do this ('It wouldn't have really hurt anyone, would it?'). As cheating went, it probably seemed a fairly mild example to them – the equivalent of a slightly theatrical dive in a football match, perhaps, or keeping quiet about an incorrect line call that works to your advantage in tennis. They had clearly never heard the one about the bloke who comes into the clubhouse and announces that the bloke who sneakily kicked his ball out of the rough in last month's Saturday Medal has just been sentenced to thirty years in prison after being convicted on multiple counts of rape, GBH and arson ('He kicked his ball out of the rough?' responds the Greens Committee Chairman. 'Right! He can think again if he thinks he's playing here again in the next decade!').

Golf's indiscriminate abhorrence of all cheaters had

been ingrained in my psyche since I had taken the game up.

'You might as well praise a man for not robbing a bank,' Bobby Jones, the thirteen-time major championship winner, famously said when he was congratulated for calling a two-stroke penalty on himself in a tournament.

I wasn't quite going to go that far – unless we were talking about a small, unusually depleted bank – but had I carried on and not admitted my mistake, I would have been in for a world of self-loathing and a lot of sleepless nights.

The following six holes resembled that period where a love affair has ended but neither party is quite able to admit it. Michael, Grant and I couldn't really see how my situation could be rectified, but since this was professional golf, we needed to find a man in one of those red car-dealer's jackets driving a buggy, who needed to radio another man in a red car-dealer's jacket to make my fate official. In the meantime, I played on, somewhat desultorily and, it must be said, shockingly poorly.

'It's probably for the best,' I said to Michael. 'I haven't been feeling very well for the last few days anyway.'

'Yeah, I know what you mean. I'm stuffed with antibiotics myself.'

I watched, a moment later, as he pummelled a drive thirty yards beyond mine. How far, I wondered, did he hit it when he was healthy?

'It's a tough tour,' said Grant. 'Everyone's scrabbling for survival, it's expensive and there's hardly any prize money. But that will probably work out well for you, because it means everyone's dosh runs out later in the year. I wouldn't worry. You'll still get some invites to tournaments.'

As we reached the ninth green, a buggy pulled up, and from it emerged a Europro Tour official. He said his name was Steve Cox. I wondered if he drew little apples on his golf balls, but, from looking at his stern demeanour, decided he would deem such an activity far too frivolous. After I'd explained the exact course of events, he reiterated what the three of us already knew, and offered me a lift back to the clubhouse. I weighed up my options. On the one hand, I would have quite liked to have continued watching Grant and Michael – who were at that point standing respectively at level par and one under – serenely going about their fairway-splitting, flag-peppering business. On the other hand, there was nothing to play for, and I hadn't been in a golf buggy since 1991.

I loaded my clubs into the back. As we motored back past the first green, I replayed a dewy-eyed, dewy-fairwayed montage of my one *bona fide* completed hole as a pro: the duck-hooked drive, the scruffy wedge that clawed its way up onto the green, the almost-birdie-putt, the frankly quite dull tap-in that followed. I smiled to myself: the first hole was supposed to be the hardest, and at least I could give myself a pat on the back for completing that. As if on cue, my clubs fell off the back of the buggy.

Five minutes later, in the car – I'd avoided the clubhouse and locker room, unable to face my beloved leaderboard, with its 'DISQ' alongside my name – I thought of the four hundred or so hopeful young Euro-pros, here in Essex and at the other three Stage One

Qualifying School venues, in Bedfordshire, County Durham and Cumbria. Most of them still had two rounds to go – five, if they were lucky enough to be one of the 240 players who made it to Stage Two of qualifying, at Frilford Heath in Oxfordshire. But for me it was all over already. On the other hand, my contemporaries were on a cold golf course, battling with their minds, whereas I was in a warm car, the most pressing thing in my immediate future the question of whether I would spend an unexpectedly free half-day reading the new John Irving novel, catching up on sleep or rewatching a couple of Will Ferrell fil . . . Crapping hell! What in God's name *was* that smell?

I'd first noticed it when I was loading my clubs into the boot. In fact, now I came to think about it, maybe it had infiltrated my nostrils quite a while before that, when I'd been too busy with more pressing matters to properly take it on board. Edie had been suggesting I change my golf shoes for a few months now, but I was pretty sure it wasn't them. Not quite damp enough. It had a slightly oaky quality to it . . . yet it was sort of . . . acidic, too. You might almost have mistaken it for cat piss. I leaned around the headrest and put my nose a little closer to the canvas of my flimsy Maxfli bag – the one I had bought from Bluewater shopping centre in a half-price sale two years ago, and which I still thought of as 'brand new' – and gagged slightly.

Replaying the moments before I'd left the house this morning, I began to put two and two together. In fact, I began to put three and two together. The way Bootsy's tail looked unusually *upright* when she came into the entrance hall. The subsequent, sniffing arrival of her cretin brother,

Pablo, and finally of my oldest cat, The Bear, aka Colostomog, never a big advocate of change in any form. It was entirely possible I could be dealing with more than one brand of urine here. Maybe if I'd been equipped with a stronger sense of smell, or hadn't been so focused on my golf, I would have detected the transgression earlier, but perhaps it was for the best that I hadn't. After all, I could have taken it for a negative sign, and as everyone knows, that kind of thing can really mess up a person's round.

Three

Patch Work

To: puffyswing@tom-cox.com
From: amarilis.espinoza@guinnessworldrecords.com

Hi Tom,

Thank you for your enquiry.
I've had a look at our database and there is no such record as 'Shortest Ever Pro Golf Tournament Debut'. I've also discussed the idea with our record management team and they feel the idea is too specific and more of a unique occurrence rather than a record.

I hope this information is of your help.

Thanks,

Amarilis Espinoza

Communications Officer
Guinness World Records
184–192 Drummond Street, London, NW1 3HP

If my first performance as a pro golfer had been something of a let-down, I at least felt I had made an impact. Obviously, being known as That Bloke Whose Golf Bag Smelled of Wee or That Bloke Who Played the Wrong Ball – or, more probably, both – wasn't quite the sort of notoriety I'd envisaged the previous summer, but it was important not to be picky at this early stage. And while I'd hoped that my thirty-one minutes of legal play might have been commemorated by more than the 'D/Q' alongside my name on the Euro Pro Tour website, it wasn't my fault if the people at Guinness were a touch on the fickle side (I wasn't quite sure what made 'Shortest Ever Pro Golf Tournament Debut' any less of a record than, say, the officially recognised 'Shortest Computer Instruction Manual' category).

I had been the subject of a freak sporting occurrence. I couldn't blame myself for that, could I? OK, well maybe I could blame myself a little bit, but in the days that followed I found myself in a surprisingly positive state of mind. As Michael and Grant had told me, even as a non-qualifier I was still likely to get invited to other Europro Tour events. The hope of The Open remained, too. I would have a nervous wait to hear about all that, but I think I'd known, ever since I embarked on my golfing quest, that it was always going to be a matter of playing it slightly by ear. That was OK: I could 'do' flexible, as anyone who had watched my still somewhat undisciplined practice routines would testify. Besides, it was April – a golfing month when, even in the face of an uncertain future, it's hard not to be optimistic.

Not only is April the time when the golf season begins in earnest, it's also when The Masters, the game's most sumptuous tournament, is played, with its greener than green fairways and concordantly coloured winner's jacket. The truth is that an archetypal April in British golf is a time of winter greens, muddy tees and hip flasks. But it takes only one look at Augusta National, where the US Masters is played – one snatch of its ever-present birdsong, one glimpse of its blooming azaleas or its legendary water hazard, Rae's Creek – to give the most pessimistic, soggy golfer the deep-seated conviction that summer is here, and from now on everything is going to be OK. Even in my lost golfing years, the tournament had still excited me. My *Best Shots of the Masters* video had been one of the few survivors of my Great Golf Video Purge of 1996, and ten years on, as I fished it out of a box of other arcane golfing paraphernalia* in my loft, I gave silent thanks to my former self for his foresight.

At the time of writing, it is not possible to buy a new copy of *Best Shots of the Masters* on the Internet, but you can get a used one on amazon.co.uk for £1.23. It is, all told, not the most sought-after golf video of all time, and I for one am not holding my breath for the lavishly packaged DVD reissue. Released in 1988 – the year I was first seduced by The Masters – and presented by the veteran golf pundit Renton Laidlaw, who could ooze more respect for Augusta only if he got down on his hands and knees and began to slurp gently from Rae's Creek, it is peppered with such 'Did-he-really-say-that?' type statements as: 'It was in 1983 that the club first allowed the professional players in The Masters to use

---

* What exactly is a 'swing incubator'?

their own tour caddies [cue shot of former Masters champion George Archer's wife, Elizabeth, in a white boiler suit], even if, *ahem*, she happened to be a *woman.*' In fact, let's not beat around the bush here: it's appalling. Fawning, muzaky, creakingly edited. My own copy is even worse, in that it's so worn that it now features coverage of a rarely reported snowstorm that interrupted Seve Ballesteros's victory in 1983.

My illogical love of *Best Shots of* . . . sums up the relationship that I, and countless other golfers who grew up watching the tournament in the eighties and nineties, have with The Masters. Most of us know Augusta is intrinsically a pretty despicable place: a club full of self-important George Bush supporters with outdated, unswerving notions of manners and decorum; an enclave so closed-minded it didn't agree to admit its first black member until 1990, and still outlaws women. Nonetheless, starved from a winter of golfing frustration, we allow ourselves to be seduced. We permit ourselves to imagine driving up Magnolia Lane to the bright white clubhouse, then taking a juicy, blasphemous divot out of the sixteenth tee and watching as our seven-iron shot takes the right-to-left slope of the marble green and drops into the hole, just like Tiger Woods' miracle chip did the year he almost lost to Chris 'fascinating' Di Marco. Never once do we question the wisdom of expending all this energy fantasising about a tournament whose ultimate prize is an item of clothing so irredeemably naff that our grandparents wouldn't have looked twice at it had it been on the '60% off!' rack at Littlewoods in 1986.

A few months previously I'd been comparing notes

on Masters madness with James Day and David Ford, from the hi-tech Urban Golf facility in London, and the golf writer Dan Davies. The four of us had grown up in vastly different parts of the country and our birth dates spanned almost a decade, yet our adolescent memories of the fervour surrounding Masters week were almost identical. We remembered those Saturday afternoons after the televised highlights of the first two rounds had been shown on *Grandstand*, and how, unleashed onto our home courses with these pictures still fresh in our heads, we would hit more stylish, spectacular shots than we'd believed possible. Did we feel any different now, as adults? No. Our Masters adrenalin was still there. It was just that we no longer had a proper outlet for it.

With this in mind, the four of us came up with a plan. What, we wondered, if we inaugurated our own tournament, that tried to recapture the lawless enthusiasm and instinctive creativity of those junior golfing days? What if we held it on the Saturday of The Masters? What if it combined all the short-game-orientated magic of Augusta with none of its elitism? Shortly afterwards, the Cabbage Patch Masters was born.

The inaugural Cabbage Patch Masters arrived at a perfect time for me. Not only would it fill a gap in my pro schedule, while I was waiting to find out whether I'd get admitted to the British Open qualifiers and further Europro Tour events, it also promised a relatively pressure-free environment in which I could give my ailing chipping and pitching a much-needed MoT. It was to be held at Biddenden, a pitch-and-putt course deep in the Kent countryside that had played host to the 2005 British Pitch-and-Putt Championship, and it marked an amalgamation of the Society of Secret Golfers, which I had founded the previous year with James, and the Cabbage Patch Open, the cult, anarchic pitch-and-putt event that Dan and David had been holding on a rough patch of ground in Devon since the turn of the decade.

Maybe it was something to do with watching those guffawing gaggles of men who'd turned up at my home clubs in the past, reserving the tee under some dull-yet-exotic corporate banner, loudly monopolising the course and seeming to have so much more fun than mere club golfers, but I'd always wanted to be a member of a golf society. Since it seemed unlikely that I was ever going to work for a major exporter of chemicals or sell photocopier toner for a living, starting my own society had seemed the easiest way to solve the problem. There was nothing all that clandestine about the Society of Secret Golfers, really. The name simply came from my conviction that there was an ever-growing group of people out there like James and me: people who didn't quite fit the archetypal image of a golfer, who didn't give a hoot whether golf was credible or not, who loved the game, who even loved many of its traditions, but still felt alienated by its perverted dress codes and cliquey customs.

To date, the SSG had been a rather hit-and-miss, ramshackle endeavour. We'd only managed to hold one event, at Stoke Park in Buckinghamshire (best known as the venue for James Bond's golf scene in *Goldfinger*), at which 30 per cent of the competitors had played the front nine without being informed of the day's scoring format, and whose official shirts had shrunk in the wash.

During the SSG launch, the chasm between the characters of its creators had quickly become obvious. As I worried whether people had the right directions to the club, forgot where I'd stored the prizes, lost my clubs and got my ball stolen by a fellow competitor's dog, James played the solid esplanade to my flapping organisational seagull. Over the ensuing months, our relationship continued in a similar fashion. When he was just twenty-three, James had founded his own underground golf centre: a state-of-the-art, subterranean clubhouse, where it was possible to play three dozen of the world's top courses without the hassle of going to America, walking several miles with a bag on your back, or hacking about under trees looking for your ball. In the sport of Urban Golf, a player swatted his or her ball – and, oddly for a golfing environment, there usually *were* plenty of hers here – off delectable Astroturf into a soft screen, then watched as it became computerised and soared away on a frighteningly authentic virtual vista. If he or she was feeling really extravagant, they might order a Budweiser, and perhaps some olives to munch on as they watched their playing partners smack the ball over the cliff edge on the eighteenth at Pebble Beach.

James might have had a similar, disorderly golfing upbringing to me, and have felt ashamed about confessing his love of the game to his schoolmates, but at almost six years my junior he was a product of a different age: the age that I had popped out for a cup of tea and missed, which also happened to be the age when, technically and socially, golf had gone through its most dramatic changes ever. I'd imagined that, with the knowledge of shaft flexes and ball compressions that I retained from long-gone afternoons in the back of the pro shop of Cripsley Edge, coupled with the odd phrase like 'over the cellophane bridge',* I could get by as a jargon-speaker in the Brave New Golf World. However, an hour spent with James in front of one of Urban Golf's infra-red ball scanners soon gave me my doubts. These doubts became even more extreme in February, when the two of us travelled to Birmingham for my official club-fitting at the Taylor Made Matt headquarters – a sort of robot's version of a clothes shop changing room, only with clubs, not garments – and James got into a technological conversation with my fitter, Anthony.

Since my golfing rebirth I'd plodded along with an armoury consisting of a mid-nineties Callaway driver, a 1970s persimmon Hogan three-wood that I'd had 'on loan' from my mate Ollie since February 1992, a 1980s Ping Anser putter, of the kind once favoured by Seve Ballesteros, and the Ping irons I'd purchased, in the first flush of my reunion with golf, without regard to loft, lie or shaft, from the Piccadilly Circus branch of Lillywhites. I'd been a bit bashful about showing these to James, who from what I could work out had already updated his clubs four times since the beginning of the year. Upon first inspecting my weaponry, he had made a couple of clucking noises in the back of his throat, of the sort you might hear from a mechanic at an Aston Martin dealership if you asked him to service your rusting Morris Marina. These days, he argued, a good golfer

---

* Used to acknowledge a putt that miraculously goes straight over the hole without dropping. Or, in the case of my former playing partner, Ernie 'The Luck's Not With Me Today' Wilton, a putt that misses the hole by seven feet, never remotely looking as if it might drop.

would rather hit a ball around his local municipal dirt track with a walking stick than use a set of clubs that hadn't been custom-fitted to his exact height, weight, stance and swing path. That sounded fair enough, but I hadn't realised being 'custom-fitted' would mean wearing knee and shoulder pads and a helmet, and having numerous little pins stuck to my body.

It was bewildering enough having to stand with my arms spread like the old *World in Action* logo as a computer learned intimate information about my physical make-up. It was more bewildering still to watch as the computer at Taylor Made took this information, then used it to create a sphere-heavy parody of my swing and body, and compared it with that of Ian Poulter (it turned out my computer man had a swing speed 6 mph slower than Ian's, but his computer man seemed to have much more hideous trousers). Most baffling, though, was the discussion taking place a few feet to my rear as all this was going on.

'What system is that you use? Zonar?'

'No, we're just on basic infra-red.'

'What about those 560s, though?'

'I know, well cool, aren't they? I've heard Nike might be incorporating them.'

'What's the torque like on these? The ones to the right.'

'Which? Blue dot or red dash?'

'Blue dot. Squiggle, though, not bracket.'

'Pretty good. I prefer the previous model. But maybe that's because I'm a bit lateral from the top.'

By accompanying me to Birmingham, James wasn't just playing the role of a technologically savvy friend, he was also acting in a (sort of) official capacity. The previous summer, when I'd announced my intention to turn pro, he'd offered, somewhat surprisingly, to act as my manager. 'I'm thinking of getting a stable of up-and-coming players together,' he'd explained, as if already picturing his first ultra-thick £20 cigar. Immediately, I'd questioned the wisdom of this move. Did he not have enough on his plate with one branch of London's most popular indoor golf franchise to run, and another, in east London, due to open in the summer? Did it not raise any alarm bells that, in all our games on the simulators at Urban Golf, I'd beaten him just once, and even then, only at Pebble Beach, my lucky course, when he'd had a hangover and I'd snuck in a cheeky practice round beforehand? Surely he realised the lack of potential financial benefits here? But he was adamant, and, I had to admit, I was flattered. James was, after all, a PGA-qualified pro himself, who'd flirted with the tournament circuit and grown up with Luke Donald, Britain's best young player. If neither of us was sure what exactly his role as my manager would entail, he could at least pass on his insights into the competitive mindset. Failing that, he could tell me some interesting anecdotes about Donald pretending to listen to his iPod on the practice ground to keep people from disturbing his concentration, or the nasty side of Phil Mickelson.

I asked James what he thought had been the difference between him and Luke. Both had been good junior golfers on the Home Counties scene, both had gone on to turn pro. But now one owned four houses, spent half the year in America, and was being touted as the European golfer most likely to break his major championship duck, while the other spent much of his time playing pretend versions of Spyglass Hill and St Andrews with people who thought it was perfectly OK to buy their clubs from Lillywhites.

'Luke was always one of those people who was great at everything he tried,' said James. 'I have a video from primary school where he's singing hymns, and he has the most perfect choirboy voice. You can see how amazed everyone in the room was. He's got the perfect level kind of temperament, he's never had a bad patch, and he doesn't let anything worry him. But I think in the end it's about commitment. Maybe I just didn't want it enough.'

I pondered this for a while. I also thought about a story James had told me, in which he and a bunch of friends had posed to one another the question, 'If you were forced to make a choice between sex and golf, which would you give up?' and James – a man not without carnality – had answered, without hesitation, 'Sex!' In what earthly way, I wondered, could you be more committed than that?

One of the refreshing things about the Cabbage Patch Masters was its unlikely inclusivity. Pros and amateurs crossed paths and joined teams in pre-tournament pro-ams, but they rarely competed in singles formats for the same prizes, and particularly not in pitch-and-putt events. Here, three pros – one of whom, I had to keep reminding myself, was me – would battle it out, every man for himself, with a field of seventy players from 'the other side of the fence'. The flaw in this idea was that some of the handicaps were of a less than official nature – 'I think I'm about a thirty-two,' I heard one competitor announce, immediately before slam-dunking a forty-foot practice putt, using a hockey grip – but in the end, playing in what was quickly becoming known as 'The Real Masters' wasn't about the winning. In fact, it wasn't even really about the taking part. What it was about – as became evident from the moment the participants stepped off the coach and made their way over to the canopy and DJ booth that had been set up beside the first tee – was drinking vast quantities of alcohol, shouting a lot, and messing about in a way you hadn't done on a golf course since you were fourteen. If, in the process, you won one of the shirts or hats that had been donated by several of golf's numerous new streetwise fashion labels, great. And if, when you got it home and tried it on, you decided you felt a little bit too much like something used to alert people to a traffic hazard, that was great too. You could always sell it on eBay.

Having tested out my event-organising skills at Stoke Park and found them wanting, I'd suggested that other members of the SSG committee take the helm at the Cabbage Patch, with me in a 'back-room' role as Official Champagne Pourer. This seemed a satisfactory solution for all concerned, since it meant competitors would be well lubricated, yet properly informed of the scoring format and directed to their correct starting tees. It also meant I would get time to scope out the course before my round. After being coerced into a game of football on the eighteenth green with the greenkeeper's nine-year-old son, I sneakily threw a couple of Titleists onto the putting surface in order to test its condition. On the stimpmeter, the device used in golf to measure the speed of greens, a top-quality fast green usually runs at 9 or 10, a slow one around 7. During Masters week, Augusta's routinely read at around 12 or 13. Biddenden's, from what I could work out, were more in the region of 4, but I could see that, on the hard-baked patches at their edges, where the daisies weren't so much in bloom, they could probably get up to at least 6½. I knew James and I weren't too anxious about our professional status being undermined by a course where 'in-built irrigation system' probably meant 'really big garden hose', but I was a little concerned about Andrew Seibert, the other pro on the start sheet, who was over here on injury-provoked sabbatical from the Hooters Tour (a more lucrative American equivalent of the Europro Tour). Andrew, a fellow pupil of Steve Gould whom I'd first met at Knightsbridge Golf School the previous summer, had come all the way from Florida to play in the event. Anyone who played his most serious golf on a tour with the word 'hooters' in the title would need to be in possession of a sense of humour, but I didn't want him to be too disappointed in a tournament that billed itself as a rival to the most prestigious in the sport. As he walked over to greet me, he already looked slightly pale, although that may have had something to do with the purple plus fours being sported by the man to his right.

'How's the pro life treating you?' he asked as we shook hands and moved away from the DJ booth and the deafening sound of Primal Scream's 'Movin' on Up'.

I gave him a brief summary of my season's curtain-raiser, leaving out the cat wee.

'Ah, that's tough, dude,' he said. 'I remember my first year on the Hooters Tour. I was *not* used to the lifestyle.

I probably averaged eighty shots per round for the whole season. I even ended up crying one night when I missed the cut. My mom wanted me to quit. I got my game back, but it took a while. It's a hard life out there.'

Like virtually every tournament pro I'd spoken to, Andrew tended not to refer to being on Tour as 'being on Tour' or 'playing in pro events': he called it 'being out there'. The phrase brought to mind some vast, untameable landscape, where one might have to kill for one's lunch.

I mentioned that I'd been surprised, in my brief flirtation with the pressure environment of tournament play, at just how sombre the atmosphere was.

'It's a lot tougher out there than you think,' he said. 'Too many people seem to think it's a lifestyle, but it's a job. The fact is, most guys out there have to be pretty self-centred to get to the top. Have you heard of Charles Howell?'

'Of course.' Despite his possessing a frame that looks as if it could easily topple over in light winds, Howell's drives go further than some of my more outlandish day trips. He had been one of my favourite players on the PGA Tour for a few years, but at this point hadn't quite lived up to the early hype.

'Well, Charles is kind of a geek, and a really nice guy, and I think he was shocked when he got out there and people didn't talk more. They were all kind of doing their own thing. You can have a social life out there, but not much of one. Nick Dougherty is a good example. He loved the Tour life, enjoyed the parties, and he started to lose his game. But after a few years he got it together. You have to realise how physically demanding being a pro is. It takes sacrifices. Remember, Tiger Woods missed out on a childhood to be where he is.'

I picked up my wedge and began to loosen up.

'So. Let's see it, then. The Cox action.'

Andrew and I had talked frequently over the past year, and our dialogue might, to an outsider, have sounded like that of two hardened Tour survivors. We'd reported our eagles to one another, we'd warned each other not to think too much about our games. He'd told me of two caddies he'd seen fighting in a Nationwide Tour[*] event, when one wouldn't look for the other's player's ball, and of the girl who wanted to marry him, whom he'd left because golf was more important. I, meanwhile, told him of my three-birdie finish in the Thetford Golf Club Scratch Cup. However, none of this disguised the one yawning cavity in our relationship: neither of us had ever seen the other hit a shot. As I stood over the ball and began to move, something happened that I was beginning to get used to in pressure situations: I stopped thinking of my swing as a swish or a carefree swat, and instead began to perceive it as a never-ending arc of infinitely complex movements involving countless tiny bones and muscles, an impossible piece of timing and co-ordination. Nonetheless, the ball took off fairly impressively, landing somewhere near its target, a hundred yards away.

'It's quite a retro ball flight you've got there,' said Andrew. He said it was 'kinda loopy' but added that I shouldn't feel bad, since a lot of Europro Tour players

---

[*] The Hooters Tour's similarly sized rival tour – presumably for the more serious-minded struggling pro.

find it quite hard to control their trajectories in the wind. 'Watch this.'

With a short, lazy punch of a swing, he flicked a ball in the same direction. The shots ended up in the same place, but that was all they really had in common. It was like comparing a stone dispatched by a quarter-extended catapult to one that had been thrown, somewhat shakily, underarm. It was also another moment where the enormity of what I was trying to do came into sharp focus. I was thirty years old, and happy simply to strike a wedge shot out of the middle of the clubface and get it somewhere near the flag. Andrew was twenty-six, and had been beyond that for years. Yet, in the half-decade he'd spent on America's more minor circuits, he'd had relatively little success – one eleventh-place finish and a round of 64 in a charity event.

If he thought my ball flight was a bit dodgy, I feared the worst about his views on today's venue. But I asked him for them anyway.

'It looks very nice. Sort of cute. It's not normal golf, but it's nice to just focus on the short game sometimes. There's too much emphasis on macho power in the modern game.'

It was true: Biddenden, in its modestly manicured way, was sort of cute. The last time I had played pitch-and-putt had been almost two decades ago. I had played it not out of choice, but because I had not been powerful enough, or well-off enough, to play any other form of golf. As soon as I'd been admitted into a proper golf club, though, I'd dropped it. Getting out onto a full-length course had felt like getting the stabilisers off my first bike. And who ever bothers putting stabilisers back on? But now I wondered if this abandonment had been an act of heartless networking, the cruel abandoning of a supportive, humble friend. As I negotiated Biddenden's opening nine, I began to remember the feelings accompanying my nascent rounds at Bramcote Hills, a par-three course three or four miles outside Nottingham. Sure, hitting one of those bright orange balls they'd sold at the shop had been a bit like hitting an onion, and some of the holes had had very silly names,* but hadn't Bramcote been the place where I'd first hit upon golf's enduring mystery? Not the mystery of blasting the ball as far as humanly possible, but the mystery of contours and hollows and the angles of a clubface. I often claimed that I wasn't interested in the short game these days, but perhaps that was because, much of the time, I was not in an environment where I *had* to be interested in it. At Biddenden, a course where the longest hole was barely over a hundred yards, and there was no opportunity for show-off drives, you couldn't really do anything but get interested in chipping and putting. As a result, my chipping and putting quickly improved.

By the time I reached the sixteenth it was obvious, both from the profusion of high handicappers and the ever-rising cheers ringing out from elsewhere around the course, that I was out of the race for the title. Nonetheless, I was enjoying myself more than I had on a golf course at any time in recent memory. This was partly because of the sequence of delectable wedge shots

* It would be interesting to find out exactly how many pitch-and-putt holes in Britain played between two hills are called 'Dolly Parton' – I'd be willing to bet the number is in triple figures.

I'd hit over the last few holes, and the vicarious thrill that came from watching one of my partners surge to the top of the leaderboard (or, rather, the champagne-stained paperboard).

In the Cabbage Patch Masters, there was no 'draw' as such. Competitors played, by and large, with the people they were most suited to play with. On the official entry form, I'd been asked to submit details pertaining to my golfing life, including my favourite pro (Fred Couples), my career highlight (sixteenth tee, Nottinghamshire Boys' County Championship, 1990: three pars needed to go into play-off with Lee Westwood), my career lowlight (eighteenth tee, Nottinghamshire Boys' County Championship, 1990: birdie needed to come fifth, four strokes behind Lee Westwood) and my on-course motto ('Don't Piss Down My Back and Tell Me it's Raining'). This data had been assessed and, as a result, I'd been put together with my Richmond friends, Scott and Simon, and a man called Ricky who kept pretending to ride his putter as if it was a horse.

One of the many enduring joys of playing with Simon and Scott is witnessing their ever-more creative line in swearing, as their rounds falter. In Scott's case, in particular, my respectful desire to see a mild-mannered friend play well is all too often countermanded by my desire to be entertained by a tragicomic drama of profane brilliance. Watching as he gets himself into another fine mess in a bunker was, I feel, a little like witnessing my own private episode of Laurel and Hardy, with Scott as a much skinnier, curly-haired Hardy, and his sand-iron as Laurel. A few weeks ago, before the tournament, I'd seen him worry terribly after breaking a cafetière in my kitchen, and with this in mind I'd been slightly concerned about the effect the tricky back nine at the Masters might have on his nerves. Today, however, he had brought with him what an American commentary team might have called his A-game. After holing a spectacular bunker shot for birdie on the seventeenth and securing his par on the eighteenth, it was clear that, at four under par, he was somewhere close to the lead, if not in it. A tense wait followed, with Scott, Ricky, Simon and me nursing bottles of Budweiser while the scores were totted up. As, in a voice evocative of a self-deprecating Scottish woodland animal, Scott repeated the phrase, 'I won't have won, you know,' you would have had to have been made out of reinforced steel not to share his excitement.

Sadly, he was right to be pessimistic. I have no idea what caused twelve players to end up on four under par in the Cabbage Patch Masters. Drunkenness? Cheating? Laziness? A practical joke? Whatever the case, at three beers past my best, and not particularly relishing the prospect of bringing my iffy maths skills out of hibernation in such a raucous environment, I wasn't going to be the one to stand up and demand a recount. My heart, however, went out to Scott.

Everyone loves a play-off in golf.* On the whole, 'play-off' – whether the five-hole kind employed to decide The Open, or the more universal sudden-death version – means the most extreme, nerve-biting thrills available to a sport fan. It means a pumped-up Greg Norman

---

* The possible exception being the eighteen-hole kind used to decide the US Open, which always seems blighted by the special kind of downbeat atmosphere only otherwise experienced after a social gaffe at an inter-village bowls match.

throwing away the 1989 Open by driving into a bunker he didn't think he could reach. It means 'We apologise to viewers expecting to see the director's cut of *Amélie*, but due to extended coverage of the golf, the film has been cancelled, and will be shown at a later date.' It means Peter Alliss almost losing it and, for the 368th time in his commentary career, talking about the prospect of 'a cavalry charge down the first extra hole'.

Of course, you never see anything that *genuinely* resembles a cavalry charge in televised golf. That would be far too undignified. In the more crowded play-offs – the 2002 Open's, for example, featuring Steve Elkington, Ernie Els, Thomas Levet and Stuart Appleby – the players tend to be split into two separate groups. There was no such faffing around at the Cabbage Patch Masters.

If you haven't seen twelve inebriated men playing a golf hole at the same time, let me tell you, it's a fearsome sight – the kind of thing that, if caught on tape and mailed surreptitiously to the R&A, could give the coronary ward of St Andrews Hospital a busy night. Here, striking out in unison, in dangerously close proximity to one another, was every swing in the book (but not, almost certainly, in the textbook). Long swings, stubby swings, exuberant swings, fearful swings, swings that looked as if they were digging for rare coins. Peering through the swaying, jeering crowd in the failing light, it was often hard to spot Scott's signature action – an action that always seems to say, 'There is an invisible precipice six inches ahead of me, and if I follow through properly, I may tumble into the deathly, nettle-speckled chasm beyond it' – but it was apparent, as others fell by the wayside, that he was hanging in there. By the time the skirmish reached the fifth play-off hole, I'd offered my caddying services – I'm sure Scott didn't need any help carrying the three clubs he'd brought out with him, but I felt I could at least offer a calming word or two and some advice on Biddenden's trickier putts – and it had become a two-horse race. The coveted first prize (I made a note to myself: find out what the first prize was) could only go either to Scott, or to a Leeds United supporter called David with a rowdy fanbase and a swing that was beginning to show its mechanical shortcomings. With both players having executed their second shots, and Scott on the green and David ten yards left of it, the signs were good. The pressure doubled for my man, however, after David chipped to within two inches of the flag. Scott hit a poor first putt, and was faced with a three-footer which he needed to hole to keep the tournament alive.

When reading the contours of a green, it's important to get down as close to the putting surface as possible. Normally, this dictates a squatting position, since to flatten one's body against the green is considered uncouth. But this was an exceptional situation. As Scott took a couple of tentative practice strokes, I pressed my stomach to the grass and eyed every nuance of the slope.

'Get the fuck up off the grass, Coxy, you hairy twat,' shouted one of the crowd.

I turned to Scott. 'Left lip. Firm,' I said.

I walked away and rejoined Simon at the side of the green. Twenty yards away I spotted Andrew Seibert, who like the other two pros in the field had taken a back seat in the day's action. I tried to acknowledge him, but he was too wrapped up in the moment – all Hooters-related thoughts momentarily forgotten.

Scott crouched over the ball, took one practice stroke, then set it on its way. It started left, and stayed left, blowing a kiss at the hole on its journey past. As a dozen Leeds supporters charged onto the green and held their man aloft, Simon and I watched as ours turned to the heavens with a familiar expression. It was the same expression we'd seen not long ago, hovering above my deceased cafetière. The kind of expression that a million middle-aged mums would want to take home and bake something for.

Afterwards, we returned to 'the tented village' (i.e. the canopy covering the DJ booth and the area stretching four or five feet beyond it), where I was immediately accosted by Jim, a friend of a friend, and one of the more boisterous members of the crowd. When I'd first met him three years ago he'd been a bit dismissive about golf, but now, he told me, he was blowing £100 a week on proper lessons and it was his new favourite sport. 'All my footie mates are playing it,' he'd told me earlier.

'But what about you?' he asked. 'I thought you were supposed to be good. Shouldn't you have won this thing easily?'

'Well,' I said, 'it's not that simple when people have high handicaps and you're p . . .'

'Sounds like a crap excuse to me!' he interrupted. A bit of drool had escaped from his mouth, and was working its way down his chin. Within a matter of seconds, it would land on one of his old school Adidas trainers. 'What did you score?'

'I think I was seven over par altogether.'

'That's bloody shit, innit!'

Before I could answer, he turned and lurched in the

direction of the barbecue, where there were some more interesting people to talk to – many of whom were beginning a singalong of the popular football-themed hit, 'Here We Go'.

By this point in my golfing life, I was accustomed to having vaguely unpleasant experiences in the aftermath of a disappointing round. Over the years I'd been told to tuck my shirt in, informed that my 'training footwear' (i.e. a pair of undramatic brown leather Velcro-strapped shoes from the Next sale) was not welcome in the Men Only Bar; I'd even had a man take me aside for 'a quiet word' and tell me that the Handicap Chairman at my old club believed the 'disgusting' golf book I had written about my misspent adolescence 'shouldn't have been allowed' – but never once had I been told that the round I had just played had been 'bloody shit'.

That's the thing about golf, at its most conventional level: it might dress like a complete tool and possess the political and social outlook of a 1982 *Daily Express* headline, but it always respects a man's sporting dignity. Maybe today I was seeing the new face of the game: not so picky when it came to dress codes and staying quiet while the other bloke took his address, but a real, boorish stickler when it came to *competing like a man*.

Did I like it? I thought so, but I wasn't completely sure. What I did know was that the SSG was sliding away from my initial vision of a quiet get-together with an emphasis on sexual equality,* lawless attire and

---

* Despite several beseeching emails and phone calls, and a plea in the *Independent* newspaper, the Cabbage Patch Masters included only two female competitors.

competitive high jinks. But then, perhaps I'd felt that from the moment I'd founded it. Every anti-establishment golfer had their own ideas about what constitutes a satisfactory break from the staid golfing norm and, as a median of those ideas, the first alternative Masters could be judged a success.

As Renton Laidlaw says in *The Best Shots of the Masters*, 'From small beginnings, great things are born.' It's a fairly vacuous statement, when you think about it – from small beginnings a lot of completely inane small things are born too. On a brighter note, though, you have to ask yourself just how many of those small, inane things allow you to play golf with your shirt untucked, shout a lot, and change your shoes in the course car park without fear of getting a bollocking.

Four

Wind of Change

'It's not how, it's how many,' is one of golf's most commonly used phrases. The point being that you can play sophisticated three-A-level golf from tee to green, make it look as fetching as possible, but what ultimately counts is the score, and nothing else. An ugly birdie is still, in the end, a birdie.

My feelings on this issue have always been: fair point, but as a sportsman, does one not have at least some duty to crowd-please? As long as I've loved golf, I've always loved the players who take a stadium-rock attitude out onto the course. The sporting accountants who grind out their scores with dollar signs for eyes – the Bernhard Langers, the Nick Faldos, the Padraig Harringtons,* the Tom Kites – have always held negligible interest for me. I'm not all that fussed about the plodding classicists either: the Luke Donalds, the Jack Nicklauses, the Jeff Maggerts. What I want out of my pro golfers are very specific requirements:

* Not only is Harrington an accountant-like player, he actually trained as one, not long before turning pro and joining the European Tour.

1. The ability to play miraculous escape shots (yet not in a way that could fall under the unattractive heading 'Scrambling').
2. A classic swing (but one that works in a natural, flowing way, rather than a join-the-dots way).
3. The capacity to hit the ball vast distances and to be always close to, if not at, the top of the driving stats (but always with an ultimate sense of having more firepower in reserve).
4. The power to make vast numbers of birdies and eagles in a row (but without ever looking as if putting could be described as one of your strong points).
5. A constant, lingering feeling of unfulfilled promise (but with the odd, heroic, against-all-odds victory thrown in).

Am I asking too much? Maybe. Does all this make me the golfing equivalent of an aesthetic fascist? Perhaps. It also makes for frequent heartbreak as an armchair golf fan, and probably goes some way to explaining why my favourite five golfers ever – Angel Cabrera, Eduardo Romero, Fred Couples, John Daly and Sergio Garcia – have amassed, at the time of writing, the piddling total of four major championships between them.

So, now *I* was a pro, was I really expecting the same swashbuckling standards of myself? Well, sort of. In all my dreams about playing professional golf, I'd always been less interested in the victories and the scores I would shoot to secure them, and more interested in the artful shots I would perform along the way. Since my life as a pro so far only amounted to two and a half holes of tournament play and an eighteen-hole pitch-and-putt tournament, it was probably too early for an attitude autopsy, but I had already noticed a significant difference in my approach to that of the pros I had met – something about it that was a little less . . . mathematical. I had imagined that 'It's not how, it's how many' was something I would leave behind upon leaving amateur golf, along with rants about extended tee times on Ladies' Day and snide comments about my untucked shirt. It was an ugly, mustn't-grumble kind of phrase that I associated mainly with Roy-ish types who liked to kid themselves that their manifold golfing failings – e.g. inability to hit the ball more than 198 yards, propensity to swing their sand wedge as if involved in major garden-clearing project – did not matter in the grand scheme of things. But, slightly surprisingly, pros said it too.

In the professional golf world, though, the INHIHM mantra takes on a much more serious meaning. Here, in a kill-or-go-broke environment, one could not afford to put style first. The priority was doing whatever it took to get the ball in the hole in as few strokes as possible. Pros were *very* interested in 'how many'. I, on the other hand, remained a great advocate of 'how'. When I'd come away from the Cabbage Patch Masters, what stuck with me and pleased me was not the birdie I'd made on the twelfth hole (reasonably struck wedge to fifteen feet, pretty good putt) but the sumptuously struck tee shot on the following hole: the one that felt like liquid velvet and flew the green by twenty yards. Similarly, if I hadn't quite revelled in my drive so much on the second hole at Stoke-by-Nayland, maybe I would have been able to get on with the more important business that followed: hitting the green, two-putting for a bread-and-butter par,

86

playing the right ball . . . that kind of thing. Even in the better practice rounds I'd played at Diss, my memory of my scores had quickly drifted away (a 71 here, a 74 there, or was it a 73?) as I'd stewed happily in the shots that had felt nicest. I rarely worried that these shots were often the ones that had left me in the most difficult predicament.

When I related all this to James, he shook his head even more gravely than he had done the first time I'd showed him my twenty-five-year-old Ping putter with the bent shaft. He explained that in order properly to survive on Tour, I needed to put all this out of my head.

'What you have to realise,' he explained, 'is that, in pro golf, nobody is really interested in the details of your round, how many birdies you made or what massive drives you hit. All they want to know is whether or not you've beaten them. You need to be the man who can walk into the clubhouse and be able to answer the question "What did you shoot?" with the words "Sixty" and "eight". Nothing more. That's it.'

There was no doubting James's wisdom, but he was, after all, only twenty-five. Additionally, I knew that if he was being totally honest, he wasn't averse to a few 'It's not how many, it's how' moments himself. What I felt I needed was a bit of time with one of the steady men of pro golf: someone who had seen it all, someone who wasn't going to let wedge shots that felt like liquid velvet and went twenty yards over the green distract him from the important business of plotting his way calmly around the course. Someone a bit like Ken Brown.

I had never met Ken, but a friend of a golf friend knew him, suggested that he might be amenable to giving me a pep talk about pro life, and gave me his number. A couple of weeks after playing in the Cabbage Patch Masters, I built up the courage to give him a call, and he cheerfully invited me down to his home club, in Harpenden, Hertfordshire. To say this was an unexpected boon would be an understatement: not every Europro Tour rookie in his early thirties got the chance to get free advice from a five-time Ryder Cup player. With the exception of Fred Couples, I couldn't think of anyone whose easy-going golfing demeanour I would want rubbing off on me more than Ken's. Always the most patient of players, he had quit tournament golf when he was only thirty-four, owing to a wrist injury and 'pushing myself incredibly hard for fifteen years before losing the desire'. Before that, he'd been one of the most astute golfing strategists of the seventies and eighties, a willowy swinger – 'Without,' he said, 'a lot of weight behind the punches' – who made up for the weaknesses in his long game with Zen concentration skills and a demon touch around the greens. The good points about his game, in other words, probably doubled as an easy-to-use guide to the bad points about mine.

When I suggested to Ken that some players must go out there with the intention of thrilling the crowd first and thinking about the score later, he shook his head and looked at me as if I'd just told him that I enjoyed composing action paintings in the middle of the eighteenth green.

'Nobody goes out there with a mission to entertain,' he said.

I searched my brain, sure I could think of at least one player who was the exception to the rule: to be specific, one gambling, long-hitting, guitar-playing, chain-smoking, cheeseburger-gobbling player.

'Not even Long John Daly?' I asked.

'Not even Long John Daly,' Ken said.

It seemed far-fetched, but I had to take his word for it. He tends to be right about most things, after all. In his role as BBC golf's resident trivia nerd, Ken is always being asked questions like 'Who got defecated on by a pigeon in the 1986 World Matchplay?' and 'What is the name of Darren Clarke's thirteenth-favourite sports car?' by his colleagues, and is alarmingly quick at coming up with the answers.*

Perhaps it is the combination of little Britain (the concept, not the TV comedy) ambience, spongy grass verges, perfectly maintained windowboxes and abundant 4x4s, but Harpenden is the kind of place that would seem downright odd without a golf course – a bit like an old-fashioned stockbroker who'd lost his bowler hat. In fact it has three courses, all within an easy three-wood of one another – as I found out, to my cost, on my way to meet Ken.

Harpenden Golf Club was like a lot of exclusive commuter-belt golfing hideaways: security keypads that rendered entering the clubhouse and exiting the car park complex military procedures; a disapproving, square-jawed man in the car park, eyeing the Led Zeppelin sun visor in my car with distaste; architecture that you knew you'd be hard-pressed to remember three minutes after you last saw it. It was something of a

---

* I like to think this isn't *just* down to a swift-fingered research team and an extensive database.

relief to find out that this was not where Ken played his golf. 'Ken Brown?' the moist-headed youth in the pro shop had said, scanning his computer printout of the club membership. 'Nope. Can't see him.' After a couple of minutes we got our wires untangled ('Oh – Ken *Brown!*') and I was directed to the neighbouring Harpenden Common Golf Club. This was an altogether more welcoming enclave down a leafy, Camberwick Green-ish lane, with open doors, an overfed resident cat and a period clubhouse full of smiling, chattering grey-haired women, all of whom I immediately wished were my grandma.

There was something very Ken Brown about all this, and not just because the course at Harpenden Common is only 6200 yards long – a length that seems commensurate with the reputation for 'placid' driving that Ken developed during his playing days. In the commentary box, Ken might not have the endearing non-sequiturs of Peter 'Voice of Golf' Alliss, or the sarcasm of Mark 'Jessie' James,* but there is something perennially warm and welcoming about him. He is neither old guard ('I don't see any harm in someone playing golf in a pair of jeans,' he told me) nor new, simply a man whose passion for the game runs so deep and pure that he can't help but calmly radiate knowledge about it. It seemed appropriate that, unlike most other members of his generation of the ex-pro British golfing establishment, his home club was not a semi-fortress in deepest Surrey.

* This might go some way to explaining why he has not yet been awarded his own fake middle name in inverted commas.

He was quick to dismiss my suggestion that he was uniquely unflappable as a player. 'You'll find that most pro golfers are surprisingly calm people,' he explained. 'That's why you don't tend to see them going off the rails in the way you might other sportsmen. You have to be on a pretty even keel because you have to concentrate for forty seconds, seventy times a day, over the course of four hours, for four days running. That existence doesn't allow for instant adrenalin rushes or terrible depressions. I suppose Ian Woosnam gets a bit wsssh wsssh sometimes, but that's about it.'

'Wsssh wsssh' – which I took to mean 'overexcitable' – was, I was beginning to realise, about as near as Ken Brown got to slagging off his peers.

After our interview, we headed out onto the eighteenth green – clearly the old 'no practising on the course' rule didn't apply to former Irish Open champions – so he could have a look at my putting and chipping strokes. Strangely, he didn't seem to think either was a total travesty. I told him that I struggled on both. He asked me if I thought I was being honest about my game.

'Are you blaming your putting for other faults in your game? Do you tell yourself you're hitting the ball to the right, when the real fault is that you're hitting it to the left? It's easy to con yourself. You've got to be brutal in your analysis. The way that you're not deluding yourself is by consistently having rounds of 69 or 68.'

I decided not to tell him that the previous week I'd only just scored better than that at a pitch'n'putt venue barely more than a quarter the length of a normal golf course.

'When I joined the Tour [in the mid-seventies], there

weren't more than ten people making a living of any description,' he continued. 'But because there are now two hundred or more people in Europe in a position to do that, it has got harder to get there. There are more people than ever trying to rush up and give it a go. Players come through with better role models, better advice on fitness and psychology. That and the new technology has made everyone that much more tightly packed. Giving yourself an edge, no matter how small, is that much more important.'

I hit another bunker shot, being sure to take a lot of sand, so as not to send the ball bulleting over the green in a way that might decapitate my temporary mentor. I wondered if Reminding Yourself to Hit the Sand Before the Ball so as Not to Kill Anyone counted as the kind of 'edge' he was referring to. Probably not.

Before I left, Ken offered one more nugget of advice about the pro game. It sounded familiar.

'The thing you have to understand about professional golfers is that, unless something really exceptional happens, we've heard it all before. We don't want to know if you holed two bunker shots. So what?'

'What about if I holed a five-iron from two hundred yards?' I asked.

'Hmmmm . . . Not really.'

'What about if the five-iron ricocheted off a passing blackbird before it went in?'

'Well, maybe. That's certainly more like it, anyway.'

Thanks to a kindly passing member, I came away from my encounter with Ken Brown with a photograph of the two of us. This showed me putting, with a cake-eating grin on my face, and Ken behind me, checking my alignment. It had been an extremely cold day, and I'd worn my thickest woolly hat, partly in tribute to the tea-cosy-like headgear Ken had been renowned for sporting in his early European Tour days. It wasn't the most stylish of golfing looks, perhaps, but I was surprised at the illusion of competence that my posture gave.

'It looks like he's teaching the village idiot how to play,' said Edie when I handed her the picture.

Actually, I continued to be amazed at how supportive my better half was of my new career. Not only had she been quick to rush in with the Febreze after my Europro Qualifying School disaster (some of the odour had subsequently vanished, but there was still something undeniably oaky in the region of the pocket where I kept my pitchmark repairers), she'd also been surprisingly swift to pick up the complex lingo of a game which, if not for my peculiar passion for it, would undoubtedly have held zero interest for her. There had been the initial, anticipated mix-ups to shed light on – e.g. me having to explain that, no, I didn't fancy taking my parka out with me to the golf course, as it would restrict my back-swing, and that, yes, it was weird that the captain of a club often tended to be one of its worst players – but it wasn't long before she got the gist, even if she still wasn't too keen on the accompanying dress sense and complex-ions. 'Hmmm. Tradesman's entrance,' she'd comment knowledgeably as Fred Couples' birdie putt at the Nissan Open narrowly snuck into the rear side of the hole, before turning her attention back to her newspaper. Or later, as Jim Furyk took his repulsive, jerky backswing in the

Honda Classic: 'What was that? It was horrible! It looked like his arms were attached to invisible pulleys!' (a real 'That's my girl!' moment, that one.) Before long, I began to see where the golf commentary teams of the world were going wrong. What they really needed was a bit of feminine input:

'Thanks Jim! Stone the crows . . . Davis Love III just *spun* that ball like he had *air-brakes* on that baby, I'm telling ya. Now, it gives me great pleasure to introduce a new member of the ABC team, Edie Cox. Edie, welcome.'

'Thank you, Gary. I'm delighted to be here, even if I am a bit confused as to why you speak in that weird voice, where you say some words very slowly and others very quickly, as if to make them sound funnier and more dramatic than they really are. Here we have Darren Clarke, putting for a whatdyamacallit, the one that's one better than a birdie. Anyway, whatever; he's putting. Stroke looks pretty smooth, but . . . it doesn't look like he's exfoliated since at least 1998. And . . . OOOH, over the cellophane bridge, leaving him a tricky one coming back. I wonder if it would have gone in if he'd accessorised a little better. Maybe a bit of serum on that hair might have helped. We'll be back, hopefully with some factor fifty suntan lotion, after these messages, including the one about the steakhouse where the food will probably give you some pretty bad meatsweats.'

Edie had been to the driving range with me a few times and, with very little instruction, had hit impressive, lofty shots beyond the hundred-yard marker using the lightweight Lynx seven-iron I'd bought her.

But I knew that she viewed golf in the same way as most other women in their twenties and thirties: as a closed-off, sombre, sexist island, somewhere a few miles off the coast of 1981. Since that was pretty much what I thought about golf too, I wasn't going to try to persuade her to fall in love with it. It seemed unlikely she ever would, particularly now that she had hit some pure iron shots without having any major existential epiphanies. All I could hope was that I didn't bore her to death with my tales of show-off drives and insouciant eagles. Or bankrupt us with my pro ambitions. Or damage too much furniture with my sand wedge.

Even when I was only playing golf twenty times a year, I had frequently arrived home from a few holes of practice, walked into the living room and announced to Edie, 'I've found it!' in a manner that suggested something that would turn our world upside down, only to proceed to describe a new grip or pre-shot waggle. Playing almost every day, these revelations came with even more lunatic regularity. 'I've realised it's all about keeping my swing shorter!' I would proclaim, after a particularly perky nine holes before dusk. 'It's all become clear now – I'm getting too narrow, not completing my arc,' I would announce three days later, ingenuously, following a brisk morning birdie barrage. More irksome still must have been my tendency to see golf in all of the life around me, and evaluate it incessantly. I tried not to talk constantly about my swing, and sometimes succeeded in finding distraction in a nice meal or a quality sitcom, but it soon became obvious that a good pizza topping was a bit like a good golfing attitude – you needed all the ingredients just right, but it was important not to overload it – and that while Joey, Chandler and Ross from *Friends* obviously represented a neat overview of the three predominant types of modern male, they just as obviously represented the three predominant types of golfing persona to be found on the PGA Tour.

'It's quite a nice evening out there,' Edie would say, as I theorised on the way that Buffy and Angel could never be truly together in *Buffy the Vampire Slayer*, and why it was a metaphor for the way you could never play a perfect eighteen holes, and would never ultimately want to. 'Why don't you nip down to the club and work on your long irons? Take your time. No hurry to be back here at all. Maybe pop into the driving range on the way back. While you're at it.'

I probably *was* spending a little too much time indoors. One major indication was that I'd begun to succumb to a deadly strain of Golfcommentaryitis P72. Telltale symptoms included finding myself staring wistfully at squabbling ducks and saying, 'Steady on now, steady on,' in a half-senile granddad voice; suddenly referring to people on TV whom I had never met by their complete names (e.g. 'Jonathan Adam Belushi, you do crack me up!'); overusing the phrase 'Cor blimey O'Reilly'; and throwing screwed up bits of paper at dustbins, missing, then discussing where the missile 'finished' and how 'You just can't legislate for that.'

There are plenty of good things to be said for an indoor golfing life – even if it does subject you to a lifetime's worth of Muzak and make you talk like a human cardigan. With a truly grotty spring churlishly following one of the mushiest winters in recent East Anglian memory, I was glad of such time-honoured living-room classics as Wifey Foot,* Coffee Shotty,† Curly Matt Ball‡ and, on the computerised side of things, Mario Golf.** I was also glad to have the chance to catch up on my golf-movie watching.

In truth, most golf movies are a bit like most rounds of golf: they have their great moments, and they have their embarrassing moments, but they never quite get within reach of perfection. It's as if golf's natural up-down pattern is so all-pervading, it can't help invade the quality of its fiction, too. I've probably watched *Caddyshack* – frequently proclaimed as the greatest ever golf movie – almost as many times in my adult life as I've bought new shoes, but even I would be forced to

---

* Involves the player putting into a small gap between his or her partner or spouse's feet. Every time he or she 'holes' five putts in a row, the gap gets smaller. Simple, but surprisingly effective.

† Like normal sand-iron keepie-uppies, *à la* Tiger Woods in the Nike ad, but with the addition of a low-lying glass coffee table beneath the player, and a steaming mug of freshly-ground in their non-club hand. Generally recommended only to those of a nine handicap or better.

‡ A classic. Can be played on a normal Astroturf putting mat with a gentle upward curve, but for proper authenticity it's best played on the mouldy, dog-eared one bought for me by my parents for Christmas 1991. Extra points go to those who can successfully negotiate the bit of dried yoghurt stuck to the surface about a foot from the hole.

** This landmark of Supernintendo gaming might not be as sophisticated as Tiger Woods PGA Tour 2007. It does, however, let you pretend to be a dragon while playing a course with cactuses taller than your house. Metal Mario, the most advanced of the competitors on offer, hits the ball over three hundred yards: a remarkable achievement for a man wearing dungarees.

admit that, without the bits featuring Chevy Chase (that's Cornelius Crane Chase to you, Golfcommentaryitis sufferer) and Bill Murray, its 'Hey, you old squares – loosen up and dance!' humour would be as badly dated as a Tupperware party. *Happy Gilmore*, its spiritual descendant, is more consistent, but is marred by an underlying suggestion that life isn't about golf at all (arguably true), but actually about finding a lover who resembles Anthea Turner (almost certainly untrue). *Tin Cup* has its gnarled charm, and its line 'You can't ask for advice about the woman you're trying to hose from the woman you're trying to hose' is probably one that will stay with me into my dotage, but it's spoiled by all those cruddy bar songs about double bogeys, and Kevin Costner overdoing the rough'n'ready shtick. Then there's the more gravitas-heavy *The Legend of Bagger Vance* and *The Bobby Jones Story*. I could just about excuse Matt Damon's chronically bent left arm on his backswing in the former, but did anyone really ever talk like this, even in the golfing American South of the early twentieth century? To watch these two swollen monuments to the age of the plus four and the necktie-constricted swing in the same day is to slip into an alternative dimension, where it's hard not to find yourself wanting to accompany even the most mundane acts with inflated, gentlemanly dialogue. For example:

Edie: 'Oh, that's nice, Tom. You've made me a cup of tea.'

Me: 'Congratulating me for making that tea, missy, is like congratulating me for not robbing the local branch of Nat West. You call it good honest tea, but the truth is, I would not know how to make tea any other way.'

That said, there's a surprising amount a budding pro can learn from fairway-based cinema. I liked Will Smith's advice to Matt Damon in *Bagger Vance* about good golf being all about learning how to 'stop thinking without falling asleep'. And while the bit in *Caddyshack* where Chevy Chase gives his caddy a lesson by blindfolding him and telling him to 'Be the ball' is highly amusing, his advice can in fact be seriously useful, if carried out in the correct way. I didn't much fancy venturing out onto the practice putting green at Diss with a scarf over my eyes,* but I found that the technique improved my feel for mid-length living-room-carpet putts no end. That 'Be the ball' thought, meanwhile? Dynamite. It worked like a charm for me at the driving range, anyway – although that may have had something to do with the fact that it had rained for eight days straight, keeping me off the course, and by that time my brain was so accustomed to hitting range balls that it probably *had* begun to believe that it was a small, white, dimpled object with 'STOLEN FROM DISS DRIVING RANGE' stamped on it in big green letters.

---

* It wasn't that I was embarrassed to do this in front of the members of the actual club, who, being golfers, and eternally in search of The Secret, were probably as likely to imitate me as take the piss. My trepidation came more from the fact that the practice green was a matter of a few feet away from one of the town's main roads. A road used frequently by gangs of young people in souped-up, brightly coloured Peugeots, some of whom had, only a few days ago, complimented me on my bucket hat in a manner that I wouldn't want to repeat in front of an elderly relative.

Perhaps the moment that I fully realised I'd over-dosed on the many varieties of indoor golf training, however, was when I found myself watching the Golf Channel.

In theory, the Golf Channel should have been a Godsend to someone like me, who'd once been the proud owner of more than three hundred home-taped golf videos: a twenty-four-hour channel, all about golf. But I'd always been a bit suspicious of it. There isn't an important golf tournament these days that you can't absorb via Sky Sports or Setanta or the BBC, so what could it have to offer, I wondered, other than lots of fake walnut wood-panelling, oodles of instruction, and adverts for weirdly shaped plastic things that are supposed to turn you into Phil Mickelson when you attach them to your arms? The answer turned out to be a tough yet necessary stage in my golfing development, a sort of golf viewer's boot camp.

'Sure,' the Golf Channel said to me, 'you think you're obsessed, but are you obsessed enough to watch thirty minutes of presenter Megan West's bright pink blouse when all you're getting in return is a slightly bland interview with the winner of the 1997 Buick Invitational?'

'Fine,' it said to me, 'you think you're tough, but are you tough enough to stick out the ninety-minute coverage of self-congratulatory speeches at the Golf Hall of Fame and stay calm, even though you feel that if you hear it said one more time that "Golf is now a global game" your head will explode?'

There are four stages that a mere mortal goes through

when subjecting himself to an initial overdose of the Golf Channel. First, there's Denial. Watching the adverts, the profile of a typical Golf Channel viewer emerges. He is male, in his forties, has experienced significant sun damage, drives an Audi, and holidays in Spain and Portugal. When he sees America in his head, he sees Florida and some other indistinct bits of land surrounding it. He flies business class, uses American Express, is preternaturally impressed by gadgets, and all the women in his universe are blonde.

'This is not me!' I fumed, as Stage Two, Rage, set in.

Then came Stage Three, Stupefaction. 'Hmm. This Dave Pelz bloke is all right,' I found myself thinking as the short-game guru clipped yet another neat wedge shot onto one of the greens of his Colorado hideaway. As his strangely bland and scientific way of speaking hypnotised me into a false sense of security, I even began to appreciate his unusually roomy slacks.

Finally, Stage Four, Acceptance, set in. 'Now I come to think of it, perhaps the living room could do with a bit more walnut,' I said to myself as I watched former Masters champion Ben Crenshaw make a speech about some new course that was going to save the world's orphans (he didn't actually mention orphans, but it was obvious from his tone that he was talking about them). 'Perhaps a pewter figurine of a 1930s caddie, too? A couple of carriage lamps? And maybe a few framed, sexual-innuendo-based cartoons, depicting women in bunkers in a state of undress?' If I'd thought I was in the golf zone the previous July, when I'd worn a groove in the sofa from watching seven hours of The Open without moving, I now realised that I had been nothing but a naïve pretender.

Was any of this helping my game? I hoped so, and if not, it was at least helping me to brush up on my technobabble and prepare me for the furthest excesses of golfiness that the pro scene had to offer. I was also making some headway at the driving range, working on what James called 'getting into a strict drill at address' ('You need to address the ball in exactly the same way every time,' he'd said, 'because then, when the pressure's on, your routine will stand up, and you'll go onto autopilot'), but I wasn't quite managing to imbue my practice routines with the discipline I'd promised myself. One only has to look at the entries in my golf diary for this period to see how easily I was allowing myself to be distracted.

April 19th
Two hours' practice at Diss. Swing thought for the day: 'Maintain the Position'. Placed my practice-ball bag fifty yards ahead of me to use as a target, with the intention of working on my short pitch shots. Realised, after ten minutes, that I'd forgotten I was aiming at it, and had instead been blasting away to several entirely haphazard points 130 yards in the distance. Went to retrieve a ball from trees to left of practice ground, but did not realise club committee had recently installed barbed wire at shin level. Large purple bruise, with some bleeding. Checked trousers ripped. Will probably still wear them, though, since it's not often you find a fit like that for a tenner in the Top Man sale. Saw that dog again in the car park – the one that nobody seems

to know who owns – and it tried to get in the car with me.

April 20th

Just an hour at Diss today. Good to see so many kids at the club – makes a change from the last place, where the 'Junior Organiser Needed' notice stayed up in the locker room so long it had almost gone yellow. More wedge play and a few seven-irons. Worked on James's address routine. Decided to go for 'Look at target, do a waggle, address the ball, thump it,' but got confused after ten minutes and started doing 'Address, target, waggle, thump' instead. It worked better, somehow, but I returned to 'Target, waggle, address, thump' on the basis that its acronym – TWAT – is more memorable. Nice juicy divots, owing to rain, but plenty of mud – and at one point a pebble – splashing up into my eye. Is that Ben Hogan ball in my practice bag that goes 40 per cent the distance of my other balls really the same one I used in the 1991 Taylor Cup at Cripsley? Surely not. Swing thought for the day: 'Will the Circle be Unbroken?'

April 21st

More rain. Stomach bug. Stayed in and rewatched my old *Seve: A Study of the Ballesteros Legend* video. Had totally forgotten it had Leroy Gomez and Santa Esmeralda's ace disco cover of 'Don't Let Me Be Misunderstood' on its soundtrack: kind of makes up for Sandy Gall's presenting skills and Tony Jacklin's use of the word 'delish' to describe a good shot. Broke off after twenty minutes to dig out the album. Swing thought for the day: *'Eau de Golf'*.*

April 22nd
More rain, intermittent. Wonder if they still make those crystal pouches that warm up when you pour hot water in them and that you can put in those big furry plastic mittens between shots. Come to think of it, wonder if they still make those big furry plastic mittens. Must do some chipping practice soon. Decided to head over to the practice green but turned back after I spotted that bloke who always tries to get me to talk about cricket even though I drop lots of subtle hints about not being interested. Opted for driving range instead. Three teenagers in tracksuits stopped behind me while I was driving the ball almost over the back fence and said 'Woi!' and 'Fuckin' *hell!*' Pretended to be too profession-ally ensconced in my routine to notice. Couldn't decide what was more gratifying: that the word 'Woi!' – a provincial, slightly backwards version of 'Wow!' used by my friends and me when I was growing up – is still in circulation, or their amaze-ment at my long hitting. Swing thought for the day: 'Oily'.

---

* A steal, this, from Simon, who during our last game at Richmond had found great poise and fluidity from imagining a brand of golf perfume while in his address position. Even my speculation about what *Eau de Golf* would smell like in reality – a mixture of teacakes, damp inner soles, sweat and pipe smoke – had not detracted from his fantasy.

The weather had been bad for weeks, but I had only myself to blame for my lack of discipline in practice. It was that aesthetic stubbornness again. Ridiculous as it might have seemed, coming from someone who hadn't had a sub-par round in getting on for a year, I couldn't seem to shake it. An innate feature of all my loose-cannon pro fantasies had been that I would be the kind of player in whose direction pundits would make harrumphing noises with regard to his lack of practice and unfulfilled promise, yet marvel at his natural rhythm and moments of mercurial brilliance. Yes, when I came back from the Cabbage Patch Masters and shanked eight chips in a row on the practice ground, I *should* have made myself stand there until I sorted the problem out, but the thought of the driving range, with its whooping teenagers and easily impressed pensioners, was just too tempting. It also seemed, in a way, truer to the long-held idea at the heart of my pro mission: that this was only worth doing if I did it in the most flamboyant, enjoyable way possible.

I had a suspicion, though, that at some point soon my attitude was going to come back and bite me. With the weather still distinctly wintry, I was happy to go to the Cabbage Patch Masters and be taken aside and told by the editor of *Golf Monthly* in reverential tones that I had 'a really lovely swing'. I liked visiting Urban Golf and being informed by Owen, one of James's co-workers, that my action resembled that of Ian Baker-Finch, the 1991 Open champion. Better still, I liked being told that 'It's not a golf writer's swing, that's for sure.' Nonetheless, pretty soon I was going to have to start putting a caption to the picture. A caption, preferably, that read, 'Cox currently stands at a fluent six under par, yet he barely seems to have got into second gear.'

After a few enquiries, I had had no luck finding sponsorship ('Er . . . we're trying to move away from our image as a golf label, so I think it's unlikely,' said a lady in the marketing department of Penguin Clothing, awkwardly), and the leads that James had pursued (did strip clubs really sponsor golfers?) hadn't come to anything either. I'd put my writing career temporarily on the back burner, but there was only so long I would be able to keep turning down offers of paid journalism and using the term 'work' to refer to driving a mile down the road and standing in a glorified field pretending to be Sergio Garcia. One day, very soon, it was suddenly going to be summer, and when it was, I was going to find out exactly what Ken Brown meant about 'being brutally honest about your game'. I'd had word from the Europro Tour that an invite to the GMS Classic at Mollington, near Chester – one of the less heavily subscribed events on the Tour – would soon be forthcoming. Competing in the greatest championship of all, The Open, was still also a possibility – albeit a possibility that I couldn't even think of without my stomach dropping somewhere south of my knees. Still, I was sure that it was only a matter of time before I received a letter from golf's governing body thanking me politely for my interest but explaining exactly why they didn't let dirty hippies/former five-handicappers/ pissy golf-bag owners like me into their hallowed institution. But in front of me more immediately – and perhaps even more improbably – was another tournament: my first pro-am.

I have to make a small confession here. As a writer who every so often got to compose newspaper and magazine articles on his favourite sport, I had been able to build up a list of (fairly paltry) contacts in and around pro golf. I knew these would do little to help my playing career, even if I utilised them. If anything, my golf-writing background would probably be more of a drawback than an advantage – after all, most pros viewed journalists with the utmost suspicion – and I'd vowed that I would try not to mention it to my fellow competitors during tournament play. This wasn't just because I didn't want their attitude towards me to change; it was also because I felt it would be a distraction from my own game. Obviously, the fact that I wrote about golf wasn't going to be something I would be able to hide from the Europro Tour, but I had decided to play the fact down whenever possible. That said, things weren't going too well so far in my rookie year, and when I received a call from my editor at the *Daily Telegraph*, asking if I would like to compete in the Morson International Pro-Am Challenge, a European Challenge Tour event just outside Manchester, and write about the experience, I was faced with a dilemma. With its far-flung locations and considerably sexier winners' cheques, the European Challenge Tour was a level up from the Europro Tour. It was owned by the European Tour, populated by many regular European Tour players – sometimes people even *called* it the European Tour. Unless my Europro Tour fortunes took a dramatic turn for the better over the summer, it was unlikely I'd get another opportunity like this.

Did I decline, explaining that I wanted to stay 'authentic' in my pro mission? Or did I take the view that this was my one Get Out of Jail Free card? By accepting an invite to the Morson event, I reasoned, wouldn't I just be using my status as a writer to make up for the decade or so of golf that I'd lost – the same decade that other pros my age might have been using to do their own networking and build up sponsors' invites? It was a fairly shaky argument, but I decided that, just this once, I would take the easy option.

As it happened, 'the easy option' didn't turn out to be quite as easy as expected. First of all, I had to track down David Brooks, who worked for International Sports Management, the company organising the event. Brooks was one of the elusive movers and shakers of corporate golf, the kind of administrational whirlwind who had clearly sat down at some point and – without any unnecessary dawdling, naturally – worked out that he could do monumental, productive things with the 22.8 hours of extra lifespan he would have if he cut out such pointless platitudes as 'Goodbye' and 'How are you?' from his everyday existence (he still had time for 'Hello,' but I had a feeling it could happily get the push in a more frantic week).

'Of course,' said Brooks, when I finally got to speak to him, 'because we're extending this privilege to you, you'll have to wear the clothes we give you, with Morson's logo on them – hat, trousers, shirt, jumper, golf bag. I assume this won't be a problem with your sponsors?'

'I would have thought I'll be able to square it with them,' I said.

I knew that I shouldn't have been feeling too pleased with myself, since none of this was down to my playing merits, but I was elated. Here I was, one of the casualties of the Europro Tour Q School, getting to play a pro-am, followed by at least two full rounds in a proper European Tour-affiliated event . . . and one which didn't require an aeroplane journey, at that. Surely there had been some mistake? Well . . . yes. It turned out there had. It could have been something to do with the brief conversation I'd had about my amateur record with Brooks ('Dammit,' I thought, 'I knew I shouldn't have mentioned my final-hole blow-up in the 1990 Breadsall Priory Junior Open!'), or perhaps he'd taken time out from his busy schedule to do some research on me, or maybe we'd just got our wires crossed, but three days before the competition started, I found out exactly what function I'd be performing during my weekend in the north-west, via a phone call from his PA.

'I'm just ringing to confirm that you'll be teeing off at 8.11 in the pro-am,' she explained.

'That's great,' I said excitedly. 'And do you have the times for the tournament itself? Or will I receive them when I arrive at the course?'

'I'm not quite sure I understand what you mean.'

'Well, obviously there's the pro-am, but that's just practice, really, isn't it? A bit of fun, and a warm-up. Not that that won't be great, and there won't be some prizes, but I just wondered about the stuff that comes afterwards.'

'I'm sorry, but I'm afraid Mr Brooks only has you down to play in the pro-am, not the tournament.'

The Morson International Pro-Am Challenge might have made a big deal about the pro-am in its name, but in truth the pro-am bit was strictly a sideshow to the main attraction. Like most pro-ams, it took place a couple of days before the real competition, and involved each pro accompanying three amateurs, to form about a hundred four-man teams. The news that this would be the full extent of my Challenge Tour debut was deflating, but I soon realised that my appearance at Worsley Park, inconsequential as it was to my overall pro record, would come with its own unique pressures. In the event proper, after all, I would have been playing just for myself, but here, in the preamble, I'd be beholden to others – a position in which the pro golfing loner rarely finds himself, outside of Ryder Cups. Most amateurs paid a pretty penny to compete in pro-ams, on the basis that they would be spending a day with the golfing elite, picking up handy technical hints, and getting supplied with an even handier stash of anecdotes about How the Other Half Golfs to take back to their local nineteenth hole and impress their mates. Whether I liked it or not, I was going to be the star here.

Thankfully, there were signs of winter finally coming to an end as I drove up the M62 to Worsley Park the evening prior to my first round, and I had little difficulty getting into a relaxed frame of mind. After a laid-back stroll around the periphery of Worsley's accompanying hotel under a low, toasty sun, I managed to squeeze in fifty laps of its swimming pool, changed my clothes while listening to a couple of dawdlingly naked men discussing what separated Great Sportsmen from Good Sportsmen ('But that's the *thing*, Colin: it's not about doing one thing 50 per cent better than everyone else, it's about doing everything 1 per cent better than everyone else . . .'), then settled down in my room to watch a documentary about the Argentinian national football squad which, to my delight, featured plenty of footage from their 1978 victory against Holland's classic 'total football' team, one of the prettiest sporting units of all time. Before going to bed I dwelled on the changing-room blokes' conversation and what their (rather dreary) '1 per cent' rule might say about my approach to golf, but got off to sleep with no trouble, satisfying images of orange-kitted, rippling-maned sporting flamboyance playing behind my closed eyes – the kind of sporting flamboyance that might not actually have gone into its chosen profession with a primary mission to entertain, but certainly looked as if it did.

I woke about five and a half hours later, with a feeling of trepidation – a feeling that only got more extreme when I peered out of the window.

Contrary to popular belief, spending the most pliant period of your life – i.e. your teens – inhaling and exhaling golf doesn't just tend to make you good at golf. It also tends to give you an uncanny ability to act as a talking weather vane. To someone who had never breathed pure golf, the early morning scene outside the Worsley Park Marriott Hotel might have looked accommodating enough: a light breeze flicking the top of the copper beech outside my window, a grey-blue sky getting lighter by the second. I, on the other hand, knew better. Call it groundhog-like climatic sensitivity, call it a certain unmistakable, irritable clarity to the air, or call it rank pessimism . . . Whatever the case, I could sense something nasty on the horizon.

'It's going to lash it down,' I told Edie an hour later over the phone as I unloaded my clubs from the car. 'And when it's not lashing down, there's going to be a gale.'

'Is it raining now?'

'No, it's quite nice.'

'So how do you know?'

'I just do.' (Couldn't she remember that she was talking to a person who could judge the median wind strength of the coming fortnight just by taking a passing glance at a conifer? Had she forgotten that day last summer when we'd been on the way to the coast for fish and chips and, despite a clear blue sky, I'd been able to predict with almost perfect accuracy that an hour later we'd experience approximately three quarters of an hour of showers, but that they'd clear up and make way for an evening of soft, heavy stillness of the kind that makes you think you can smell freshly mown grass, even when there's none in the vicinity? Did she not know me *at all*?)

'Well, that's OK, isn't it? Maybe the bad weather will take the pressure off you a bit. Anyway, you can wear your waterproofs. You have got your waterproofs, haven't you?'

'Yes, they're right here, in my bag.' (I didn't own any waterproofs. In fact, I hadn't since 1992, on the grounds that they rustled a lot and restricted my swing.)

'What about your umbrella?'

'Yep, it's just here, next to me, in the car.' (This was not, at face value, a lie. At that moment, the pocket-sized umbrella with 'PURINA ONE' emblazoned across it which I had got free with some cat food a couple of weeks previously was sitting in the footwell next to me. And that was exactly where it was still going to be sitting in forty-five minutes' time, when I teed off.*)

Sure enough, in the twenty minutes that I spent on the range, an air quality that the man who'd given me my scorecard dismissed as 'Just a draught' mutated into the kind of 'draught' that, in May, I'd only normally expect to feel if I was standing next to an angry dragon who'd got bored and traded in his fire for ice. Just to get the comic timing right, whatever cruel meteorological god was watching my golfing ordeals chose to wait until I reached the opening tee of the day before pelting me with his first fat, disdainful beads of rain. I clung to the small consolation that, somewhere in their administrative process, ISM had forgotten that they'd wanted me to wear their sponsor's clothes, and that this was all still better than a proper job, but when I added up all the little factors of the morning – the weather; the old wrist injury that had recurred on my final few shots on the range; the fact that, unlike the other pros playing today, I wouldn't be competing in the main event; the unaccountable dirty look I'd received from Sam Torrance's son in the clubhouse while eating my breakfast – I had to admit that, for the first time in my pro career, I was feeling a mite

---

* I might not have been too interested in conforming to golf's prevailing fashions, but since I was already wearing ripped trousers, I didn't want to look *completely* as if I'd just come from a part-time job at the waste disposal centre. Besides, unless you've got a caddy, umbrellas only make your hands wetter when you're playing golf.

pissed off. Nonetheless, I did my best impression of a cheerful host as I met the amateur members of my team. These turned out to be three chunkily built Welshmen called Gary, Gordon and Nathaniel, who did something called 'financial structuring' for a company that made umbrellas.

'So,' said Gary, unleashing an enormous fart, 'looks like you'll be putting up with us for the day.'

'Oh, I don't know about that. I'm going through a bit of a bad patch at the moment. I think you'll be the ones putting up with me!' I replied lamely.

'Well,' said Gordon, 'just don't let Gary's arse put you off. He ate a bit too much Chinese last night.'

I was obviously going to need a bit of practice before I got the hang of the whole pro-am banter thing.

Over the years, I'd heard plenty of pros discussing pro-ams. They talked about them in the way computer-software salesmen talked about dull yet necessary oral presentations. From what I could work out, it was all about doing your bit for civilian golfers – turning up, smiling, adjusting their grips, saying 'UN*LUCKY*!' as if you really meant it when they missed an easy putt . . . that kind of thing. A bit of a drag, but ultimately a day of rest from the cut and thrust of tournament play – which was probably all very well, if your experience of the cut and thrust of tournament play amounted to more than two and a bit holes in total. As I squelched my way through the front nine at Worsley Park, I began to suspect I hadn't been prepped with the full pro-am picture. Nobody, for example, had told me that one of the traditional obligations of being the pro in a pro-am fourball is marking the card for yourself and each of your playing partners, then subtracting their handicaps, then converting them into stableford points,* then working out which of those two scores are the best, and adding them to the team aggregate.

I was so busy doing sums, attempting to keep the sole collective scorecard from turning to papier mâché, worrying about the shooting white-hot pain in my wrist that was getting more extreme with every shot, and keeping up with Gary, Gordon and Nathaniel's banter, that it wasn't until I reached hole seven or eight that I began to look up and properly notice the course. When I did so, I couldn't say I was massively impressed. I probably should have known Worsley Park would not exactly be Pebble Beach, from the concise conversation I'd had about it with David Brooks (when a tournament organiser describes the venue for their tournament as 'not bad' you've got to be a bit sceptical), and it turned out to be the kind of place that, if you'd been dropped on one of its fairways after a blindfolded secret car journey, you could have mistaken for any one of several hundred newish, tidily arranged, unimaginative parkland courses in Britain. It was also extremely long, particularly when

---

* Not so much an alternative golfing scoring system as an alternative golfing language, created half out of a mission to speed up play and half out of boredom. In truth, stableford is just like normal strokeplay in disguise (one point for a bogey, two for a par, three for a birdie, etc.), the only difference being that double bogey or worse doesn't score, allowing the more unfortunate player to pick up his ball and move on. Often confused, in my youth, with Stapleford, a suburb of Nottingham where I drank my first bottle of Thunderbird and stole some milk bottles – possibly for the reason that its existence is very nearly as pointless.

you were playing off the pro tees, set twenty to fifty yards behind your playing partners', to fairways so wet that anything other than a skulled long iron was likely to embed in them upon landing.

The idea of a pro-am is that the professional is the rock of the team. The amateurs may weigh in with the occasional birdie or better, aided by their handicaps, mixed in with a few disasters, but the pro will always be steadfastly not far away from par. By the back nine, I'd contributed to the team score on only three holes. The best thing I could say about my performance was that there were some truly great shots in there – about four in total. Concerned as I was as to whether my playing partners would think they'd got their money's worth, on a purely personal level my poor form didn't bother me. I'd long since decided that today was not about scoring well: it was about managing to stick out eighteen holes of dripping, snivelling and shivering without making too many whimpering noises.

On the second hole (our eleventh of the day, owing to the 'shotgun start' – each team had teed off simultaneously, utilising all eighteen holes), after a particularly muddy bunker shot, I cracked slightly, admitting to a probing Gary ('Is this all you do, then, play golf?') that this whole pro thing was new to me, and that only a few months ago I'd been playing off five handicap. That, at least, took some pressure off. Gary and I had a stress-free conversation about the social differences between golf and rugby, which he'd once played professionally for Cardiff ('They're a bit solitary and, what do you call it, introspective, aren't they, pro golfers? Us rugby lads like to have a drink and a laugh'). I then had three slightly less stress-free conversations, where I found myself having to explain separately to Gary, Nathaniel and Gordon exactly why I didn't wear waterproofs. Each dressed in high-quality virtual wetsuits, they listened thoughtfully to an argument that no doubt would have stood up better if: a) they hadn't been experts in raingear, and b) I hadn't made it whilst wearing a synthetic 1970s jumper from C&A and a sodden REO Speedwagon trucker's cap that was dripping water onto my nose like a burst pipe. I then borrowed some of Gary's Titleists, after losing the last of the half-dozen I'd bought from the pro shop ('Did you not get one of the goodie bags from the clubhouse with the free ones in?' he asked), Gordon offered to mark the card for the last three holes, and Nathaniel loaned me his umbrella. By this point the score was the last thing on our minds, as I'm sure would be obvious if you'd seen the picture of us smiling through dripping, gritted teeth taken by the Morson International Pro-Am Challenge's corporate photographer ('Tom, can you just pretend to be pointing at that flagstick and laughing at a joke Gary's just told you?') two thirds of the way through the round.

After we'd finished the ninth hole – our final one of the day – Gary, Gordon and Nathaniel decided it would be logical to play the tenth, since it was clear of other players, and it led to the clubhouse anyway, but I bowed out. It was obvious that, with a total of 58 points, nothing short of a miracle would put us in the running for a prize. I knew I'd feel slightly guilty about my escape later, but the guilt of not having gone for a sociable drink with my Zentex Fabrics teammates was easily conquered by the same urge that I'd had after my Europro

Qualifying School mishap. It was that old instinct to flee from golf – from all it represented, from all it inflicted – overriding everything again. I thanked my teammates and shook their hands, wondering just how miserable I might have felt if I *hadn't* been playing with three admirable, easy-going human beings. Nathaniel kindly offered to hand our scorecard in on my behalf. I deliberated, for a split second, over giving him that tip I'd been intending to about aiming not quite so far right, to help cure his violent hook. Then I thought better of it, and headed for the car. On the way there, I noted, as well as my humming wrist and a slight twinge in my lower back, my right hip had begun to ache and make a clicking sound when I walked, not unlike the one my dishwasher made when I blocked its cleaning arm with inconveniently tall crockery.

Six hours later I arrived home and opened a letter informing me that, in a few weeks' time, I would be competing in the world's most illustrious major golf championship.

Five

Banality Check

The documentation certainly looked authentic enough. If this was a cruel ruse concocted by Scott and Simon, I had to admire their professionalism. There was the unmistakable Open logo – the silhouette of the sacred claret jug – and a letter from Peter Dawson, Chief Executive of the R&A, wishing me 'a very enjoyable and successful championship', followed by the obligatory sheaf of rules, in migraine-inducing point-size, that tends to accompany any golf tournament of substance. I could be found a couple of pages further on, listed in the thirty-fourth group of the Hollinwell branch of regional qualifying, with a 1.18 tee time: 'Tom Cox, representing Diss,'* paired with John Ronson from Tydd St Giles and Michael Hempstock from Doncaster. Possibly such information might not have seemed quite so overwhelming if I hadn't

---

* Of course, I didn't actually represent Diss in any official capacity. I did not even represent Zentex Fabrics. I represented me. Whatever the case, since my Europro Tour debut, I had clearly been demoted from representing 'England'. Perhaps England had complained.

received it whilst still feeling like the survivor of a minor shipwreck, but I would still have needed a lengthy horizontal moment to digest it. Me. Playing in. The Open. Very soon. Maybe if I rearranged these facts, they would make more sense? The Open. Very soon. Playing in. Me. Nope: it still sounded implausible.

Obviously, competing in the regional qualifying stages of The Open is not quite the same as competing in The Open itself. To play in The Open as recognised by armchair golf fans the world over – the seventy-two-hole part, in mid-July, due to take place at Hoylake, near Liverpool, for the first time in thirty-nine years – I would need to pass through the regional qualifying stage by occupying one of the top nineteen places at my allotted course, then travel to Merseyside, play a further thirty-six holes in the local* qualifying stage, and defeat my fellow Stage One qualifiers and hundreds of their international equivalents to grab one of twelve coveted spots. But does the unfancied reserve for the Bulgarian national football squad, called up out of the blue for a World Cup pre-qualifying clash, ring up his mates and say, 'I've just been called up to play in a World Cup pre-qualifying match!'? Of course he doesn't! He says, 'I'm playing in the bloomin' World Cup!' By the same logic, I was playing in The Open. I had sent my qualifying form off to the R&A two months ago, and it had been smoothly processed, along with several thousand others from around the globe.

So who, or what, was responsible for this admin-

---

* Local, in this instance, meaning 'local to the course where The Open is held', as opposed to 'local to the player'.

istrative cock-up? Famously, in 1976 an out-and-out hacker called Maurice Flitcroft had attempted to qualify for The Open, ticking the box on the entry form that said 'professional', and gone on to shoot 121 – the worst round in Open history, and, alongside a couple of particularly bellicose streakers, one of the most humiliating moments in the R&A's history. Flitcroft had returned under a variety of pseudonyms in later years – e.g. Gerald Hoppy, Gene Pacecki (pronounced 'Pay-chequey') – only to be rumbled by officials and pulled off the course. I'd imagined that security might have tightened up since then. But no. Here I was, without a professional top-ten finish – without a professional *finish* – to my name, and golf's governing body was only too happy to take my £110 entry fee. Could my seventy-six-year-old non-golfing nan have done the same thing, if she too had agreed to relinquish her amateur status?

As a veteran, bemused observer of unnecessarily long-winded golf paperwork,* I'd been surprised by how simple filling out my Open entry form had been. I'd pictured the most long-winded job application form imaginable, asking for all manner of information about my golfing background, from 'best round' to 'biggest divot', along with references from my last three Handicap Chairmen, my school PE teacher and the Secretary of the Norfolk County Golf Union, but in reality it had just been a matter of submitting a modicum of banal personal details, stating which tour I played on, which one of the

* e.g. 'Minutes of the Thetford Golf Club AGM, 2004', aka 'How We can Solve the Badger Problem on the Tenth Fairway: A Ten-Page Treatise'.

sixteen regional qualifying venues around the country I would ideally like to compete at, and my debit card number. Somehow unable to convince myself that I'd done enough, I added 'PLEASE!' next to the box where I nominated Hollinwell in Nottinghamshire as my preferred course.

The reasons why I wanted to qualify at Hollinwell were threefold. Firstly, it was only half an hour's drive from my parents' house, meaning convenient, free accommodation. Secondly, it was possibly my favourite golf course of all time: a heather-speckled paradise bowl ringed by Forestry Commission land, from whose heavily guarded fairways one could easily convince oneself that one was entirely removed from twenty-first-century life. Finally, and most crucially, it and I had a little bit of unfinished business to settle. When I was sixteen, I'd had an unsuccessful trial for membership there. I'd never found out what I'd done wrong, but since I'd beaten my handicap in my test round, I suspected the reasons for my fruitless application were not golfing ones. To qualify for The Open at the same course, fifteen years later, in my first visit back, would constitute a fairytale bit of score-settling.

The Hollinwell debacle had been a fork in the road of my adolescence, coming at a time when my deferred rebel years were catching up with me and I needed to decide whether I was going to get serious about my golf, or loaf away my days in the back of the pro shop, drinking too much Coke and serving an apprenticeship in low-grade pyromania. Moving from my soft, slack south Nottinghamshire base to a club in north Nottinghamshire, where the fairways and the juniors were made of flintier stuff, had seemed an obvious way to take my game to the next level. I'd often wondered what might have happened if I'd handled myself differently that day in 1991. What if the man from the committee hadn't seen my dad's ancient car with its CND sticker and moss growing up the wheel arches? What if I'd had headcovers without rips in them, had cleaned that big mud stain off my bag, and not stolen the honour from my playing partner on the thirteenth? Would I now be Lee Westwood?

As a boy, Westwood played his golf at Worksop, a neighbouring course to Hollinwell, not dissimilar in character. For a short time in the early nineties the two of us had been teammates on the Nottinghamshire junior side, but I'd always been a bit too intimidated to get to know him. The grim, gritty spirit of north Nottinghamshire mining country ran through his sporting veins. Like most good north Nottinghamshire players, he was big and immoveable-looking, particularly in the posterior and head, and had an odd way of nodding at the ball, as if in dogged self-encouragement, upon initiating his downswing. He always looked, even at his most crestfallen, like the kind of dependable competitor who'd happily sell his teeth for a birdie.*

There would be no regional or local qualifying for Lee this year. As a member of the world rankings top fifty, his

---

* Not that teeth were necessarily thought of as a major asset in north Nottinghamshire. My own grandma, who was from that neck of the woods, had got rid of hers when she was in her early twenties. 'There wasn't anything wrong with them,' she once told me. 'It just seemed more convenient to be done with them. And I knew a nice man who could do it on the cheap.'

place at Hoylake was already assured. Naturally I hoped that the two of us might get paired together in the third round when, as we vied for a place in the hallowed final group with Tiger on Sunday, we'd josh about old times and compare experiences as former winners of the Lindrick Junior Open. Just in case that didn't happen, though, I needed a back-up plan, as I felt it was an important part of my rookie year to compare notes with a man who in many ways was a grown-up, parallel-universe version of Teenage Golf Me. Pro-am day at the British Masters – a tournament that's never quite been as prestigious as it's promised to be, but nonetheless remains an important part of the European Tour calendar – seemed to be the perfect opportunity. Lee, I was informed, would be in a relaxed frame of mind. Maybe, I speculated, I might even be able to tap him up for a lesson.

'You'll get ten minutes, and that's all,' said David Brooks when I called him from my mobile upon my arrival at the Belfry, the British Masters venue.

I was beginning to doubt whether I'd chosen the right route to Westwood. Because Brooks had extended the invite to the Morson event to me, and also happened to be Westwood's manager, I'd decided to arrange our meeting through him. Yet a simple call to Bob Boffinger, my old club's former junior organiser, who still shared many mutual acquaintances with Westwood, might have resulted in a less potentially fraught encounter. Nonetheless, I couldn't complain. I was at a tournament that featured nearly all the stars of European golf (my nemesis Sergio was the one distinguished absence), I had an access-all-areas badge, and the sun was out. I got out of the car, stretched my legs and let out a satisfying yawn. Immediately, I spotted a grey-haired man. He was scratching his head, and his eyes, while notable for their deep unshakeable wisdom, looked disorientated. I recognised him as Dave Musgrove, one of the legends of the caddying world.

I'd never met Dave before, but I'd spent the first decade of my life living two miles from him, and had watched him countless times on TV, bent double beneath sporting luggage almost as big as him. Now retired, he'd been one of the most sought-after caddies in the business, having won major championships with Seve Ballesteros, Sandy Lyle and Lee Janzen. When I was having a revelatory near out-of-body experience watching my first US Masters in 1988, Dave was there at Augusta, giving Lyle the perfect yardage for the unforgettable seventy-second-hole bunker shot that set up his winning birdie. I'd been told by golfing peers that there was no man alive with better insights into the pro game.

I introduced myself. Dave said he was looking for a friend's car, where he was supposed to deposit some books that he planned to sell later.

'I'm damned if I can find it,' he muttered. 'They all look the bloomin' same.'

I looked around. If someone (other than me) had decided to stray from the norm and *not* drive a BMW 7 Series, they had obviously parked it at least two hundred rows away from where we stood. My miniature, dented Toyota was used to hanging out in car parks where every other vehicle cost more than itself; a car park where every other vehicle's *hubcaps* cost more than it, though? That was a new one.

After caddying for very nearly the whole of his walking life, Dave hadn't quite grasped the idea of retirement. He was here this week, a day early, to scout out the course for his employer, Gary Evans. Was he going to The Open? 'All depends if my man makes it.' Evans, a player whose up-and-down form had established him over the years at a level just above 'journeyman', had come spectacularly close to winning the 2002 Open at Muirfield, but this year he would have to battle it out with the baseball-capped masses in the qualifying rounds. I told Dave that I was scheduled to play at Hollinwell.

'That's where I started when I was a kid, me'oad,' he said. 'When I was ten. Used to get paid a shilling a round. Still bloomin' love it. Always will.'

We compared notes on growing up in the north-east Midlands. Did I live near the pit when I lived in Brinsley, Dave wanted to know. Yes, I built a den in the woods next to it, just before they closed it down. He said he'd built a den in the exact same place, three decades earlier. Few regions do hard-faced taciturnity quite as well as the one stretching from D.H. Lawrence's birthplace to the Yorkshire border, but Dave was the most accommodating person I'd met on the pro scene, if not on the golf scene as a whole. He was also the first person I'd met for sixteen years who used the phrase 'me'oad' in the place of 'mate'.

He invited me over to the range, where we sat behind five teenage boys, all in matching J. Lindeberg belts and hats, and tried to get a view of the long-hitting, lazy-swinging Argentinian Angel Cabrera. Dave said that although he had a pass to go behind the ropes, he preferred to take a back seat unless he needed to be with his player.

'All this has changed so much in the last twenty years, me'oad,' he said. 'You get all these cling-ons now. In the old days it just used to be a player, a caddy and maybe his coach. Now you can't turn up unless you've got your sports psychologist, your physical trainer, your dietician and your bloomin' hairdresser.'

It was true: the practice ground was thick with bodies. As players arrived with baskets of gleaming Titleists, many of them had to spend several minutes trying to find a spot between caddies, swing technicians and numerous other red-faced men in polo shirts, none of whom seemed to be doing anything directly related to golf, but all of whom succeeded in making the process of text messaging and eating burgers appear of extreme consequence. There were probably three hundred people in our eyeline, and it seemed that almost every one of them – including the players – was frantically speaking or typing into a small piece of technology. Off to the left, in the logo-spattered trucks now ubiquitous at European Tour events, other, bigger bits of technology waited to do miraculous things to some of these men's backs and shoulders. And straight ahead, a magical tractor, fitted with a protective cage, waited to pick up their balls. Dave told me how different this was from even the most sumptuously catered European Tour events of the seventies and early eighties. In those days it had been his duty to stand at the opposite end of the practice ground collecting his player's missiles, in slight fear for his life. He'd just gone on to talk about his favourite experience in golf, the 1986 Masters, when he and Lyle had been paired with the resurgent, victorious Jack Nicklaus – the noises that greeted Nicklaus's birdie putts on the back nine were 'the loudest I'd ever heard on a golf course' – when he was interrupted by another, possibly even louder noise: a booming voice, coming from our left, steamrollering the low buzz of conversation around us.

'I TOLD YOU I WAS ON MY FUCKING PHONE. DON'T YOU DARE TALK TO ME WHEN I'M ON MY FUCKING PHONE!'

'Oh, right, here we go,' said Dave, as we watched a famous, formidably built British golf pro storm into our eyeline, pursued apologetically by a man in his seventies with a look of *The Wind in the Willows* about him.

'What do you think happened there?' I asked Dave. 'Do you think that bloke was hassling him when he shouldn't have?'

'Oh, I dunno,' he said. 'Probably not. He's usually having a go at someone or other.'

For a couple of minutes, our end of the range became muffled and chilly and muted, and people moved more slowly than they had done before – as if a fog had descended on us, carrying all the implicit elements of fog, apart from the fog itself – but not many people looked very surprised at the big pro's outburst. Pretty soon, normal service was resumed. The exciting Swedish player Henrik Stenson continued perfecting his Boeing 747 ball flight. The cavalier Argentinians Eduardo Romero and Ricardo Gonzalez continued to share a joke (why did the Latin players always look as if they were having the biggest laugh?). Ian Poulter sent another text message. Some teenage boys behind him dressed in bright pink trousers pointed at his bright pink trousers. Some rotund men in front of them ordered some more burgers, and received a couple more text messages (from Ian Poulter?). To all intents and purposes, I had never been more 'inside' as a golfer than at this moment. Here I was, a professional, sitting with a living legend, at a club that had staged four Ryder Cups, within putting distance of some of my favourite players, about to meet one of Britain's best ever players, having just got a rare insight into another's social skills, yet I'd never felt more like a bemused outsider. I sensed that I wasn't the only one.

'Do you think of yourself as a golfy kind of person, Dave?' I asked.

'Not really. My wife doesn't like it, for one thing. She can't stand the clothes.'

For the first time I noticed Dave's outfit, which was casually stylish, well fitting, and helped to make him look about a decade younger than he was (i.e. about fifty-three). You wouldn't exactly have called it a statement against typical golfing attire, but it definitely didn't look as if it been bought entirely from a pro shop – which was more than you could say for almost every other person in our eyeline.* It was an unending source of mystery to me that the vast majority of golfers chose to stick to golf brand clothing when a) 95 per cent of the

---

* The notable exceptions were Ian Poulter, who gets his clothes tailor-made, and the spectator in his early fifties standing just to our left modelling the 'Golf Hipster in Mid-Life Crisis' look: fluorescent bri-nylon orange shirt, jeans and golf shoes. You could put the combination of the first two items down to mere male menopausal disarray, but not the footwear. Why on earth was he wearing them? Was he hoping for a spot in the tournament?

time it was still hideous, and b) unlike uniforms for most other sports, it was no more athletically advantageous than outfits that could be purchased more cheaply from any number of high street stores. I hoped, when I took my game to the next level and qualified for The Open, that I might finally get a handle on this.

'So I suppose a lot of stuff associated with the game gets on your nerves?' I continued.

'Yeah, quite a bit.'

'But you love it?'

'Yep.'

'And you'd never not want it in your life?'

'No way, me'oad. I'll always love it.'

'Me too. It's weird, isn't it?'

'What do you think of the course this week?' I asked him.

He took a thoughtful look out into the bright green yonder and paused, as if weighing up the much-improved Belfry of today against its previous incarnations: in 1985 it had been dismissed by some as 'a glorified potato field'.

'Well, it's a shithole, isn't it?' he said.

Having met a few full-time bag carriers over the years, and read *Four-Iron in the Soul*, Lawrence Donegan's terrific book about being a European Tour bagman, I'd already suspected that nobody in pro golf told it straighter than the caddies. Even with this in mind, though, meeting Dave had been unexpectedly refreshing. I wasn't expecting any such candour from Lee Westwood, who, being a top Tour pro, would no doubt have an inbuilt mechanism enabling him to answer even the most probing question with a statement that was a cliché wrapped in a platitude.

I don't wish to denigrate the higher plateaux of the golfing profession here. I understand that in a sporting environment not without its history of blackballing, where you're rubbing shoulders with the same people week in and week out, there is little social sense in making a controversial statement about your contemporaries. I also understand that the mindset that comes up with choice *bon mots* is not necessarily one that is able to roll forty-foot putts stone dead under pressure. All the same, would it be such a tragedy if *someone said something interesting in an interview sometime?* It wouldn't even have to be about golf. It could be about go-karting, or kettles, or iceberg lettuce. During the periods I'd spent watching televised golf in 2006, I'd sometimes questioned my motives for turning pro. Maybe I did want to put my golfing ability to the ultimate test. But perhaps I really just wanted to put myself in a position where I could subvert the post-round interview custom of answering every question with one of – or a slight variation of one of – the following three statements:

a. 'Well, you know, it's all just about making a few putts. And today I didn't make any putts.'
b. 'Well, it's all just about hitting the greens. And today I didn't hit any greens.'
c. 'We'll just see how it goes. I've just got to take every shot as it comes, and not really think about tomorrow.'

People think politicians do the ultimate line in interrogative stonewalling, but they have nothing on golfers.

If you listen carefully, there's actually a great skill to it. It's as if, at some point on their road to stardom – possibly shortly after perfecting their standardised 'I'd like to thank the greenstaff for the condition of the course' amateur victory speeches – the whole lot of them have been sent to secret seminars with titles like The Use of the Phrase 'Y'Know' as a Delaying Tactic, Appearing to Evaluate Your Disaster on the Back Nine When Really You're Just Spouting Hot Air that Could Apply to Any Round of Golf, and (a favourite of Colin Montgomerie, this) The Merits of 'As it Were': How it Can Make You Look Articulate, When You're Saying Something Quite Obvious and Dull. Long were the hours I'd spent dreaming about bringing my own brand of answers to the mix:

'So, Tom – 67 today. That puts you just three shots behind Paul Casey, tied with Woody Austin. Still hope for tomorrow, then? And I suppose it could have been better still had you not had that bit of bad luck in the Road Bunker?'

'Well, Julian, you could call it bad luck, but the truth is, I bollocksed it up! Totally my fault! Should have knocked it on the green, but I got distracted. The problem was that I'd sort of drifted off and started thinking about how much I wanted a packet of Monster Munch.'

'Er . . . right. Were you thinking about the roast beef or pickled onion flavour?'

'Oh, pickled onion, naturally.'

'Well – remarkable! So, a birdie barrage on Sunday?'

'I'm buggered if I know. Probably not, I suppose, if I keep swinging like something halfway between Lee Trevino and that mushroom-headed creature you get on

Supermario Golf. Also, I'm not that pleased about being paired with Woody Austin. He looks like a right bad-tempered git. Did you see him beating the crap out of himself with his club that time he missed that two-footer? I'm just looking forward to the next interview with you, to be honest. Which reminds me, I've been meaning to ask: are Dougie Donnelly and Colin Montgomerie actually the same person, and if so, how do you get them in the same camera shot together?'

To be fair to Westwood, there were far less effusive pros out there, and I'd probably have done better if I'd caught him outside office hours (even if a pro-am is a kind of 'wear your flip-flops to the office day' in the working week of a pro golfer). My main problem was that he'd obviously been briefed for our encounter in an 'A golf journalist wants to interview you' kind of way – with the possible addendum 'He says you've met before' – rather than 'A fellow pro who's a bit lame but who used to play on the Nottinghamshire county team with you would like to talk to you' kind of way. Again, I reminded myself that I must remember to keep my journalism out of my pro life. One mention of the 'j' word and, to Lee, I probably instantly became part of the amorphous, untrustworthy, badge wearing creature top pros refer to through gritted teeth as 'the *press*'.

I'd not expected Lee to recognise or remember me. I'd only ever spoken to him once when we were kids – well, more like mumbled, actually – and although we'd eaten sausage, egg, chips and beans* at the same post-county-

---

* Fact: all county-funded junior golf meals consist of sausage, egg, chips and beans.

match table a couple of times and I'd watched him thank the greenstaff for the condition of the course in a dozen wooden junior winner's speeches, I knew that the first rule of talking to famous sportsmen is Assume They Don't Know Who the Hell You Are. What was surprising, though, was that he didn't seem to remember our mutual Nottinghamshire acquaintances either.

'So you used to hang about with Pete Langford?' he asked.

'No,' I said. 'I was pals with Robin Walters. He once played in the same Notts Boys vs Notts Police match as us, I think. But I doubt you'd remember him.'

'No, I can't say I do. Sorry.'

'Ooh, but of course you know Jamie Daniel. I was mates with him.'

'Who?'

That Lee didn't recall my old golfing rival Jamie, whom I'd actually witnessed partnering him in at least three events, and sharing a laugh with him in a couple of Midlands clubhouses, was a surprise. 'How could you not remember the former Next You!?' I wanted to shout. But then I thought about just how many people Lee must have met over the course of the last decade. A few minutes previously we'd walked from the range to the putting green, and throughout the hundred-yard journey his hands had not been without an autograph pen for more than a second ('That would have been on eBay tonight,' he said to me after refusing to autograph a photograph of himself and Colin Montgomerie at the 2004 Ryder Cup, thrust at him by a woman he was certain he'd already signed for. 'Does your fuckin' 'ead in'). Before that, I'd watched a man of roughly forty-nine years of age stand next to the gate to the practice chipping green and say, 'How are you, Ian?' to Ian Woosnam,[*] then, having got his answer ('Ah, y'know, I'm all right'), thank him, and go literally skipping off to report the good news to his wife, who was waiting on the other side of the barrier, looking slightly uncomfortable ('Ian is all right! YEsssss!'). When you play the kind of golf Westwood and Woosnam do, everyone wants a piece of you – whether that piece is in the shape of a photo sanctified with your handwriting, or one of your broken tee pegs, or the more transient confirmation that you're all right or that you'll take every shot as it comes and see what happens and that it's all about holing some putts, in the end.

When Lee and I passed beyond the ropes to the restricted-access area beside the putting green, the wanting didn't stop, it merely took on a slightly more dignified form. As Lee stood there, and I tried to find some conversational space, endless well-wishers arrived from all angles. Of these, only the golf-mad pop singer Ronan Keating acknowledged my presence – or rather, my minidisc recorder's presence – and said, 'Ooh you're doing an interview. I'll come back and have a chat later.' Others arrived and Lee spoke to them about his tournament schedule and his new, wispy sideburns ('I'm taking tips,' he said, pointing to my bushier ones), and how he'd sent 'the wife off shopping for the day'. It was not, perhaps, the chat you'd expect of a man whose

* Holder of the record for the Most Frequent Use of the Phrase 'Y'know' in a five-minute period (see US Masters, third round, 1991, BBC archives).

manager had said he could only spare ten minutes for an interview, but maybe it *was* the chat of a man who *needed* that manager. Going on this evidence, a Westwood who took care of his own diary would never make it to the tee on time.

When the area finally cleared, I wasted no time in getting straight to my most important question: what did Lee think was the single most important attribute that a fledgling pro could take with him on Tour? But as soon as he'd given me the answer – 'You need a complete belief that you fit in and that you're good enough' – I knew that my *real* important question was coming next.

'But if you've got that belief, surely it needs to be so strong and all-pervading that it will take over the rest of your life?' I asked.

He gave me a frank sort of look, and half a shrug. 'Yeah, totally. You can't turn it on and off.'

His answer, I suppose, was not unexpected. After all, this was the man who, when asked what he wanted most out of his golfing life, had responded without hesitation, even at the age of sixteen, with six simple words: 'I want to be the best.' Nonetheless, it troubled me slightly. Obviously, there was no point in going out on a golf course and telling yourself you were rubbish, but if you acted as if you thought you were the best away from the golf course too, what kind of person would that make you? I had a feeling that this was a question that might be troubling me a lot more once I'd had time to ponder it properly.

We talked for a few more minutes (to be fair, the total was more like seventeen than ten). I asked him what he remembered about winning the Lindrick Junior Open (not much), and told him I'd won it with the precise same score the following year ('Hmmmph'). I asked him if he thought there was such a thing as a 'Nottingham swing' (he didn't). I wondered if he could apologise to Mark Foster – another Worksop junior who'd gone on to success on the European Tour, and a good friend of Westwood's – on my behalf for keeping him waiting on the tee at the 1991 Midlands Boys' Championship (a nervous I'm-not-quite-sure-if-you're-serious laugh in response to this). I asked whether he remembered a fork in his adolescence where he'd had to choose between messing about with his mates and long, lonely hours on the practice ground (he looked at me as if I'd asked him if he dropped an E before all his tee shots, or just some of them). Focusing on my technical obsession of the current month, 'light hands', I asked him to hold my hands as if they were a golf club and demonstrate what he thought was the ideal grip pressure for a golfer (he was really starting to give me a 'Jesus – Dougie Donnelly never asked me to do this!' stare now). He asked, slightly brusquely, 'Is that it? Are we done?' I wished him luck on his round, and he went off to hit some putts, watched by his loyal dad, who had once taught at the same school as my uncle (I at least had the restraint not to bring this up).

When I was fifteen and Westwood was seventeen, I'd been in awe of him. I'd had plenty of chances to start a conversation with him but hadn't, for fear of distracting him from more important business, like cleaning the mud off his golf shoes or eating his sausage, egg, chips and beans. Now I'd finally done so, and probably irritated him slightly in the process, but I felt strangely unconcerned about it. In fact, in a way I felt as if I *had* been talking to his seventeen-year-old self – or at least someone much younger than me.

Certainly, he was a great golfer, and he had that Ready Brek glow about him that all great golfers had, but on another level he was just a very ordinary bloke who liked a good bit of meat, hadn't read a book since school, and felt the *Sun* fulfilled all his daily news-based needs. What made him different from other ordinary blokes, perhaps, was that he'd been smoothed into a wondrous half-adulthood by courtesy cars and prize money and luxury hotels and a management company which (as one of its representatives had explained to me earlier) would gladly take care of the fiddly business of household bills and accounts if it meant he could concentrate on the thing he was best at: hitting a small white ball into a hole. The result of our meeting for me – and seventeen minutes is hardly ample time for a full character assessment – was that I felt pretty much the same about him as I had done before: he seemed nice enough, and I knew I'd continue to root for him when I saw him on TV. But as I left the Belfry later that day, I could not ignore the fact that a few voices in that little choir in the back of my head singing 'What could have been?' had piped down.

That night in bed, I made a list in my golf diary of my immediate priorities, as informed by my trip to the Belfry. I was very tired from the drive back to Norfolk from Birmingham, and from the two hundred balls I'd hit at the range on the way, trying to groove in that 'light hands at address' technique, so I fell asleep before I'd completed it, but I think I got the main points down.

1. Before every round, repeat this mantra: 'I belong here. I belong here. I belong here.'
2. Remember to take suntan lotion to tournaments to avoid 'golf skin'.
3. Perfect that Henrik Stenson 747 trajectory.
4. When meeting top pros for the first time, don't get too 'forward'. Keep touching to a minimum and try not to freak them out by concocting weird theories about geographical swing trends.
5. Achieve Ready Brek glow (but not, preferably, from the more extreme symptoms of 'golf skin').

During my adolescence, June had always been a frustrating golfing month: a time when good weather had usually arrived, but the junior tournament season hadn't quite kicked in in earnest. I was used to spending large chunks of it on the practice ground, and that's what I attempted to do now. As a kid, I would skip school and college to spend periods of four or five hours ensconced in the repetitive task of hitting thousands of wedge shots at my umbrella. I didn't have an umbrella any more, of course, but I was pretty sure that wasn't what was making my attention wander while I was on the practice ground. I loved hitting balls, but I could no longer lose myself quite so completely in the process. Bagger Vance would not have been impressed: I couldn't stop thinking, and I sometimes came dangerously close to falling asleep. All too often I'd manage thirty wedge shots and find myself wandering over to Diss's ninth tee, abandoning practice for a distinctly less beneficial match between 'Garcia' (Titleist 3) and 'Couples' (ancient Pinnacle 5). Even when I was alone, swallowed up in the peace of an early-summer evening at Diss, I would get jittery just thinking about my next professional tournament. This was The Big One. More than likely, after I had played in it, I would have a fair idea of whether I had any remote chance of pulling this pro thing off. In two weeks I would be playing in The Open, and, lying awake in bed, I had already rehearsed the opening tee shot roughly five hundred times. And when I'd got it safely away, I usually rehearsed the shot after it, and the shot after that. By mid-June I had been round Hollinwell in 65, 67, 64 and driven the green of its par-four sixteenth twice. I had been suffering from sporting insomnia all year, but now I had taken it to new levels.

I'd arranged to play two more rounds before the biggest golfing day of my life, and despite my baggy-eyed state, I was looking forward to them both enormously. The second of these was to be a practice round at Hollinwell itself, but the week before that I drove to Woburn, near Milton Keynes, to meet Stephen Lewton and his dad, Mike – something I'd been promising to do for several months.

If the 1988 US Masters had been the first intoxicating snifter of my golfing life, then the British Masters, played at Woburn's Duke's Course a few weeks later, had been the invigorating chaser that sealed the deal. The British Masters had long since moved on to pastures new – or rather, pastures a little bit bland but long enough to stand up to the increasingly powerful equipment used on the European Tour – but the Duke's still seemed like a Valhalla of a course. Cut through a pine forest on the private estate of the Marquess of Tavistock, it was green, mean, walled by trees, and an ideal way to ease myself towards the longer, more penal Hollinwell. This was where Lewton, a plus-four handicapper on the cusp of turning pro, played a lot of his golf, although, as the recipient of an American college golf scholarship, for nine months of the year he was based in North Carolina. Our mutual friend Peter Gorse, who ran the Golf Refugees clothing label,* had been trying to get us together for almost a year, and I'd finally stopped using the fact that I 'needed a bit of time to hit my best form' as an excuse to put it off. I also thought it would be interesting to meet a golfer who was taking a very different route into the pro game to those I'd already seen first hand – a route whose (then admittedly scant) existence I hadn't even been aware of in my youth.

Lewton was lucky: his scholarship was of the 100 per cent variety, worth £30,000. His main living expenses were in the form of his airfares to and from America. The owner of no fewer than six high-spec golf bags, he couldn't remember the last time he'd had to pay for any of his equipment. 'They throw all sorts of stuff at me,' he said, pointing to his latest pair of £200 golf shoes. 'The coaches out there tend to have deals with all the big manufacturers, on top of their salaries.' He made a beeline for my bag and began to finger my clubs suspiciously. 'What do you think of these Taylor Made RACs?'

* Sample product: 'Cheat' golf pants, replete with a hole in their pocket, to enable players to drop new balls in the rough when their partners aren't looking.

I frowned and pretended to consider the question for a second, then said, 'I like them!' This was a stock answer that I'd had the chance to perfect during the fourteen or fifteen times, since the end of winter, that James had asked me the same question. The truth was, since I'd got my new irons, I hadn't really given a lot of thought to their 'performance'. The way it seemed to me was that they were golf clubs and, like most other golf clubs, if you swung them well, they would help the ball go more or less where you wanted it.

'Driver's nice. Maybe put a bit of lead on the shaft? Putter looks kind of offset.'

Four years ago, Lewton had played as an amateur in a couple of Europro Tour events (amateurs of two handicap and better can enter tournaments, although, not being able to win any money, the incentive is low), and had also missed out on qualifying for the European Tour by a shot. He hadn't enjoyed the former much ('I didn't find it very friendly – people seemed to keep themselves to themselves'), and the latter had proved to be a blessing in disguise, as it allowed him to take up his scholarship at North Carolina State University.

'I love it out there,' he said. 'The courses are in out-of-this-world condition and the practice facilities are like nothing in the UK. The greens are about 13 or 14 on the stimpmeter. They're so fast that sometimes the ball will roll away if you don't press it into the grass when you mark it.' Being on a scholarship (the academic part of his degree was in Business Management) meant that Steve would have to wait longer than many to start earning money as a golfer, but one only had to look at the career of Luke Donald – a former American college golf number one, and now one of the top ten players in the world – to see the benefits of this kind of golfing apprenticeship.

When Steve was at school in the UK, he'd known it wasn't wise to admit that he liked golf – particularly to girls. In America, he said, it was very different. 'When you say you're on the golf team, the women out there are like, "Cool."' They love my accent as well. But it's not quite like being one of the American football guys. They can have virtually any girl they want. And they've got the biggest gym you've ever seen all to themselves. We have to share ours with the basketball team.' He said he worked out five times a week on average – three times under supervision, twice on his own.

I knew that the notion that golf wasn't an athletic sport was one that had become outmoded somewhere between Tiger Woods's first green jacket and Craig 'The Walrus' Stadler's final season as a PGA Tour regular, but Steve's intrinsic sportiness still surprised me. It wasn't just that he had all-round talent – he'd considered becoming a professional footballer too, and had only chosen golf after sustaining a knee injury whilst skiing – but that he was a completely alien golfing being to the ones I'd been taught to idolise while growing up. I'd already noticed that the world's best golfers were fitter and taller and more positive than they had been when I was in my youth, but my game with Steve was the first time I'd been up close to someone with the whole package: pure-bred confirmation that the days when a belly was OK providing it didn't impede your swing and the ideal golfer's height was just under six foot and long hitting wasn't necessarily an advantage and it was considered 'bigheaded' to talk about your inherent greatness were long gone.

Steve was six foot three, he hit his drives well over three hundred yards with an ease bordering on the comical, he talked frankly about how 'Every time I stand up to the ball, I just know I'm going to hit a good shot' . . . and it was obvious that every one of these things worked hugely in his favour. If I didn't add anything to my post-Belfry golfing to-do list after meeting him, it was because doing so would have been too depressing: achieving that Lee Westwood glow was a mere enigma; growing three and a quarter inches was a biological impossibility.

I played poorly at Woburn. It was one of those days – with which I was becoming worryingly familiar – when I had so little sense where my hands were at the top of my swing that, for all the good they were doing, they might as well have been back at home, twiddling the keypad on my Nintendo. Only minutes after my round, though, I looked back at it and found that, oddly, I couldn't remember much about it at all – not even the destructive bits. Had I scored 76? 78? 81? There was the pleasing moment on the eighteenth when Steve had told me to widen my stance, and I'd promptly belted my drive three hundred yards (only about forty yards behind his, that time). And then the moment before that when his dad, Mike, showed me a famous bit of tree trunk that looked like male genitalia. And . . . that was about it. Had I actually been on the course, or just haunting it from the sidelines, an appreciative ghostly spectator to Lewton's languorous birdie-making and Mike's fond tales of his son's endless childhood brilliance?* I couldn't be sure. Whatever the case, I'd had a great day.

There should have been something terrifying, mortifying about playing with Lewton. And, on some level, I knew the facts. I knew that he was bigger than me, stronger than me, more technically adept than me, seven years younger than me. I knew that, although I'd had rounds under 70, and (two) rounds with seven birdies in them, I had never had a round under 70 with seven birdies where I had been able to say, in all truth, that I could easily have had seven more. I knew that he had a dad who believed in him so much that he'd never made him do a day's work in his life. I knew that, for Steve, golf made everything else go out of focus, in a way it didn't for me. I had first-hand experience of appendicitis, and I knew that suffering from it and still managing to shoot two rounds of 75 in a tournament, as Steve had done, was an achievement of mind-boggling stamina. I knew that he was *that* good – so good that, just last year, he'd been tussling with the new star of the PGA Tour, Camillo Villegas; so good that he was in line for a Walker Cup call-up next year; so good that he'd been given a scholarship that thousands of other young British golfers would have killed for – and he *still* wasn't sure if he was going to be able to make a career in golf pay. And I knew that *all of that really should have been*

---

* e.g. The time when Steve was twelve and he won a junior tournament at Wentworth and Ryder Cup captain Bernard Gallagher, who was announcing the final European line-up on TV from the club's putting green that day, pretended that Steve was one of his two captain's picks.

145

telling me something, and that it was enough to cancel –
no, not cancel, STOMP – out all those moments when
I'd played with a pro and beat him or hit the ball more
sweetly, and thought, 'I could do this!' And, finally, I
knew that the most worrying thing of all was that none
of this dampened my spirits or detracted from the fact
that it was perfect golfing weather and it wasn't often
you got to see ball-striking of that quality for free and I
was lucky to be playing Woburn.

But, like I said, I really did have ever such a nice day.

It's only later that you're able to take a balanced look
at what happened. Only later that you think about statements like 'I really did have ever such a nice day' and
'I felt lucky to be playing Woburn.' Only later that you
ask yourself, 'Do these honestly sound like the statements of a man who is about to show no mercy, wrestle
the rest of the Open qualifying field to the floor and beat
his chest in victory?' That's where before and after are
like two separate camera angles: the close-up, showing
the man walking into the cave, which he thinks is a little
bit scary and stalactitey and damp but sort of cosy too;
and the long shot, which reveals the cave to be not a cave
at all, but the mouth of a gargantuan extra-terrestrial,
ready for its supper.

Six

Welcome to Par-adise

There are some great golf courses – St Andrews, for example – that announce themselves matter-of-factly to the world. Others demand a grand entrance. Hollinwell, like Augusta and Wentworth, is among the latter. It is reached by driving almost a mile down a private lane, through a five-hundred-yard wall of pines so opaque it formed a convenient hiding place for one of Nottinghamshire's most infamous modern-day murderers. However, you don't ever really just 'reach' Hollinwell; you always *arrive*. The trees clear dramatically, and from an elevated vantage point you look down a hill to a characterful, if slightly spooky-looking, clubhouse built in the 1930s (the underacknowledged heyday of nineteenth-hole architecture). To your left and right, enough of the cascading third and eighteenth holes are visible to offer an immediate assurance that this is true golfing terrain – if not built by the gods, then considerably nudged along by them.

I'd had numerous dreams about that moment at the top of the hill, and had spent considerable time mentally preparing myself for it. It was no surprise that, when it finally arrived, it gave me a cold feeling in my throat, as if I'd just gone for a jog after eating a packet of Fox's Glacier Mints. What I wasn't prepared for was the realisation that over the years, the vista had not shrunk. Hollinwell still seemed vast, important, not the kind of course that squeezed its holes parsimoniously into the smallest possible amount of space. It might have had attitude, but unlike most other restricted golfing hideaways, you could sort of see its point. Much as it pained me to admit it, I had to face up to the fact that if I was a golf course like this, I probably wouldn't want some south Nottinghamshire ne'er-do-well sullying my environs with his stinky golf bag and his dad's rotting car either.

I used to imagine that a day would come when I'd feel a sense of bold belonging upon arriving in the car park of a golf club, but it has yet to transpire. Time has taught me that, in the same way that most car accidents happen within a mile of home, most golf bollockings happen within a minute of parking your car. At times like this I am unable to distinguish between pre-tournament nerves and pre-authoritarian nerves – it is all one heady, terrifying cocktail. It is, however, one of golf's many contradictions that the more prestigious the tournament, the less suspicious that tournament's venue is of outsiders. Had Hollinwell merely been playing host to the Captain's Greensome Stableford, I'm sure that as I drove past the pro shop the man standing outside it with the blazer badge and comb-over would have already been on the phone to the local constabulary about my breach of headgear regulations or contravention of Local Rule 136.13: Minimum Permissible Visiting Vehicle Engine

Size. As it was, he barely twitched a buttery jowl in my direction.

In fact, on practice day for The Open Championship Regional Qualifying, Hollinwell took on a reposeful, almost welcoming quality. As I drove vigilantly past the clubhouse entrance, careful not to run over the golf bags of any immediate past captains, a couple of youths cleaning the grooves on their irons with tee-pegs outside the shop even smiled at me. I smiled back and, seeing that one of them was my old friend Jamie Daniel, waved.

Jamie gave me a 'Who the fuck do you think you're waving at, you bum onion?' kind of look, and returned to his grooves.

I then noticed that he wasn't Jamie at all, but a facsimile of a younger Jamie, only with louder trousers and soggier hair.

It seemed appropriate that in considering what my old golfing adversary would look like, I had not factored in the ageing process. Youth, after all, had once been his Thing – in the same way that smoking a cigar or being sarcastic might be other people's Things. He'd honed it, become renowned for it.

Jamie Daniel and I had begun playing golf properly on the same day. Sure, we'd both had the odd knockaround on Bramcote Hills, the local pitch-and-putt – we'd later note that we had both ricocheted off the same tree on the first hole and, in lieu of knowing what 'out of bounds' was, played our second shots from the car park – but our first serious shots had been struck side by side at the Saturday junior lessons at Cripsley Edge Golf Cub. For the next four years we'd stayed more

or less neck and neck, me managing to get my handicap a shot or two lower than his, Jamie winning the
Notts County Boys' Championship, me pipping him to
become the first of our band of juniors to win the Cripsley
Edge Club Championship. But, being born in August
1977, he always had a two-year head start on me – sometimes more, if the local newspaper was to be believed.
When I'd walked away from golf, he'd persevered,
reducing his handicap to scratch where I hadn't, then
turning pro and attempting to work his way up to the
top level of the game via satellite tours and Midland
PGA tournaments. When I pictured him, it was not as
a twenty-eight-year-old, but as a forever young prodigy:
the same one I'd only seen once since the day, aged
eighteen, that I had explained to him that I was never
going to pick up a golf club again.

'Yeah, right, Cox,' he'd said, back in 1993 as we sat
on the steps outside Cripsley's clubhouse, watching our
friend Mousey retain the under-eighteens' hold on the
club's Scratch Cup. 'I believe you. *Honest.*' It was a scene
encapsulating a relationship in which it had long been
Jamie's role to look on in a cool, collected and slightly
sceptical manner as I made yet another hyperbolic statement about my latest seen-the-light drive or triple-bogey
calamity.

I was a little apprehensive about meeting up with
Jamie. In my first book, *Nice Jumper*, I wrote about the
distance I had often felt between the two of us. I had
also been – I thought in retrospect – a little bit unfair
about the competitive role his parents had played in his
golfing life. I knew he'd read *Nice Jumper*, but when I
phoned him to tell him I'd turned pro and to see if he'd

like to meet up for a game, I found him instantly congenial – much more so, in fact, than I remembered.

It had been seven years since I'd last seen him, leaping around a dancefloor with his mum at his twenty-first-birthday party, and that had been only briefly. My image of the evening had been blurry enough at the time, and had since become considerably blurrier, so now, as I made my way over to the practice net, I wasn't quite sure what to expect. A few minutes later I noticed a broad-shouldered, loping figure with thinning hair making his way in my direction. I decided not to risk a wave this time until he was two feet away at the most.

We shook hands and grinned at one another. 'Ahhhhrg. Knackered,' said Jamie.

'Ahhhhrg. Knackered' might appear an odd way to greet a friend you haven't seen properly for thirteen years. In Jamie's case, though, it worked as a more familiar version of 'Hello,' and gave me a pleasant warm little feeling in my chest. In the old days, 'Ahhhhrg. Knackered' had simply been what Jamie said, every time he saw you. I'm sure it didn't always mean that he *was* knack-ered. It just meant that he was there, in his lethargic, gladdening way, and ready to play some golf.

'So what are you playing off now?' he asked.

'Well, I'm not playing off anything. I don't have a handicap any more; I'm a pro, like you,' I said.

He squinted, raised one eyebrow a quarter of a millimetre, and took a moment to digest this informa-tion. He looked like a man trying out a new pair of jeans, noting that, though the leg and waist were the correct size, something was wrong with the fit – possibly a bit of bagginess around the rear. Perhaps he hadn't heard me properly when I said I was a pro during our phone call. Or maybe he'd thought I was using the word in a different sense – as in 'pros and cons', or 'I'm a real pro at making this cheesecake now.'

While I'd been waiting for him to turn up, I'd been into the pro shop to sign in for our practice round. The assistant professional there had informed me that Jamie and I would have company: 'We have to send everyone out in fourballs, because the tee is only booked for so long and we have to make sure everyone gets round.' I wasn't quite sure if I saw the logic behind this: the course looked deserted.

'Yeah, fuck that!' said Jamie, marching in the direction of the first tee. 'Let's go out on our own. I've played in loads of these things, and a lot of the time you get paired with complete wankers who give it the big "I am".'

From the age of eighteen to twenty-six, Jamie had played on the Europro Tour, the South African Sunshine Tour and the (now defunct) Hippo Tour, in pro events of all shapes and almost all sizes. He'd had success – and even one victory, in South Africa – but not enough, and he'd now put his playing career indefinitely on hold and taken a teaching-pro job at a driving range in Nottinghamshire. There were a few things he missed about being on tour, and a lot he didn't.

'There are a lot of people out there who won't speak to you,' he said, after flipping a four-iron 250 yards up the par-four first hole, in the manner that many people might flip an omelette. 'They think they're the best and that they're above you. But in a way that's how you've got to be when you're out there. I used to get quite lonely.

I remember going on this massive train ride up to the top of a mountain in Switzerland and then having to play a practice round with these two complete wankers who totally blanked me, and wondering, "Why am I here?"'

'And then there were the hotels. Formula One are the worst. They were where I stayed mostly when I was on the Sunshine Tour. The bathrooms aren't big enough to turn around in, and you have to share a bed with a complete stranger, but that's all you can do when you can only afford eight quid a night. I'd always get a snorer, too. At times like that the only way to get to sleep is to drink about eight pints, which is no good when you've got a 7.30 a.m. tee time.'

The Jamie I remembered from my childhood had had a cool, reserved competitive edge that everyone around him seemed sure would take him far, but his older incarnation was open, candid and self-deprecating. Perhaps a little too self-deprecating. 'If you're not a cocky so-and-so, you may as well give up, really,' he said. 'And I don't think I can be that way. I don't want to be a twat.' The ultimate dampener on his pro ambitions, however, had been financial.

'It's hard out there when you're standing over a putt knowing that holing it's the difference between getting to play the next week or going home with nothing and having to go and put cones out on a motorway in the middle of the night. It's like my mate Stuart, who's still doing it and has God knows how many credit cards. One day he's at Gleneagles playing with Sam Torrance, the next he's working on a road crew. It gets even harder when you know that there are guys out there who have trust funds, or who are supported by their parents, and it doesn't matter so much to them. I know you said a bit of stuff in your book about my parents wanting me to be the best, but the truth is, I wanted to go out there on my own and support myself, and I did. It fucks you off, though, when you can hear rats under your bed and you know some of the other guys are in the Hilton.'

Jamie's last big playing year was 2002, when he made it through Regional Qualifying here at Hollinwell, then shot a 69 in the opening round of Local Qualifying at North Berwick. That year's Open, at Muirfield, had been just one good round away, and with it the probability of more prize money than he'd ever won in his life, invites to European Tour events and who knows what else. But a second-round 75 had put paid to all that. He said he'd still love to play in The Open, but even if he qualified this week, he would have mixed feelings about going to the north-west and playing Local Qualifying at one of the courses near Hoylake. 'The way you have to look at it is that once you've factored in accommodation and travel, it's another five hundred quid. And that's more than a week's wages for me.'

Now Jamie had cut down his schedule to Midland PGA events and The Open Qualifying, he said he was playing the best golf of his life. 'The pressure's off now, and golf's just a stroll again and a good laugh, like it used to be when we were at Cripsley.' He said that since he'd stopped pushing so hard, he'd started to get on better than ever with his wife; he'd also started to sleep without nightmares for the first time in years.

As we negotiated fairways that were not only narrow but dangerously crispy from a month of non-stop sun, he looked supremely relaxed. He asked me if I still listened to 'all that weird shouty punk music', and I asked him if he still listened to smoochy R&B (the answer to both questions was no). We reminisced about the time I'd chased him around Cripsley town centre after drinking nine cans of Red Stripe (neither of us could remember why).

When I hit a bad drive on the seventh, he told me that I looked as if I was 'desperate to get it over with'. I noticed that his swing, meanwhile, sent the ball huge distances yet gave an impression of being in slow motion. It was as though his arms were saying, 'Look, I know we're not going to stop halfway through our downward movement and make a cup of tea, because that would be silly, but that doesn't mean we couldn't if we wanted to.' I observed, too, that it was a wider, more modern action than the one I remembered.

'Yeah, I did some work on it five or six years ago,' he said. 'It's weird, though – yours hasn't changed a bit. It's sort of like an old-fashioned swing, isn't it?'

I had hoped that my work with Steve Gould at Knightsbridge might have brought me a bit closer to the present day – if not right up to the beginning of July 2006, then at least, say, March 1998. Clearly not in Jamie's eyes. But then, next to him, I suppose I'd always felt like a bit of a relic.

I mumbled something about my hand action always having been 'a bit unpredictable'.

'That was always the thing with you,' he said. 'You could always make a lot of birdies, but you could be all over the shop too.'

By the time we came off the course, I wasn't quite

sure I'd lived up to Jamie's memory of me as 'The Birdman of Cripsley Edge'. I'd made two birdies in my workingman's round of 77 to the four that he'd made in his artisan's 71. I still felt out of sync, stuck between three conflicting swing thoughts and hesitant around the greens, but it wasn't a bad display, considering my recent form and the fact that Hollinwell was probably at least three shots more difficult than any other course I'd played in the last year. In the fortnight since Woburn I'd hit even fewer practice balls than normal, having panicked slightly about mortgage payments and accepted a couple of journalism assignments. I felt that by getting these out of the way, I'd have optimum opportunity to be wholly golf-centred in the week before my Open debut. In my diary, I had meticulously blocked out each day between now and then, using a colour-coding system for each of the components of my game that required work. It had felt energising, and as I'd done it, the theme to *Rocky* had played on my internal jukebox.

When Jamie and I went into the clubhouse for a post-round drink, though, I received a nasty shock. A shock, in its own way, more disorientating than the one I'd received examining my ball on the third hole at Stoke-by-Nayland.

It came not long after the two of us had got into a conversation with Charandeep Thethy. Jamie had pointed out Thethy, a Kenyan pro, earlier in the day, as we passed him on the practice putting green. 'I used to see that bloke everywhere,' he told me. 'He seems to be able to spend his whole life playing golf. I think he's some kind of African prince.' Intrigued to find out more about a man who appeared to live the golfing life of Riley – not for him the struggle to find the next entry fee – I'd approached Thethy in the Men's Bar and asked him if he liked the course. He said he did, but he was amazed at how much the fairways had been tapered in, particularly when they were so bouncy. After a few minutes of further dialogue, in which I found out that Thethy was currently employed part-time at a driving range near Nairobi and that this week he was staying on the couch at his brother's house, down the road in Bestwood,* it became clear that either Charandeep was a man who played down his exalted lineage, or Jamie's royal assumption was considerably wide of the mark.

'Have you been playing much?' Jamie asked him.

'No,' said Charandeep. 'This is only my second tournament of the year. It's so hard to raise the cash. I played a full season last year, but that was only seven events. It's just not enough to get into a rhythm. There's so much riding on everything you do. It's not just another round of golf, that's the problem.'

A couple of men in dark-blue blazers arrived in the bar. Both, I thought, bore a resemblance to Bagpuss, the cloth cat from seventies children's TV. The one who looked a lot like Bagpuss, rather than just a little bit like Bagpuss, asked us what we thought of the course. We told him we thought it was wonderful, a genuine test, which is probably what we would have told him even if it had been an ill-groomed mudtrack. They departed,

---

* A name that still strikes terror into the heart of my dad when he recalls his career as a supply teacher. Typical local news headline: 'Third Bus Driver Quits as Local Thugs Continue to Pelt Routemaster with Stones.'

chuckling in that particular male, middle-aged, self-congratulatory way endemic only to golf club men's bars and the Radio Four quiz show *I'm Sorry I Haven't a Clue.* Jamie and Charandeep shared a couple more stories – about the island green that Vijay Singh (Charandeep's hero) owns in the sea next to one of his mansions, and the time a hard-up Jamie played with Mark Roe in The Open Qualifying and snuck back out onto the course to retrieve the barely-used Titleists Roe had thrown away in the bushes.* We all wished each other luck in The Open, and Jamie asked Charandeep what his tee time was.

'Eight oh six,' said Charandeep.

'Shit. Pretty early. What about you, Tom?' said Jamie. 'What time did you say you were off tomorrow?'

'Oh, I'm off right now, I think. I'll probably head straight back to Norfolk.'

'No, I mean your tee time.'

'I don't think I know what you're talking about.'

'Your *time*. In The Open Qualifying. Tomorrow. What is it?'

OK. I admit it. As golfing schedule cock-ups go, it was fairly sizeable. Who knows what would have happened

---

* This was in 2002, the year before the veteran Roe went on to lead The Open, only to be disqualified for filling in and signing the wrong card (the one belonging to his playing partner, Jesper Parnevik) in the third round – the incident for which he is best known. Karma telling him to be a bit less cocky? Or just a desperately unfortunate incident? It's hard to say. Whatever the case, those 'Shit! I've got Mark Roe's card!' jokes were good in Monthly Medals across the country for at least a fortnight afterwards, and for that, perhaps, we should be thankful.

if Jamie hadn't said anything? Perhaps I would have driven the 120 miles home and then that night, in bed, whilst going through my Open paraphernalia and savouring my day at Hollinwell, caught sight of the date on the start sheet and noted my mistake, then prepared myself for an early-morning drive back across country. Or perhaps I would have remained oblivious. The qualifying event would have come and gone, the scores would have been posted, and, six days later, in accordance with my diary, I would have arrived at Hollinwell and enthusiastically made my way over to the first tee, only to be told by a couple more of those Bagpussy blazer-badge men that I was six days late and that if I didn't get off the premises within five seconds flat they would shoot me and mount my ashen features in the trophy room.

There had been a time, once, when I'd been a great one for planning out my tournament schedule. Since then, I'd got caught up in the mess of adult existence, and realised the immutable truth that life isn't ever going to be ordered, no matter how much order you impose on it, and with this in mind, there isn't much point in trying. My approach to important dates these days tended to be more freeform, and worked like this: I wrote them down in the margin of a newspaper or some junk mail, then, a few hours later, threw them into the recycling. Nonetheless, like I said, I'd really made an effort to plan out what I presumed was the week before my Open campaign, and I'd been sure – *sure* – that the tournament was being held on 10 July. It was only after being put right by Jamie that I began to ask myself questions like, 'Well, perhaps it would be more logical to have the qualifying event the day after its practice day, wouldn't it?' and 'If Local Qualifying was on the tenth, and Local Qualifying was only for people who got through Regional Qualifying, it would be a bit difficult to hold Regional Qualifying on the tenth too, wouldn't it?'

My first task, after picking myself up off the tarmac outside Hollinwell's front entrance and taking a few deep breaths, was to phone my parents and tell them there had been a change of plan. Would it be OK if I stayed over at their place tonight? It would. Might I be able to use their washing machine? I might. Next, I called Edie. Could she manage without the car tomorrow? She could. Finally, I spoke to one of my editors. Could I have a twenty-four-hour extension for the television review I was due to submit tomorrow afternoon? No problem. Within ten minutes, I was feeling distinctly rosier. I thought back to that unforced afternoon last summer, when I'd had my hole-in-one. I hadn't been expecting to play golf that day either, had I? Perhaps the unanticipated nature of tomorrow would work in my favour.

I'd got to the top of Hollinwell's long, winding drive when I remembered the final piece to the puzzle: Pete Boffinger. Pete, the son of Cripsley Edge's tireless ex-junior organiser Bob Boffinger, had offered to caddy for me in the competition, and now almost certainly wouldn't be able to. I could hardly expect him to drop everything and take a day off work at less than twenty-four-hours' notice, could I? I pulled over into a layby, and dialled his number, fearing the worst.

'Yes,' he said, after I'd explained my mistake, 'I know it's tomorrow. You're teeing off at 1.18. I know I'm not a proper caddie, but I'm not *completely* useless.'

* * *

The most important day of my golfing life dawned in a way that most summer-loving Brits would describe as 'a bit muggy and overcast' but wind-fearing golfers like me call 'perfect'. I hadn't slept well, owing to my mum and dad's clanky boiler, the *Pet Sematary* yowling of their senile cat Daisy and a greatest hits montage of golf-based nightmares* playing behind my eyes, but the weather calmed my fluttery innards. Having ridden out some parental fussing,† I left for the course in good time.

* Now expanded into deluxe form to include not just The One Where the Ball Keeps Falling off the Tee-Peg but also The One Where No Matter Where I am on the Course There is Always a Hedge Impeding my Backswing and The One Where I am Holing Out to go to Seven Under Par and Have to Leave the Course After Realising I have Forgotten to Sit my GCSEs.

† My parents had always seen the moment when I decided to give up my pro ambitions as the moment when I came to my senses and rejoined my original, intended path in life. Now I'd started all that silly 'sticks and balls' business again, they were perplexed. Nonetheless, they tried their best to be supportive, asking such infuriating but ultimately well-meaning questions as 'Are you sure you're OK with just one glove?' and 'Would you like to take some of last night's chowder to eat on the greens when you're not teeing off?' My dad had even expressed an interest in driving to Hollinwell and watching my round, but I made noncommittal noises about the idea – partly because I knew he'd probably forgotten how little, on the whole, he enjoyed the company of golfers, and partly because of a potentially prophetic vision from another one of those nightmares. In the nightmare, every time I'd gone to play a shot, my dad had been blocking my path to the flag, sitting on a weird umbrella-seat contraption he used to take to tournaments when I was a kid, and talking to me about novelty calypso songs from the 1950s (I had no reason to suspect that he still owned the umbrella-seat, but I'd already been asked for my opinion on at least four novelty calypso songs this morning, so I felt it was best not to tempt fate).

Upon arriving at Hollinwell, however, it became clear that there was going to be another unforeseen bump in my road to Hoylake.

The first thing I noticed was that the fairways were empty. The second was that there was a gathering of a couple of hundred people outside the clubhouse. All of these people seemed either to be muttering grimly into their mobile phones or engaged in terse, one-sentence-per-minute conversations with one another, whilst frowning in the direction of the sky. I did not have to use any master eavesdropping skills to grasp the situation.

'They're saying at least a two-hour delay . . .'

'It's been two hours already, yoof . . .'

'I heard them saying the last groups won't get in 'fore it gets dark . . .'

'I don't know what I'm doing chuffin' standing here. I may as well get my van and go and shoot some more of them rabbits . . .'

'If you look, it is brightening up a bit . . .'

There was once a time when golfing authorities took a gung-ho attitude towards the threat of lightning at tournaments. Despite being equipped with bags full of what were essentially conductor rods, players would be expected to soldier on as the air crackled and fizzed over-head. Just occasionally, a couple of them would get hit and almost die,* but that was seen as another of the fundamental dangers of a round of golf: a bit like an extra-punitive bunker that had electricity instead of sand (and actually didn't resemble a bunker at all). Greater

---

* Lee Trevino and Jerry Heard at the 1975 Western Open, for example.

communications with the Met Office and the advent of the Health-and-Safety Age, however, have changed all that. It is not uncommon now, particularly on the PGA Tour, to see play suspended and players pulled off the course at the first gentle tummy rumble in the sky. For me, today might have represented perfect golfing weather; to the R&A, it probably represented several lawsuits waiting to happen.

Having signed in at the tournament office, I wandered around for a while, trying to spot Jamie. His early tee time meant he would have been one of those whose rounds had been interrupted. Noting that the driving range had, like the course, been temporarily closed, I made a brief foray into the clubhouse to try to get a sandwich – I soon thought better of it. Judging by the queue, any food order would require a long wait, and I worried that when the wait was over, the culinary options might not stretch much further than the mysterious black gelatinous substance I'd seen in the Men's Bar last evening, stuck to something that, in a previous life, might have been bread.

It was now just past midday. Judging by the estimations being made about the delay in the area of the competion office, my 1.18 p.m. tee time was now going to be a three p.m.-ish tee time, so I had ample time to kill. Remembering one of Jamie's bits of advice from yesterday – 'At a big event like this it's best not to arrive at the course until about an hour or so before you tee off, so you don't have time to think about it too much' – I decided it couldn't hurt to go for a drive.

It struck me as curious that, although I'd lived a matter of minutes away from Hollinwell for a whole decade of my life, try as I might, I couldn't remember ever eating at any restaurant or café in the area. As I steered in the direction of Nottingham, I realised that there was a very good reason for this, and that was that in north Nottinghamshire people don't sell food. Driving through town after town, forlornly looking for an outlet that might offer something pre-cooked and halfway edible, I began to see the logic to the arrangement: this was the heart of what remained of Sherwood Forest – a landscape not lacking in wildlife. Perhaps north Notts types simply preferred to forage, primeval-style, for their light snacks.

By the time I'd driven through Annesley and Hucknall and Bullwell – places that one could be forgiven for presuming couldn't possibly be as desultory as their names make them sound, right up to the moment of visiting them – I'd weighed up the options and decided I might as well head all the way into the city itself. I couldn't fail to find sustenance there.

Had there been a camera on me – and, this being Nottingham, UK capital of CCTV, no doubt there were several – the following two hours could have been edited into a useful How Not to Prepare for a Golf Tournament instructional video. It would begin, perhaps, with an introduction by Renton Laidlaw in his *Best Shots of the Masters* style, featuring a short lecture about the traditions of The Open. Then we would see footage of me going about my business, with Renton explaining just why each of my actions was not becoming of a sportsman, and bold red letters and exclamation marks stamped upon the screen to emphasise each of my cardinal sins. There would be the bit where I went to

Starbucks to get a Caramel Macchiato and said, 'No, actually, make that a medium, not a small . . . no, a large – did I say medium? I meant large . . .' (CAFFEINE CAN CONTRIBUTE TO NERVES!). There would be the moment when I decided to just quickly pop into HMV, to see if they had a Creedence Clearwater Revival album that I could listen to in the car (UNSETTLING HIPPIE NOISE TERROR!). We'd then see a shot of me realising the time and making a run for it back to the car park (NEEDLESS INCREASE IN BLOOD PRESSURE!). Perhaps finally we'd see me in the car, driving along the B600, looking hot and flustered, trying to overtake a tractor (STRESS RISING!).

When I arrived back at the course, play had long since restarted. If Jamie's philosophy was to be believed, I was now beginning my practice routine at the ideal time: almost precisely an hour before I was due to tee off. My caddie, however, was already by the first tee, waiting for me. We shook hands. Pete gave me a 'Cutting it a bit fine, aren't we?' look, and began to meticulously rearrange the pockets of my bag: separating the tees from the balls, separating the local rules sheet from a week-old banana skin, and adding various supplies of his own – a couple of energy drinks, a bath towel with which to keep my grips tacky. I knew I could rely on Pete, a former scratch player and a sturdy, calming presence. Whether he could rely on me, however, had already been cast into some doubt.

'Did you know I turned down Dave Musgrove so you could work with me today?' I asked him.

He looked at me like a man who had heard this kind of bull too many times before – mainly from me.

'OK, I'm lying. But I did ask him.'

'What did he say?' asked Pete.

'He said, "I bet it would be fun." But when I asked him again he just looked a bit nervous then suddenly saw someone he knew on the other side of the driving range.'

'Is that your London Golf Show glove on the floor over there?' said Pete.

My first few shots on the range glanced softly off the clubface, aided by my new 'light hands at address' approach. There was just one notable howler, but it was the kind you don't easily forget: a four-iron where the clubhead hit the ground a full six inches too early, sending the ball a grand total of seventy yards. Fortunately, neither of the pros flanking me – a round-faced teenager with a grimacing way about him and a backswing that reminded me of the spring device on a pinball machine, and a stocky forty-something with a home-player strut who kept making pronounce-ments on the day's outcome – seemed to notice. I moved on to the less potentially destructive environs of the putting green, and then to the tee. Here, I watched the group ahead of mine laser long-iron shots into a fairway that seemed even narrower than yesterday, met my playing partners, John Ronson and Mick Hempstock (who turned out to be the round-faced teenager from the range), declared my ball to them, memorised the dots on it, got a quick briefing on local rules from the starter, memorised the dots on my ball again, and did some breathing exercises.

A few minutes later, something happened that had

never happened to me on a golf course before: I went temporarily blind.

The transition in ocular perception didn't occur until I was over the ball, probably about thirty seconds after the starter had announced my name into his microphone. I remember taking my practice swing with my rescue club (another new concept for me: a supposedly more forgiving version of a two-iron). I remember looking up at the fairway, then realising that all I'd done was look up at the fairway, and not really picked anywhere to aim. I remember brushing an insect away, and I remember seeing the first six inches of my swing and thinking that a golf ball had never looked smaller. And then the ball disappeared. And by 'disappeared', I don't mean 'vanished into the blue yonder' I mean it disappeared before I could hit it. All I could see was grey.

Attacked by such an affliction, many people may have stopped what they were doing, walked away, rubbed their eyes . . . called for a member of the medical profession. I, on the other hand, chose to complete my swing. It only took, at most, an eighth of the second to do this. Nevertheless, possibly aided by being shut off from the seeing world, I was able to formulate a surprising lengthy and articulate internal dialogue with myself. The dialogue went something like this:

Me One: You are playing in The Open?

Me Two: I am playing in The Open!

Me One: It's a bit scarier than the Europro Tour Qualifying School, isn't it?

Me Two: What do you mean, 'a bit'?

Me One: Do you realise that you haven't practised your chipping once in the last twenty-one days?

Me Two: I realise this.

Me One: Do you realise that it would, in theory, be a lot easier to miss this ball than to hit it?

Me Two: I realise that is the truth. And I realise that it is even more the truth now I can't sodding see anything.

Me One: Do you also realise that if you were to miss this ball completely, it might scar you for life? And that people who had seen you miss it would tell their friends, and that they would tell their friends, and that you would become The Bloke Who Missed the Ball on the First Tee of the Open Qualifying?

Me Two: Yep, I realise that. Thanks for not mentioning how that coffee has probably made all this even more terrifying, or what incredibly bad timing it was for that insect to land on my ball a millisecond before I took my swing. After all, it's best not to get too negative, isn't it?

When I looked up as my follow-through twanged back on itself, I could see again. Thirty people were standing around the tee staring at me. Their silence made me feel as if I was underwater.

I turned to Pete. 'Did I hit it?' I asked.

'It's over there,' he said, pointing eighty yards right of the fairway, into a speckled quilting of heather and dogweed. Already I could see a search party of seven or eight spectators moving in that direction.

I'm sure I must have said something in the few minutes that followed, but all I can remember is staring in dumb, stunned admiration at the purples, the browns, the yellows, the richer, more intriguing greens – all the pretty colours that you get on the illicit bits of great English golf courses.

*   *   *

After that, the search party was rarely out of work. I was a generous enough employer to knock my tee shot to fifteen feet from the hole on the par-three fifth and to make a conventional tee–fairway–green progression up the par-four tenth, but these constituted rare breathers in their packed schedule.

Everyone knows about the hard graft of the caddies and the greenstaff and the scorers at a big tournament, but there are so many gestures from other bystanders that too frequently get forgotten – gestures like crawling on your hands and knees under a gorse bush just to find the ball of a complete stranger. It is these gestures that can stop a merely abysmal round of golf from becoming a permanently damaging moment of Kafka-esque despair, and I would like to take this opportunity to thank Mick Hempstock's dad, that bloke called Colin with the umbrella and the lisp, and the various other spectators who had the misfortune of following Group 34 in the 2006 Regional Open Qualifying at Hollinwell: you may not think you played a significant role in proceedings, but you did. For one troubled newbie pro, your foraging skills were a Godsend.*

Something fierce comes over men when they're searching for a golf ball. All too aware of the five-minute search limit and the looming two-shot penalty, they get a look in their eyes that suggests they have momentarily forgotten who they are and reverted to a primordial, right-brain state. One cannot be seen to be twiddling

---

* Well, OK, maybe 'Godsend' is going too far, but at least as important as those blokes who stand there at European Tour events and hold 'Quiet Please!' signs up when play is in progress.

one's thumbs at a time like this. Even if you are not really looking for the missile in question, you must appear to be doing so.* But I couldn't help noticing how the attitude of my ball-spotting team gradually altered over the course of my round. On the second hole I could see them looking at me with sympathy, viewing me as a talented, gritty competitor suffering a brief misfortune. But by the time I'd lost my tee shot off the tenth in the trees on the right of the fairway, run back to the tee, then hit the next ball into a gorse bush in the left-hand rough, I could see the light of enthusiasm dying in their eyes. At one point, when I was upside down under the bush fishing around with my driver, thirteen gorse needles stuck in my bottom, I even overheard a couple of them slacking off and taking time out to discuss Nick Faldo's potential as a Ryder Cup captain.

I couldn't blame them. I was clearly long past saving by then.

It's a mistake to think that any great round of golf can be put down to a swing adjustment or a new club or an unexpected confidence boost. When a player goes out onto the course and shoots 64 or 65, what you are seeing is not just good biorhythms or good swinging or good putting, or even a combination of all three: you are seeing a combination of a thousand little factors rubbing together and making sparks. A horrific round is similar, in a way. The only difference is that when all

---

* I find that getting on my hands and knees and looking unusually interested in stray pinecones helps. Another surefire winner is Frowning in a Way that Suggests You Have Just Received Some Bad News About a Beloved Yet Slightly Stubborn and Fast-Living Relative.

the little negative factors rub together, there are no sparks: the player just gets more and more bruised.

Later, I would spend hours wondering why I had fared so poorly at Hollinwell. I would look for answers in that ill-advised trip to Nottingham, in my bad calendar-keeping, in my lack of practice, in the pitiless nature of the course, in inappropriate glass-is-half-full thinking, in inappropriate glass-is-half-empty thinking, in my lack of sleep, in my ever-increasing back pain, in my lack of self-belief, in the way that my swing seemed to have lost its young Baker-Finch sparkle and mutated into the movements of a panicked squid. In the end, I found no one easy explanation – just an unbroken vicious circle of tiny explanations working together to create something so vile it shook me to my core.

And why did it shake me to my core? Because I knew that I could have scored considerably better even if I had gone out with just a seven-iron in my hand? Because I knew that even if I'd been *trying* to shoot a bad score, I probably wouldn't have fared so appallingly? Because it was the worst round of golf I'd played since shortly before my fourteenth birthday? No. Even though all those things were true, that wasn't quite it. *It shook me to the core because, in my heart of hearts, I knew it could have been worse.*

It was a day when I looked into the darkness and realised that there is no limit to how bad a round of golf can be.

When you're playing as abysmally as that, you feel a need to sweep yourself away from people. I imagine, for John and Mick, my partners, watching me must have been a bit like being unexpectedly introduced to someone suffering from a rare wasting illness: they presumed it wasn't contagious, but couldn't be completely sure; still, it would probably have been impolite to ask for confirmation. By the ninth green I'd already alienated my caddie, whose excuse about 'needing to get back home and bath the kids' was no doubt genuine, but probably would have been even more genuine had he not just seen me move catastrophically to eleven over par. Climbing the cripplingly steep slope to the twelfth tee, bag weighing on my back, the lost-ball fiasco on the eleventh and the resulting six-over-par ten weighing on my mind,* I should perhaps have been worrying about logical matters – like how I could muster up the strength to hit another shot, or where I could find a nice bush to hide beneath until the year 2016, when all of this would be forgotten. Instead, I could only think about what a drag I must have been to watch. I was particularly worried about distracting Mick, who was judiciously putting together a beautiful round of golf and, avoiding serious hiccups, looked odds-on to qualify.

'I'm sorry about all this,' I said to Mick and John.

They both muttered something along the lines of 'Don't worry, it happens to us all.'

But it didn't happen to us all. It didn't even happen to me, usually, and I was certain it didn't ever happen to them – at least not to this extent – and, in the unlikely event that it did, they didn't go apologising to their

---

* At another, more jolly time I might have fantasised about my post-round grilling about this ('Asked how you make ten on one hole, Cox replied, "You miss the putt for a nine!"'). Now, I just fantasised about whimpering in a cupboard.

playing partners about it. I might have been in the same group as John and Mick, on the same course, but that was where the similarities between their tournament and mine began and ended. Come to think of it, it was probably where the similarities between John's tournament and Mick's began and ended, too.

John was not what, in my short time as a pro, I had come to recognise as the archetypal modern golfing machine. If his swing had ever been on that conveyor belt Steve Gould from Knightsbridge Golf School talked about, it had clearly long since fallen off, brushed itself down, and attempted to tread its own grubby, indignant path to the end of the production line. A swing coach by profession, yet without a full PGA qualification, he had a terrier-like demeanour and a way of holding his arms aloft and looking around when he missed a putt that suggested he had decided the golfing gods held a personal vendetta against him alone. His life had become what his caddie, Paul Creasey, called 'a proper *Tin Cup* story'. Golf had broken up countless relationships and driven him 'half-bonkers'. Once, he had got so depressed during a round that he had jumped in a lake and attempted to drown himself ('I changed my mind, though, and decided to swim to the other side and tee off'). Despite all this, at the age of forty-two he was still here, giving it another go. And, while he frightened me slightly and I made sure I didn't get close when he lipped out a six-footer for par, it was obvious that the 2006 Open Qualifying was a richer event for his presence.

'John might not be a big bloke, but he's one of the biggest characters you'll meet out here,' said Paul, a sometime tournament pro himself. 'It's my job today to calm him down.'

Mick could hardly have been more different. He traversed Hollinwell's fairways with the aura of a seventeenth-century nobleman striding out onto his newly inherited acreage. For fourteen holes, he barely hit a shot that didn't go exactly to plan. When I asked him what he wanted out of his golfing life, he replied, without hesitation, 'I want to win lots of money and be in the Ryder Cup team – preferably sooner rather than later.' Did he expect to qualify for the European Tour this autumn? 'Of course – you've got to. You're a fool if you don't.'

There was nothing self-harming about Mick, who hit his three-wood about as far as Jamie Daniel hit a driver, which was about as far as I hit a club that had yet to be invented with a nozzle at the top where you poured the petrol in. He would discuss each prospective shot only in the most positive terms with his caddie, a man in his sixties also called Mick. Then, as it flew straight and true, the pair would be sure to celebrate its brilliance. It was hard not to get swept along in the upbeat rhythm of their chat:

Mick the Caddie: 'Three-wood, Mick?'
Mick the Golfer: 'Every time, Mick.'
Mick the Caddie: 'Nice and easy, Mick.'
Mick the Golfer: 'Nice and easy, Mick.'
THWACK!!!
Mick the Caddie: 'Pured it, Mick?'
Mick the Golfer: 'Pured it, Mick.'
Mick the Caddie: 'Should leave you about 155 to the flag, Mick. Perfect nine-iron distance.'

Mick the Golfer: 'Should leave me about 155 to the flag, Mick. Perfect nine-iron distance.'

Pete had done a terrific job in his half-round as my caddie, combining patience and encouragement with octopus-like club-handling skills, but I couldn't help wondering what a bagman like Mick could do for my game. He seemed like the golfing equivalent of a horse whisperer. Mick the Player, meanwhile, seemed to have a tunnel-like perception of Hollinwell as a series of beautifully mown stretches of grass and welcoming flagsticks; so different from mine – a leering wilderness of sand-traps, Brillo-pad rough and wrist-wrenching heather.

It was obvious that each of the three men in Group 34 played a game with which, to paraphrase Bobby Jones, the others were not particularly familiar. Nonetheless, as we stood on the elevated sixteenth tee, the result of all my defeatism, all John's self-flagellation and all Mick's self-belief was that we were three more men who were probably about to miss out on playing in The Open. One of us was going to miss out marginally (Mick's great run had come to an end with a quadruple bogey at the fifteenth), one was going to miss out easily, and one had never been in the running – but the end result would be the same. We were all tired, we were all miserable, and we were all going home empty-handed. As I looked across the treetops in the direction of Newstead Abbey from the tee – one of the few views in the north-east Midlands that seemed truly to merit the oft-used tourist tag 'Robin Hood Country' – I felt as out of breath as I had ever felt on a golf course. It seemed as if I had played fifty holes, not fifteen. I then looked at my score-card and had a small revelation:

Of the three of us, I probably had the most still to play for.

When people use the word 'unmentionable' in golf, what they are usually referring to is a shank: the right-veering affliction I'd felt so wary of on the Europro Tour Qualifying School practice ground. But if the shank was the good golfer's *real* unmentionable, would it be mentioned so often? I think not. Surely even *more* unmentionable, to a good golfer, is the possibility of slipping into a three-figure score for one's round. A hundred is not only the first major target the beginner strives to beat, it is the score that no pro can live down. Much was made, for example, of Sandy Lyle's fall from grace after winning the US Masters and The Open, but even though, at his lowest golfing ebb, Lyle scored in the nineties, he managed to avoid the big one-oh-oh – presumably out of some final reserve of darkest-hour pride. A hundred is, quite simply, the line that separates a freak golfing disaster from rank, unforgivable amateur hacking.

A hundred is also just twenty-one shots short of the score Maurice Flitcroft shot in 1973: the worst score in Open history.

With three holes to play, I stood at twenty-two over par. Since the overall par of Hollinwell is 72, this meant that, in order to beat the dreaded figure, I would have to play the final three holes in five over par or better. Normally, even on Hollinwell's tough closing stretch, that would not have been too tall an order. On the most errant golfing day of my life, though, it gave me something to think about. A few minutes previously I had been patting myself on the back for persevering, when it would have been so much easier to give up and card

176

a No Return. Now, though, a possibility loomed that was more *verboten* still.

Perhaps it was because I'd passed into a whole different realm of tiredness, but with this new predicament at the forefront of my mind, I immediately began to focus for the first time all day. Having holed a ten-footer for par on the sixteenth and very nearly birdied the par-five seventeenth, I hit a sweet eight-iron second shot to the eighteenth – a long par-four – only to watch, crestfallen, as it curved off the short grass and dropped into a steep-faced bunker guarding the front left edge of the green.

It was going to come right down to the wire.

The clubhouse at Hollinwell stands no more than twenty feet from the eighteenth green. In its main lounge, spectators can bag a choice view of the final stages of a tournament through a giant floor-to-ceiling window. Late in the evening on an important day like this, the window was packed with faces, many of them drooping from an intractable day on an intractable golf course and, quite understandably, in need of the kind of boost that only true *Schadenfreude* can offer. From my bunker, it would take only a slightly too-clean strike to clang into the reinforced glass. Who knew what kind of havoc a violently mishit shot could wreak? Any ball that hit the clubhouse would be deemed out of bounds, dictating that I would have to return to the bunker and add two strokes to my score. That would still give me four more shots to beat a hundred, but by that point the pressure would have doubled, and every eye in the vicinity would be on me.

If there was a dilemma here – a brief rearing of my

rebellious, smash-happy juvenile golf head – it was only momentary. There was more at stake than my and Hollinwell's shared history. If I was, finally, going to show the place what I was made of, it was not going to be in the form of vandalism; it was going to be by not making a fool of myself (or at least not more of a fool than I could possibly help).

The important thing, when executing a bunker shot of delicate length, is to take plenty of sand before making contact with the ball. I cursed the rule that prohibits players touching the sand before taking their swing: it would have been nice to have had a couple of firm, excavating practice swings in the sandtrap itself. Instead, I took a couple of swishes in the scrubby, dusty grass to the rear of the bunker, being sure to bury my clubhead deep into the turf. I then walked to the flag to inspect the slope of the green and, on my way back, as an afterthought, took one more pickaxey swish.

A giant divot flopped out of the perfectly cultivated fringe, a matter of millimetres from the putting surface itself.

I did not have to take a peek at the window to know that I had now put myself firmly in its focus.

'I'm not surprised they didn't give you membership if you do things like that!' joked John, from the opposite side of the green.

I was still chuckling slightly when I got over the ball. In my fatigue-ridden state, I wondered if it might help. All day, I had felt as if a maggot had wormed its way into my brain and was whispering evil thoughts into my ear as I swung. Maybe, I thought, I can laugh it away. But no: as I took my backswing, it was there again.

'Clubhouse!' said the maggot. It did not need to say anything more – I knew what it was trying to do. I felt sand (not enough) then ball (too much) and attempted to look up, but the flying grains impaired my vision. When the grains settled, I saw my ball just off the back of the green, twenty-five feet from the hole, and fifteen feet short of the out-of-bounds posts.

Two wobbly putts later, I was in safely at twenty-three over par: the worst score, by three shots, of all sixteen heats of the 2006 Regional Open Qualifying.

Oddly, I discovered that I did not want to leave.

Possibly it was the memory of junior tournaments I'd played in in this part of the country – tournaments where, no matter how badly you'd scored, there was always a reason to stick around, whether that reason was attending the prizegiving, inventing your own golfing assault course out back near the greenkeeper's sheds, or comparing notes on the day's woes. Whatever the case, I felt that there was something about a day like this that needed to be savoured. Mick and John, however, made it clear that a post-round drink was not on the agenda. A look at the scoreboard told me that Jamie would be long gone (his 77 would not be good enough for qualification). Pete would be at home with a glass of wine by now, his kids tucked up in bed. In fact, from what I could see, everybody apart from the four groups still remaining out on the course seemed to be leaving or on the verge of doing so.

What was *wrong* with me? I couldn't stand clubhouses usually – their prying eyes, their second-rate food, their restricted dress codes. Moreover, I had just carded the worst round of my adult life. What possible reason could there be to stick around? Surely I didn't feel as if I'd just . . . achieved something?

I did have one person to speak to before I left, and that was the scorer. Entering the tournament office, I found my path blocked by two men in dark-blue blazers. Neither looked like Bagpuss, but one did have something lionish about him.

'Can I help you?' he asked.

'I just wanted to hand my card in,' I said.

This information didn't quite seem to compute, but, slowly, he and his friend moved aside, allowing me an eight-inch gap in which to squeeze through the doorway.

A minute later I emerged from the office and took one last look up the eighteenth hole, hoping that, one day, I'd get to play it again. As I did so, a man standing a couple of feet away from me – a Hollinwell member, a spectator, or possibly a tournament organiser – asked a visor-wearing, tired-eyed pro what he had scored. Having received the answer – 'Aah, nothing good' – he began to commiserate by relating the story of another player who had been level par, only to take an eight on a par four.

'Oh well,' I said, turning towards him. 'At least he didn't have a ten.'

He twitched his cheek a fraction in my direction, as if believing a mosquito had flicked his face, then realising it wasn't a mosquito after all, but something much less significant. He then resumed speaking to the visor-wearing pro.

I couldn't help thinking back to that model golfer that James Day and others had told me about earlier in the year: the one who goes round in 68, then goes into the clubhouse and has the restraint to report his good fortune in only the most essential terms. I'd worried about how I could become that man, about whether I even knew him. It seemed so irrelevant now, laughable. It was all very well learning that when you were at the top of the pro golf world, nobody wanted to hear you crow. But no one had prepared me for the even harsher reality that when you're at the bottom of it, and sinking fast, nobody can hear you scream.

Seven

No Mouth and All Trousers

The situation, as I saw it, was very simple: the trophy was in my hands – it was just a matter of keeping my fingers from getting too sweaty to hold onto it. If I could just plonk my approach shot anywhere on the putting surface here on the par-five seventeenth, and then avoid the treacherous out-of-bounds on the eighteenth, it would probably be good enough. Two pars would clinch it. Maybe even par – bogey. Nothing fancy. Given my lowly standing on the order of merit, this was not the time for heroics.

I checked my yardage book again, took a squint at the flag, and threw a pinch of loose grass into the air: 156 to the hole. About eight yards of wind against. A medium-firm seven-iron. 'A mere bagatelle,' as Peter Alliss might say.

It had been a hot day, and a hotter battle – the kind of enthralling back-and-forth tussle that comes along once every eight or nine tournaments. There had been ugly moments (Jim Furyk's unprecedented five-putt on the fifth), infuriating moments (the bit where a crowd member came out of the clubhouse and told Furyk, Fred Couples and Sergio Garcia to tuck our shirts in because 'all the men on the veranda are talking about it'), raucous moments (Sergio Garcia's frustrated shout of 'Cock-knockers!' after slicing his tee shot on the tenth) and inspired moments (the bit where Fred Couples said he was going to 'try a new swing out' and promptly birdied the thirteenth), but the overall result was that now, in the closing stages, the Melanoma Cup was mine to lose.

As I drew the club back, I heard the maggot in my head whisper something about the stream in front of the green. Nonetheless, the ball took off and made its way over the hazard to the front fringe: a shaky sort of strike, but serviceable.

'Shot!' said Sergio Garcia. 'I was wondering . . . Do you think we're a bit old for giving ourselves pretend pro names?'

'I don't know. Maybe. But being Fred sort of makes me feel more confident,' I said. 'And I thought you liked being Sergio.'

'No, no, I do,' said Simon. 'But I think there might be something psychologically damaging about it. There's too much history of messing it up to carry around. It always seems to make me lose my bottle on the last few holes.'

A half-intelligible voice piped up from the trees to the right of the fairway. We looked in its direction and requested that it repeat itself.

'I said, I don't see why I always have to be Jim Furyk!' shouted Scott.

'Think of it as a service to Jim Furyk,' I said. 'If you're not going to be him, who else is?'

'Apart from Jim Furyk himself,' said Simon. 'And he doesn't have much choice in the matter either.'

'I think I've lost that one,' said Scott, who had now emerged from the trees, and was rooting around in his bag. 'OK if I drop another ball down here? I can't be bothered going back.'

'Go for it,' I said.

'So,' said Simon. 'What's the plan now, Coxy? Are you going to call it quits?'

It was a good question, and one to which I'd given much thought in the fortnight since shooting the worst score recorded in any stage of the 2006 Open Championship. There were endless reasons for me to admit defeat in my pro mission, not all of them relating to the increasingly destructive state of my game. I had yet to earn a penny, failed to find sponsorship, not succeeded in getting invites to nearly as many tournaments as I'd hoped, my manager had 'taken a break' from working with me,* and I'd developed some worrying lower-back pain.

As I'd learned from speaking to Charandeep Thethy at Hollinwell, it was not unusual for a struggling full-time pro to play only seven tournaments in a year, but I'd only played three – well, five, if you included the Cabbage Patch Masters and the Melanoma Cup – and entered two more, and I couldn't believe how much even

---

* Not that I blamed James for this in the slightest. 'Put your time into working on a new, bigger branch of your incredibly successful and modern underground metropolitan golf franchise, or into guiding the career of a man who can't even break ninety in The Open?' was hardly the kind of dillemma that would keep me up at night either.

that had eaten into my savings. I hadn't ventured abroad, I'd eaten basic meals and tried not to splash out on travel or unnecessary accommodation, yet when you added that to my equipment and range balls and entry fees, my expenses for my pro venture already totalled almost £5000. When I took that away from what I wasn't earning by putting my writing career on the back burner, I had a situation that could not go on indefinitely. A month earlier, Edie and I had put our house on the market. While our reasons were not predominantly related to the damage my golf career had done to our fiscal resources, it would be a lie to say it hadn't been a sizeable factor. That habit I had of stopping in front of the mirrors in the front room to check the plane of my swing? It was still just about funny. I had a feeling, though, that in a couple of mortgage payments' time it might not be.

'You're either loaded or in debt in this game,' Jamie Daniel had told me. 'And very rarely anywhere in between.'

In the times when I got most disheartened about my golf, it was Edie who kept me looking on the bright side. She seemed to have an instinctive understanding of the internal battles the game necessitated. She also knew that this was a one-time deal, and I had to at least give it a decent shot. But she had not married a golfer – that side of me had been completely dormant five years ago, when we'd tied the knot – and sometimes, when I returned from the course, I could see her wondering where the things I was talking so feverishly about fitted into the grand scheme of our life as we'd known it for six years. The phrase 'fucking golf' became an increasingly regular part of her conversations with our friends

– or it did on the rare occasions when my schedule gave us the chance to see them. 'Can we talk about something else for a change?' she'd ask when we were alone, and I'd try my hardest. But didn't everything come back to golf, in the end? I really hoped not, but it seemed that way sometimes. Golf dictated the way I planned my daily outfit, the formula I used to remember the pin number for my debit card. Golf might not have swallowed my life yet, but the mastication process was well underway. 'You can't turn it on and off,' Lee Westwood had said. I hoped he wasn't right, but I was beginning to wonder, in more ways than one.

But I couldn't leave it here, could I? Despite all my worries about golf's unhealthy power over me, despite all my increasing suspicions of my unsuitability to its social and physical demands, another, equally strong voice inside was saying that I owed the game more: more analysis, more practice, more dedication, more sacrifice. Though I was in the worst form of my life, I felt sure a change of luck was just around the corner. Having found out that I would be admitted to two more Europro Tour events in the next month – the GMS Classic at Mollington in Cheshire and (following many beseeching emails and phone calls to Europro Tour HQ, and a couple of members of the initial field dropping out) the Bovey Castle Championship in Devon – there was still the chance that I could turn things around. I'd always got annoyed in the past when people said that golf was 'a funny old game' (what game wasn't?), but now, sucked deep into its vortex, I furtively offered myself the same platitude. If I'd been a batsman who kept getting out for a duck, or a goalkeeper who continually fumbled the opposition's shots into his own net, there would have been only one course of action to take, but golf was different. Even a round as unimaginably humiliating as mine at Hollinwell had presented its teasing rays of hope.

What if I took the rhythmical confidence that had sent my drive so beautifully up that impossibly tight fifteenth fairway and applied it to every shot? It couldn't be that hard, could it? Everything I had learned said yes, it could. Everything I felt in my fingers when I waggled my eight-iron in the living room disagreed.

I had, at least, now confessed to myself that I was playing the worst golf of my life. I'd probably known this before The Open, but I had still believed that, given eighteen holes in a genuinely big tournament, everything would click into place. But now there was no getting away from it: my year so far had been crushingly, comically bad – a farcical movie script of low-rent golfing humiliation. I'd played better than this when I was seventeen and losing heart. I'd played better than this *two years ago,* when I'd been playing golf once a month.

'It's a bit like a golfing nervous breakdown, in a way,' I'd told Simon and Scott.

I'd imagined that putting a name to the horror might help, but quite the contrary. In the two weeks after Hollinwell, even my moments of practice-round hope began to vanish. My disease began to spread, too. My playing partners at Hollinwell might have been hardened and focused enough to block it out, but more inquisitive, receptive golfing beings like Scott and Simon soon got swallowed up in its dark path. The Melanoma

Cup may have been a tussle, but it was an unsightly, scabby one*. Ever since I'd talked frankly about my woes on the second hole at the Melanoma's host venue, Richmond Golf Club, I'd seen my friends beginning to unravel. A few days later, Simon had gone to Florida on a golfing holiday with his dad, and I'd quickly started to receive portentous text messages from him describing tearful 'What is it all *for*?' moments beside crocodile-infested lakes in Ponte Vedra.

Pro golfing history is full of mysterious falls from grace. Among these are some total head-scratchers featuring players with infinitely more talent than me: terrifying King Midas in Reverse tales of golfers who've gone from superhuman brilliance to sideways-hitting desolation. Having won The Open at Lytham in 2001, become one of the few men to have shot 59 in a professional tournament, and once occupied the number-one spot in the world rankings, David Duval slipped to 211th on the PGA Tour money list in 2003. Even more disturbing was the story of my man Ian Baker-Finch. That poetic victory of his in the 1991 Open at Birkdale had been the kiss of death for his career. He'd never been anywhere near as good again, and in the 1995 and 1996 seasons he'd either missed the cut, or withdrawn, or been disqualified from all twenty-nine tournaments that he'd entered. In 1997

---

* It would have been a lot less of a tussle if Simon and Scott, sympathetic to my distress, had not awarded me a special 'have your handicap back' dispensation for the day. I should probably also point out here that the 'Cup' part was purely figurative – as, indeed, was the £10 that, with a birdie on the last, Simon ended up winning from me and Scott.

he'd scored a catastrophic 92 in the first round of The Open – only three shots better than me in the 2006 Qualifying. He'd subsequently retired and become a golf commentator for the CBS network in America.*

I thought about Baker-Finch a lot as I waded through my black sporting cloud, looking for a way out. If, as Owen from Urban Golf had said, I swung like Baker-Finch, did that mean I was also predisposed to collapse like him as well? By rewatching his final round at Birkdale in 1991 so many times, had I absorbed some of his spirit, as well as his physical rhythm? These were ridiculous thoughts, but no less ridiculous than others that cluttered my mind, like 'Have I made myself into a terrible golfer merely by the act of becoming a pro?' and 'What if I read the *Sun* like Lee Westwood, would that help?' In that way, feeling depressed as a golfer is a bit like feeling depressed as a person: it makes you myopic and irrational. And, as at most low periods in life, you sometimes sense that the best way to deal with it is just to wait it out: get to that point when there's nothing left to lose, then start all over again.

When the miasma lifted slightly, I decided that there were two main causes for my devastating play. One was the Panicked Squid. The other was the Evil Brain Worm. I refrained from explaining this theory to those closest to me, for fear of prompting them to sneak out of the room

---

* Baker-Finch's commentary career has been a lot steadier than his golfing one, but it's still had its wobbly moments – such as the one where he called the American pro Billy Andrade's sports psychologist his 'psychiatrist'.

to make some discreet enquiries with mental-health charities. Instead, I examined the evidence, and tried to decide which of these two foes I needed to conquer first.

The Evil Brain Worm – formerly known as the Maggot, before it grew to unmanageable size – represented the psychological side of my game. Like all golfers, I had always had it. It lived in that fertile part of my brain that responds to the command 'Don't think of a hippopotamus!' by thinking of a hippopotamus. It had popped up every now and then in the past, when I had been compiling a good score and trying not to hit the ball into a lake, and done its duty by reminding me that there was a lake in the vicinity. On the whole, I had been able to ignore it and control it. More recently, though, I'd got interested in it, and if there was one thing the Evil Brain Worm thrived on, it was attention. 'What,' the Evil Brain Worm would ask, 'if you lined up this simple short putt perfectly, attempted to make an absolutely perfect stroke, but then I shouted "Miss It!" just as you took the putter back? Would you miss it? And, if you did, wouldn't it be weird, that I had all that power?'

But the Evil Brain Worm was not always so loquacious. Sometimes it would just have to make a noise – 'Boo!' perhaps, or 'Flunt!', or 'Unkulspagger!' – at the exact moment when I was starting my backswing, in order to do its damage. It didn't have to form proper sentences to make its intentions lucid. It really was a wriggly, insidious bastard. I suppose, though, if it hadn't been, it wouldn't have been a very effective Evil Brain Worm.

The Panicked Squid, which represented the physical side of my golfing make-up, might have been uncharitably viewed as a bigger, more hideous and tentacled version of the Evil Brain Worm. But I knew it wasn't anywhere near as malevolent. It meant well, and it wasn't its fault if it got confused. It was simply what happened when an instruction like 'Keep your swing nice and loose' transformed, in the heat of tournament play, into 'Make your swing a mad flailing mêlée of appendages.' In truth, it was probably controlled by the Evil Brain Worm, and served as its writhing, outward manifestation.

Bearing in mind that Darth Vader was nowhere near as much of a nasty piece of work as the Emperor in the *Star Wars* trilogy, there seemed to be only one way to go here, and that was straight to the source, cutting out the middleman. Or, in this case, the middle-squid.

I had been intending to do some work with a sports psychologist all year and around the time of my game at Stoke-by-Nayland had even had a couple of exploratory conversations with two members of the mind-coaching industry, Karl Morris and Peter Crone. That I had been slow to follow these encounters up may have had something to do with my confusing the role of a psychologist with that of a psychiatrist, just like Baker-Finch had. The idea of taking my sporting troubles to one of these men had seemed premature back in March: I couldn't shake the mental picture of myself lying on a couch and talking about my childhood, nor the conviction that I needed to have built up a sizeable history of angst before submitting to such therapy. Additionally, Crone had unnerved me slightly, and I felt that more unnerving – whether it was the constructive kind or not – was the last thing I needed.

'Don't take this the wrong way,' he'd told me over the phone, 'but from what you've been saying so far I gather you're a very sensitive person.' This seemed a remarkably astute observation, given that we had only been speaking for three minutes at that point: just about enough time for me to introduce myself and give him a (very) edited summary of my golfing life to date.

He didn't like to call himself a golf psychologist, preferring the terms 'spiritual excavator' or 'happiness guru'. Every time I made a self-deprecating comment, he interjected with the phrase 'Boring story!' He explained that this was one his catchphrases, intended to discourage negative thought processes. He talked metaphorically about peeling back the layers of the onion, and opening Christmas presents that were already there. 'My method is not to talk directly about golf,' he said. 'We're talking about your life here. The golf stuff will come automatically.' He was undoubtedly an invigorating force, and seemed like an intriguing character – more so when I looked at his promotional website, which featured pictures of him hugging alsatians and towelling his naked torso in the manner of an eighties Athena model – but he lived in America and didn't get over to Britain all that often. Somehow I couldn't quite convince myself that getting spiritually excavated by a man who numbered Liz Hurley among his clients was precisely what my game needed.

The former pro Karl Morris, who worked with Darren Clarke and the snooker player Jimmy White, was a similarly persuasive personality, but one in whose presence I immediately felt comfortable. When I'd met him at Urban Golf earlier in the year, he'd given me some useful hints. These included a lesson about how the fact that golf is a 'dead ball sport' makes the need for a player to train his brain more pressing – how a hypnotic trigger was needed to perform the same function that, say, a starter's pistol might perform in athletics. Karl lived not far away from Mollington, so a couple of days prior to teeing off in the GMS Classic, I drove over to his house.

Karl's office was a sparsely furnished room, containing three or four golf clubs, a couple of seats, a Tour-sized golf bag signed by Darren Clarke ('To Karl. We WILL get there. Thanks for everything, Darren') and a table on which were a couple of books: an ancient hardback called *Gravity Golf*, by Dave Lee, and *Blink*, Malcolm Gladwell's wonderful treatise on the untapped power of split-second decision-making. As I made myself comfortable in a leather chair – I took it that this was where all Karl's patients sat – he listened to my troubles in a way that suggested not one of them was something he hadn't heard before a million times. He said the question 'Why do I play so well in practice and so badly in competition?' was the one he was asked most frequently. 'And I'm talking,' he added, 'right from Darren Clarke downwards.'

I told Karl that when I was standing over the ball I wanted to get into that state of concentration that the five-time Open champion Tom Watson once compared to 'a room where everything is dim and quiet', but that as soon as I was in a competitive situation I just couldn't silence my internal dialogue. It was that old puzzler again: How could I learn to stop thinking without falling asleep?

'What you've got to realise,' he said, 'is that a golfer can't think of nothing. It's impossible, and when you try, it will make your mind wander. You need somewhere to park your attention. But it's got to be consistent.'

I told Karl about what I'd read in Bob Rotella's book on the mind game, *Golf is Not a Game of Perfect*, about how being focused on my target would concentrate my mind. Was this the kind of thing he was thinking about?

'The target works for some people,' he said, 'but it's a matter of personal preference. Some people find that by parking their attention on the target it's harder to stay in the present. I tell people to choose one of four things to focus their attention on: either the target, the ball, a part of the club, or a part of themselves.'

He handed me a putter, and asked me to choose one of the four focus points. I chose a point halfway up the shaft of the club. He then placed a cup on the floor five feet away, its rim facing me. I addressed the ball, and he twisted the clubhead so it was aiming some seventy degrees right of the target. He then asked me to putt four balls, not trying to hole them, and thinking about nothing but my awareness of the shaft.

Amazingly, three out of the four balls found their target.

'It's self-correcting, you see,' he said.

I'd heard and read plenty about the crucial golfing art of 'getting out of your own way', but nobody had yet demonstrated it in such persuasive terms. What Karl was explaining to me so eloquently was something I'd already suspected: that much of my golfing thought was carried out by an utterly superfluous part of my brain. All I had to do was find a way to shut it down. As a miracle cure, it was not just surprisingly simple. It seemed almost . . . boring.

'I wish I could tell you that what I'm teaching is something new,' said Karl, 'but there's nothing in it that wasn't said by Buddhists a thousand years ago. And then there's this . . .'

He took the copy of Dave Lee's *Gravity Golf* off the table beside us, opened it roughly halfway through, and pointed to a passage a third of the way down the page: a quote attributed to Gregory A. Mihaioff.

'In learning to make a typical multi-joint movement,' I read, 'two neurologically relevant points seem reasonably clear. First, the movement must be practised and, to be most effective, every repetition should be as true to the desired form as possible. Second, the conscious cerebral cortex control circuitry needs to be eliminated from the performance of the movements as soon as possible.'

'That says it all right there,' Karl said. 'And that's not from a golf coach. It's from a professor of neurobiology.'

For a member of the notoriously pushy and embroidered self-help profession, Karl was both refreshingly modest and refreshingly straight-talking. It had long ago become apparent to me that it was in the spiritual contract of every psychological guru to undermine the physical side of golf coaching, and vice versa. Karl was an exception, and seemed to have found the ideal middle ground between the two occupations: he had an immense understanding of the sporting brain, but – perhaps aided by his background as a playing pro – he kept the issue of hitting the ball central to all his teaching. He also gave me some good advice about practice. What was I aiming at? 'A sort of random area about ten yards wide, or maybe a tree,' I said. Was it smaller or bigger than what I would be aiming at on the course? 'Bigger, I suppose,' I said. If I was practising for a basketball game, Karl asked, would I want to make the hoop I practised with smaller or bigger than the one on the court?

'Look at it this way,' he continued. 'Is there any other sport apart from golf where the way it's practised bears no resemblance to the way it's played?*

I said I could not think of one.

'Exactly! You've *got* to make the hoop smaller.'

An hour later, I went to a driving range just off the M52, made the hoop smaller, and hit the most perfect two hundred shots of my life. When the last ball zipped off into the distance and I looked at the empty basket in front of me, I felt as if I had woken up from a brief, dreamless sleep, which was odd, given that I'd been unusually alert during my hitting. The blister on my thumb that had opened up and leaked blood on my shirt seemed a small price to pay.

I immediately noticed a sweaty man in a Ping baseball cap in the adjacent bay grinning a tooth-deficient grin in my direction.

'You must be playing in the tournament – the big one – hitting it like that,' he said.

---

* I was finding out that the long-held idea of the practice ground as a sacred place, where greater good could be done to one's game than on the course, was becoming increasingly obsolete. Perhaps I hadn't been doing myself a disservice by bunking off practice to play the back nine at Diss after all. The wunderkind Steve Lewton said he 'hardly ever practised', and now, hearing Karl Morris's thoughts on the subject as well, I was beginning to truly re-evaluate all those times, as a kid, when I'd been told by adult members at Cripsley that 'Half an hour of practice is worth three hours on the course.' If only I'd known this supposed aphorism had just been a ruse to keep me and my mates from getting in the way of the Captain's thrice-weekly fiveball sweep!

I wasn't sure if by 'the big one' he meant The Open, in which Tiger Woods had strolled to victory the previous day, or the GMS Classic. 'Er, yeah,' I said, slightly disorientated, and not wishing to split hairs. It was 33 degrees, and I was starting to smell something ripe. I hoped it wasn't me.

'Well, don't you take it for granted, mate. It's not a lot of people who can hit a ball like that.'

He limped off towards the car park.

It was a gratifying moment, as near as I'd felt to having 'arrived' all year.

Looking back, I'm glad I took a few seconds to savour it, because, little did I know, I'd already made two crucial mistakes.

The first – and possibly most telling – mistake had come before I'd even left Karl Morris's house.

As we shook hands at the front door, he'd reminded me of the importance of sticking with the brain-training rituals he'd given me, even if they didn't work at first. I promised that I would do so, then added, for good measure, 'Even if I shoot 86 on Wednesday.'

I should have kept my mouth shut.

The nineteenth-century psychologist William James once said that his most telling finding in fifty years of research into the workings of the mind was that 'People by and large become what they think about themselves'. In some ways, I have to doubt this. I mean, my friend Graham thinks he's Knight Rider, and has done for many years, but he's still a greying marketing consultant for a computer-software firm in the east Midlands who just happens to have a black car. But if you transpose William

James's theory to the world of golf, it's surprisingly fool-proof. A good example of this would probably be my performance on the fourth tee of the first round of the GMS Classic.

I'd started well at the dust-baked Mollington course. I'd hit each of the first three greens in the regulation number of shots, leaving myself two putts for par. Even though I'd missed a four-footer on the third to slip to one over, I was feeling, perhaps for the first time in my short career as a golf pro, a lasting sense of belonging. On the tee of the short par-four fourth, however, there was a delay of ten minutes while my playing partners, Tim Stevens and James* (son of the boxing legend John) Conteh and I waited for the green to clear. During this delay I began a conversation with James about his home club, Moor Park in Hertfordshire.

'I expect you probably played in the Carris there when you were a junior,' said James. He was talking about the Carris Trophy, one of the biggest under-eighteen amateur events in Britain, and one which I'd always hoped, as a kid, to get my handicap down low enough to enter.

'Ooh no, I was never good enough to play the Carris,' I replied.

Now, it's possible that there was no correlation between this negative statement and the tee shot that followed. It is, however, equally possible that had I not started talking about 'not being good enough', I might have buttered my drive 300 yards onto the green, instead of

---

* Fact: if you call your son James and live in England's Home Counties, there is an approximate 47 per cent chance he will become a golf pro.

hitting a slappy duck-hook 190 yards onto a gravel path, three feet from the out-of-bounds posts. It is also possible that I would not have gone on, in the subsequent holes, to find five water hazards.

It was the same with that 86 comment. When I'd spoken to Karl, I'd picked the figure out of the air as a random example of a suitably horrible round, but I could just as easily have said any score between 77 and 100. That 86 happened to be exactly what I ended up scoring in the first round at Mollington may have been mere coincidence. When you think of all the permutations, though, it seems unlikely. During the last few holes of that first round, my prophecy had loomed ever larger, desperate to fulfil itself. The Evil Brain Worm had sprung up and slithered back to life, with new expert maths skills: 'What if I make Tom birdie the sixteenth, then put his tee shot in the pond guarding the green on the seventeenth, then three-putt the last? What would that add up to? 87? OK, we need to give him one more shot back. We'll let him sink that awkward final seven-footer, but we'll send it round the rim a few times first, just to freak him out.'

Was I finding out The Secret after all these years? Was this what golf was all about, when it came down to it? Were all the wrist hinges and stances and grips and trigger-thoughts of 'oily' and 'smooth' and '*eau de golf*' utterly irrelevant? Was it really just a matter of believing something would happen with enough conviction and then allowing it to play itself out? If so, I wanted my money back! This wasn't the multi-faceted, unpredictable, highly nuanced game I fell in love with!

My second-round 80 was an improvement, but there

was a depressing inevitability to it. In my new, more realistic golfing mindset, to have one round in the 70s had become my target, and it had looked a very reachable target as I stood on the final tee, knowing that I needed a par for a 76. What was most disheartening about the quadruple bogey that followed was not the two nervy, foozled chip shots, or even the way that it demonstrated how easily I'd abandoned all that Karl Morris had told me.* What was most disheartening was that 80 was the exact score I was trying to avoid – the Evil Brain Worm had leeched onto that fact. Why couldn't it have made me shoot 86 again, or 95? How much did that slithering little tyrant know, exactly? Was it aware, for instance, that 80 was the exact score that I needed to come 128th at Mollington, in last place of all the competitors who completed two rounds?

At first glance, the GMS Classic looked like another catastrophic step on my pro expedition. It was another missed cut, another last-place finish, another fight with myself that I'd lost. But there was something to be salvaged from the wreckage. I'd had not only my first Europro

---

* I said that I'd already made two mistakes by the time I left the driving range. The second was to change 'awareness of the shaft' to 'awareness of the ball'. It had worked well at first, but pretty soon 'awareness of the ball' begat 'awareness of just how small the ball is', which begat 'awareness of just how many wrong ways there are of striking the ball', until, finally, I abandoned that kind of awareness altogether, and let my mind wander to other matters, like whether I was going to regrow my beard, or where in the greater Chester region one could get a caramel-flavoured iced coffee at this time of day.

Tour birdies, but my first Europro Tour eagle as well –
in the second round, after driving the green at the par-
four fourth – and even with that quadruple bogey finish,
had beaten the second-round score of one of my more
experienced playing partners. I'd at least had a go at
cutting the Evil Brain Worm down to size, even if, like
all worms, it just grew back with a vengeance. It was
hard, also, not to take solace from completing two full
rounds in a tournament that I'd feared I would barely
start, much less finish.

To say that Mollington seemed a bit ordinary after
Hollinwell is a bit like saying that having a kick-around
on a school playing field seems a bit ordinary after
playing in the FA Cup semi-finals. Situated just north
of Chester, it had an unprepossessing, barren look to
it. If not for a sign at the entrance and a few slightly
shabby-looking tee boards advertising the Europro Tour
sponsors Motocaddy and Partypoker.com, I doubt I
would have guessed it was holding a pro tournament.
What it looked like, from a distance, was a large, tightly-
mown wasteground that just happened to have some
flags stuck in it. Evaluating its yellowing terrain from
afar, I thought back to a comment Jamie Daniel had
made: 'Most of the courses I'd played as an amateur
were awesome, but as soon as you turn pro, you find
that you're going backwards in quality. If I'd been asked
to play a Junior Open on a lot of those places, I probably wouldn't have bothered.'

I was experienced enough to know that not every golf
course should be judged on first impressions. I remembered the mini-break I had taken at the Stapleford Park
golf resort in Leicestershire last summer. That had been

a similarly uncharismatic course on first viewing, but it had turned out to be stimulating enough. But when I'd arrived at the driving range at Stapleford, as an amateur nobody, I'd been greeted by a perfectly formed pyramid of brand-new Srixon balls, begging me to lay into them. By contrast, when I inserted my first thirty-ball token into the ball-dispenser at the range at Mollington, it made a noise suggestive of a severe respiratory disorder, then rasped up a single weatherbeaten TopFlite. A second token prompted a colourful eruption of twenty-two of the most abstruse balls manufactured between 1984 and 1997, all of which fell into a flimsy rubber basket that, as I bent to pick it up, proceeded to split, causing them to scatter in several different directions.

I tried to stay open-minded as I signed in, spent another £12 on another one of those scrawly mono-chrome yardage planners, and made my way over to the first tee. But as I was passing the putting green, the Geordie man from the Europro Tour who had just happily taken my £275 entry fee called me back over to the clubhouse.

He pointed to my shorts. 'I'm afraid that if you wear those on the course, you'll have to pay a £50 fine,' he informed me.

'What?' I said. 'Even for my practice round?'

'Yes, I'm afraid it's Tour regulations.'

It's always frustrating to be told to change your clothing while you are at a golf club – mainly because the person telling you to do so will invariably be dressed like your worst sartorial nightmare. But when it so happens that your clothing is clothing that you would not wear off the golf course, clothing, in fact, that you have specifically bought, against your better instincts, to appease the golfing authorities, the frustration is considerably greater. Over the years I'd frequently come a cropper in the area of shorts-related golf-club dress codes – most of which defy the whole point of shorts, by striving to make them not shorts at all, but two-tone trousers that just happen to have a three-inch gap in the middle – but I'd felt that with the baggy, dark-blue legwear I'd purchased from H&M I'd got it just right for a change. It was confusing enough when I'd been a member at Thetford Golf Club in Norfolk, and been told off for not wearing white knee-length socks with my shorts, but I'd hoped that the PGA would be more open-minded. Did the Europro Tour not realise that it was 30 degrees outside? And surely, if they were going to ban an article of clothing, their disciplinary energy would have been better focused on those nipple-clinging synthetic polo shirts I kept seeing everywhere?

'It's thought that shorts aren't gentlemanly,' said James* Holmes, a pro from Crewe who joined me for a few holes during my practice round. I hoped I detected something mocking in his tone, but couldn't be certain. He looked pretty serious.

James and I had met on the first tee, where I was warming up and he was squinting into the distance, trying to work out the identity of the player up by the green, 360 yards in the distance. He thought it was Jason Dransfield, the Liverpool-based pro he'd arranged to practise with. I thought it was Sergio Garcia. As it turned

---

* This James business really was getting ridiculous now.

out, we were both wrong. But then, this was a day when I was turning out to be wrong about a lot of things.

Another one was that little yardage book. 'Why is it that you have to pay so much more for these, when they're nowhere near as good as the colour ones you can normally get from the pro shop?' I asked James, flapping the little yellow-covered chart in his direction, though not at such close proximity that he would see the remnants of the mosquito I'd squished with it the night before.

'Oh, I think these are lots better,' he said. 'These are put together by Dion Stevens.'

His manner suggested that this explained everything. It was the same way he might have said, 'These are put together by Gary Player,' or 'These were put together by Madonna, in some spare time shortly after her *Like a Prayer* album.' I feigned knowledge, replied with an 'Oh, right!' and resolved to find out exactly what this Stevens guy was famous for.* Whatever it was, I suspected it wasn't art – at least not if his drawings of the trees at the side of the second fairway were anything to go by.

While I might have stepped fully into the cauldron of tournament play at Hollinwell, my four days at Mollington gave me a proper chance to swim around in it, take its temperature, become accustomed to the bittersweet taste of its contents. By speaking to James Holmes, James Conteh, Tim Stevens and Ian Keenan – a pro from Hoylake who, just three days before the

---

* That weekend, with the help of Google, I did. What I found out was that he was famous for making yardage charts.

comedown of practising with me at Mollington, had been awarded the privilege of playing as a non-competing marker in the final round of The Open – and others, a picture of the average Europro Nearly Man began to emerge. He tended to be around twenty-seven (*the* make-or-break age for a pro golfer, it seemed). His hair was shortish, geometric at the back and gelled (though not as heavily gelled as that of his younger peers) on top in that popular 'bedhead' style that bore only the politest resemblance to hair genuinely ruffled by sleep. He supported himself with part-time bar work, part-time pro-shop work, familial assistance or a sponsorship from a wealthy member at his local club with a gardening-equipment or tool-hire company (sometimes this would involve said member getting a share of his prize money, sometimes it would be what Karl Morris called 'one of those sponsorships that's another way of saying "handout"'). He drove a BMW or one of the sportier Volkswagens, on whose back seats he had slept on at least one occasion during his pro life. While at a golf tournament, he very rarely went out into the nearby city. He didn't drink, though sometimes, if he was one of the more sociable and prosperous players on Tour, he split the weekly rent for a holiday cottage with some of his peers and relaxed there by watching DVDs. He had at some point 'lost his swing' or 'got too technical', and was now desperately trying to regain form, with the nagging knowledge that, if golf didn't work out, he had no significant qualification to fall back on. He was a man of few words. When he did talk, the conversation always seemed to flow towards one of the following areas:

1. Michelle Wie

In the summer of 2006, the sixteen year-old, six-foot-one-inch Wie had become one of the hottest topics in the game: a child prodigy whose amateur achievements outshone even those of Tiger Woods, and who could hit the ball further than many of her male counterparts. She had also had the temerity to take a break from her Ladies PGA Tour schedule and enter a couple of PGA Tour events. This did not seem to have gone down well with the lower male pro ranks. Even the cuddly Andrew Seibert had surprised me by telling me about refusing to wear a free badge inscribed with the words 'Go Michelle!' at a Nationwide Tour event.[*] I'd overheard a couple of similar conversations at Hollinwell, and Conteh and Stevens seemed keen to air their opinions on the subject during the fallow periods in our round.

Stevens: 'If they [women] can play in our events, I don't see why we can't play in their events too.'

Conteh: 'There should be one big Tour with men and women, then they'd see. It would destroy women's golf.'

Stevens: 'Poulter reckons that if he played in women's events, he'd win 80 per cent of them.'

Conteh: 'It doesn't matter. She [Wie] will play again and she'll miss the cut again. It just means someone like us who's struggling to make a living is missing out on a place. It is equality, but it's *their* kind of equality.'

Stevens: 'Yeah, it's bullshit.'

---

[*] I assumed he meant 'Go!' in an encouraging way, rather than in a 'Bugger off back to your silly women's tournament' kind of way.

2. How Things are a Lot Harder than they Used to be in Every Way

All the Europro Tour players I spoke to seemed to agree on this. There were always more players pushing up from the junior ranks – players off plus six and plus seven who were fitter, sharper, who had started playing earlier. It was also harder to find the sponsorship and the equipment perks that made life easier. When James Holmes finished fourth on the Europro Tour order of merit in 2004 (total earnings: £24,565), Titleist agreed to give him a set of clubs, a hundred gloves, thirty-four dozen balls and two sets of shoes for the following year. Now they had stopped doing so. He also added that Taylor Made used to give every Europro Tour player who played with a Taylor Made driver £100 per event, but didn't any more ('Because they don't need to'). Other players talked about the old days, when the Tour would give the pros good-quality Titleist balls to use on the range, 'but they stopped when people started sneaking them into their bags'.

3. Quality of the Course

Player on Driving Range with Lolling Tongue and Hedgehog Hair: 'Course is good, isn't it?'
Player on Driving Range with Diamond-Patterned Jumper: 'Yeah, brilliant. Not a shithole at all. Honest.'

4. Boys' Toys and Speed

Player on Driving Range with Diamond-Patterned Jumper: 'What did you shoot last week?'

Player on Driving Range with Lolling Tongue and Hedgehog Hair: 'Fucking shanked it round. 'Mare, mate. Didn't drive home very fast after that. Honest.'

Player on Driving Range with Diamond-Patterned Jumper: 'You still got that Peugeot?'

Player on Driving Range with Lolling Tongue and Hedgehog Hair: 'Yeah. What of it?'

Player on Driving Range with Diamond-Patterned Jumper: 'Time you traded it in, innit?

Player on Driving Range with Lolling Tongue and Hedgehog Hair: 'Fuck off! I can get that bastard up to 140 on the M6. Toll bit, mind.'

Stevens to Conteh on thirteenth hole of second round: 'How long does it take you to get back?'

Conteh: 'About two hours.'

Stevens: 'Uh.'

Conteh: 'Be quicker than that after this round, though, cos I'll be driving at about 150.'

Stevens to Conteh, four holes later, upon spotting an unusually large aeroplane in the sky: 'Wonder how fast that fucker goes?'

Conteh: 'Dunno.'

5. *Clichéd Exclamatory Banter*

In-vogue examples included:

'Taxi!' (Translation: 'My putt has gone past the hole by quite some distance! It's like when a vehicle you are trying to hail doesn't bother stopping for you, but with a ball and grass instead of a car and a road!')

'Grow . . . Some . . . Fucking . . . Bollocks!' ('My putt has come up some way short of the hole, and as a result I am now quite understandably questioning my masculinity!')

'It's on the dancefloor!' ('My ball is not particularly close to the hole, but it has arrived on the green safely.')

'H_2O!' ('I have put the ball into the water. I am sad!')

'Luckier than a queer with two arseholes!' ('I did not hit a very good shot there, but, unexpectedly, it has worked out well!')

'About as much use as a chocolate fireman!' ('I did not hit a very good shot there, and it has not worked out well!')

I tried my best to join in on all of these topics, but it was obvious that I was lacking the requisite social skills. I'd never been a great connoisseur of the Bruce Forsyth brand of golf banter; I tried to keep in the spirit of things, wheeling out a few old aphorisms, but it quickly became apparent that 'over the cellophane bridge' was just, like, so 1992. Sometimes, to keep myself amused, I would invent entirely new, and utterly meaningless, golfing phrases – e.g. 'Straight off the lunchbox!' or 'Damn! That's the third Tarbuck I've hit today!' – but these didn't seem to catch on either.

The car topic was a dead loss, right from the get-go. Nobody calls a Toyota Yaris a 'baby' or a 'mutha', or talks about 'gunning' a one-litre engine, and I felt that if I really stretched myself to do the whole manly 'What are you driving?' thing, I'd only end up offending somebody by asking why, when their winnings totalled £343 for the year, they chose to drive a car worth more than

£20,000. It was an area of pro life that flummoxed me, right from the boasting about speeding to Jamie Daniel's obvious embarrassment that he 'only' drove a ten-year-old (sporty, sleek, retro classic) Mazda.

When I suggested to Conteh and Stevens that perhaps it's only right that Wie and her LPGA Tour compatriots get the chance to compete in male events, considering all the ways the male golfing establishment has tried to suppress women over the years, I was met with only awkward silence.

Golf might not have been the best social sport in the world, but I'd always felt it had the potential to be. My view on the long spaces between shots was that they were excellent opportunities for conversation: a gift that golf, almost alone among sports, could offer you. Naturally I refrained from opening my mouth whilst my partners were swinging, addressing the ball or contemplating their shots, but it was obvious that my habit of theorising about the game and constructing sentences longer than three words was viewed as something that made me 'a bit quirky'. Throughout all this, I tried to keep my backstory brief and to the point – I'd given up golf for a few years, but decided to give it another go – but sometimes, faced with an unusually inquisitive pro, I would mention that I'd written a couple of books, too. Without exception, they all asked the same question.

'How much does that pay, exactly?'

'I read a book not long ago,' Steve Lewton had said at Woburn, during the second or third version of this conversation. 'I forget what it was called now. Fucking brilliant! Shit, what was it? Ah . . . that's it. *The Da Vinci Code!*'

I was used to feeling out of place on golf courses – at one time, in my late teens, I'd even gone out of my way to play up to it. But now I was actually trying my best to fit in, to dress innocuously, to not talk about books or films or TV or any of the things that I talked about normally, or if I did, to not be too challenging or distracting – and it amazed me how easy it was to stand out. At one point on the range in the prelude to round two, I'd heard my name mentioned, and while I didn't get the context, the conversation definitely included the word 'character'. Was it so odd that I was the only person who didn't think it remotely weird to want to wear his shirt untucked in the middle of a heatwave? Was my equipment so outdated that every third person needed to inspect it and pull a confused face?* Was my straw boater so eccentric that Michael Welch, the former 'next Sandy Lyle' and eleventh-place finisher on the 2005 Euro Pro Tour order of merit, was justified in pointing and laughing at it as I walked past the putting green?† It seemed so.

I could spot my fellow GMS Classic competitors at a considerable distance, both at my hotel and at the petrol station down the road where I bought my bottles of water

---

* I'm sure this wasn't anything to do with the cat piss, which seemed to have evaporated by now. But my bag had good reason to be paranoid. If it had been a human, I feel certain that by the end of the second round at Mollington it would at least have been frantically wiping its nose, certain it was displaying some stray snot, or reaching around on its back, trying to locate the 'I do it with sheep' Post-it note that someone had stuck there.
† I checked a moment later: it definitely didn't have any snot or abusive Post-it notes on it.

in preparation for my round. It wasn't just the ubiquitous sleepy hedgehog hair and J. Lindeberg belts and fluorescent tops and shaving rashes; it was their quiet, watchful eyes and a certain dipped-head doggedness about their manner. They had their own way of walking, their own way of talking. It was unacknowledged, but it was a code that united them.

In his domain, the archetypal pro golfer was like a nerdy version of a cowboy hero: he swaggered around slowly and chewed over his surroundings indifferently and didn't say much, and what he did say didn't give much away. But outside of it, he was Bambi in spiked shoes. When he was on the non-golf planet he was so sleepy and innocent, he tended not to run into too much trouble. But when the non-golf planet crossed the boundary and came to *him*, difficulties could arise. A good example of these difficulties would be the conversation that occurred between Stevens and three teenage spectators sitting by the seventeenth tee during our second round.

'Is there any trouble over the back?' Stevens asked the oldest of the three – a kid of about sixteen, with a crewcut and a Manchester United T-shirt.

By 'trouble', Stevens meant 'bunkers' or 'water' – an extension of the pond that surrounded the front of the green – and by 'over the back' he meant 'to the rear of the green', but it was obvious that the teenager did not know this, or at least was unsure. He could have replied with, 'I'm not sure.' Instead, eager to be of assistance, he said, 'The hole used to be in a different place.' Stevens simply stared at him blankly, then teed off.

'The hole used to be in a different place' was quite

simply not what you said during a golf tournament, when everyone who knew anything about golf took it for granted that the greenkeepers moved the hole placements from day to day. If anything, you said, 'Pin's back right – about thirteen yards from where it was yesterday.' Stevens didn't mean to be rude; his refined golfing brain simply could not process a statement of such guilelessness.

I hadn't been to a football match for close on two decades, but of the five people with me on the seventeenth tee, it was those Manchester United kids with whom I'd felt the greater kinship: kids who probably tried to hit the ball as far as they could at their local driving range, shouted a lot, and got chucked off golf courses for wearing trainers. After I'd teed off and Conteh and Stevens had walked ahead, I hung back and, feeling sorry for the oldest kid, asked him if he was having a good time ('Brilliant!') and if he'd seen much good golf ('Yeah! This bloke hit it and it went about two feet away from the flag and did that spinny thing!'). As a result I was a little late getting to my ball, and rushed my second shot.

Which probably said a lot about why Stevens scored 72 for the round, and I scored 80.

If I had ever had that phlegmatic geek gaucho manner, it had long since been beaten out of me. I'd strayed too far beyond the out-of-bounds for too long. I was an outsider, and people could smell it.

Was I really all that alone in feeling a little bit alienated and lonely, though? Every player I'd spoken to who'd had any experience of playing on the Europro Tour or the Challenge Tour had talked about how solitary the experience was. 'Nobody talks much.' 'Everyone keeps themselves to themselves.' 'I find it kind of cliquey.' 'Nobody goes in for a drink after the round.' 'It's fucking bleak out there.' These comments kept recurring.

'I find it hard speaking to a lot of golf pros,' I'd been told by Paul Creasey, the ex-Europro Tour player who'd caddied for John Ronson at Hollinwell. 'Most of them are very one-dimensional. All they seem to be able to talk about is golf. I used to just spend a lot of time in my hotel room after tournaments, listening to my iPod.'

So why couldn't everyone just agree to have a better time, I wondered. Maybe go out to a few gigs together, take in a bit of theatre, kick back with a few beers? It obviously wasn't that simple. The sombreness and in-curious attitude to non-golf matters was all part of the grand sacrifice, inextricably woven in with the endless practice, the lonely travel and lonely nights, the tunnel vision, the keeping things simple, the staying out of your own way.

Maybe I'd achieve that sombreness too, if I stayed out here long enough. I felt certain it would help my game. As for what I might lose in the process? It was a big question, and one I felt I already knew the answer to. But I couldn't think about that now. If I did, I would just begin to ponder all the other elements that I was realising were part and parcel of this golf pro business. The list would unfurl and unfurl, until it smothered the positive things that I could take out of the week – like the fact that I hadn't completely embarrassed myself; the fact that I had managed to complete another tourna-ment; the fact that, in the evening after my first round, I had lain flat on my bed for four hours straight with the most crippling back spasm I had ever experienced, uncertain whether I'd be able to get vertical, much less play, the next morning. I tried to hold onto my paltry achievements, but it was hard to, as my admiration grew for the people who did this week in, week out, for how much they had forfeited.

Edie was waiting for me when I arrived home. I'd called her the previous night, when I'd been in so much pain, and I think she was beginning to reconsider some of her earlier jibes about the sedate, untaxing old bloke's sport with the balls and tees. In truth, she wasn't the only one. What was I thinking when I had remembered tournament golf as a gentle stroll that 'wasn't *proper* exercise'? I'd played almost every major sport, at one time or another, but I had never been as frazzled as this, ever, in the aftermath of a sporting event.

Her eyes scanned my seaweed hair, my sticky clothes, the bags under my eyes, my Steptoe posture, the coagulating purple mess on my ripped thumb, and gave me a 'Why do you put yourself through it?' look. 'So,' she said cheerfully, 'did you win anything?'

'No,' I said. 'But on the plus side, I did get a free pitchmark repairer.'

'Well that's all right then!' she said.

As I began to unload, she surveyed the boot of the car resignedly. We'd both long since given up on cleaning it, on the basis that until all this was over, it was futile to try to stem the flow of ingrained mud, grass, stray local rules sheets, scorecards, empty Titleist sleeves, banana skins and empty drinks bottles. 'I've, er, been watching golf this afternoon,' she said.

I was astounded. 'Really?'

'Yeah. Well, I actually had a nap while it was on. All

the sounds are so slow, they're very good for sleeping to. I did watch a bit, though. They kept talking about "the money list". Don't you think it's weird how they seem to measure achievement by how much money people have won? I mean, I know it's sort of like that in other sports too, but they're not so barefaced about it.'

'Yeah, I suppose you're right.'

'I was also thinking how "golf" is "flog" backwards. It's sort of appropriate, don't you reckon? Not just in the selling sense, but in the torture sense.'

I could only concur. Looking as flayed as I did, it would have been silly not to. We gave each other a hug, and I told her how much I'd missed her. I decided to leave it a few hours before telling her about the next, imminent bit of flogging: the bit that I had hastily arranged on my mobile phone earlier in the day. I had a feeling it was going to be quite extreme.

Eight

Agolfalypse Now

To be truthful, I'd been thinking about calling Gavin Christie all year. I'd even picked up the phone and begun to dial his number a couple of times but chickened out at the last second. As fondly as I remembered him, I also knew there was a chance that an encounter with him could crush me for good – possibly not just as a pro, but as a golfer full stop. Friends who knew him had expressed their doubts as to whether he'd agree to speak to someone who made a living as a writer (Gavin had never done an interview before, so why would he agree to do so now, at the age of sixty-five?), and told me of the nickname he'd gained when he was coaching out on Tour, 'Rhino' ('Because he's thick-skinned and charges a lot'). I could still remember the day, sixteen years ago, that he'd first appeared in my golfing life, emerging out of the fog at a driving range in Nottingham like some stubbly dry-witted ghost, to tell me that what I was doing was 'fucking craaap', then, with sleight of hand, taking approximately two minutes to get me hitting the purest shots of my life. He'd disappeared – after making sure to collect adequate remuneration, naturally – just as quickly and mysteriously. The following week I'd gone on a golfing exchange holiday to Portugal and shanked almost every shot I hit.

Bob Boffinger, Cripsley's then junior organiser, had his own theory about my shank attack: 'It had nothing to do with Gavin – the only reason you were shanking is because you fell for that Portuguese girl, Shue, and allowed it to distract you.' Bob seemed to think that my decision to reacquaint myself with Gavin was a good idea, but when he wished me luck on my trip up to Edinburgh his voice had the tone of a man seeing someone off on a journey from which they might not return. For all anyone listening in might have assumed, I could have been Martin Sheen, off into the heart of darkness to track down Marlon Brando. Bob, who now worked for the English Golf Union as a junior selector, knew only too well that Gavin's ornery genius took no prisoners. A golfer might not come back from seeing him with the same psychological defences he had when he left. As a reminder, Bob invoked the story of Steve Bow, a member at Cripsley Edge who, many years ago, had been sent to see Christie, only for his prospective mentor to draw the lesson to a close after two minutes with the words, 'Och, Steve, it's nae good – let's go inside and have a cup of tea instead.' Christie, it was rumoured, had shed his people-pleasing side since then.

Christie was at the centre of so many questions I had still to answer about my golfing life. I wanted to know if the genius I'd felt touched by that day at the foggy driving range had been real, or just a figment of my easily impressed nascent imagination. Had Gavin been the one who'd diverted me from my path to the European

Tour, or had I misinterpreted his teachings on that trip to Portugal? Was my actual mistake not seeking him out again and persevering with his methods? So many of my conflicting thoughts about my swing seemed to be dim memories of his ideas doing battle with the modern swing philosophy that I'd read about and been taught by Steve Gould at Knightsbridge. For Gavin to have met me once, for thirty minutes, more than a decade and a half ago, and to have retained this much influence – well, that had to say something special about him, didn't it? The way I saw it, if, when I arrived in Edinburgh, he told me I was 'fucking craaap', I couldn't feel any less confident about my game than I already did. And at least I would have put some demons to rest and given myself a much-needed break from my endless musing over the psychological side of my game.*

It seemed totally in keeping with my mystically tinged memory of Christie that he had not been surprised to hear from me on the phone. 'Ah, Tom,' he said. 'I remember you. You were the one who called me suave and sophisticated in your book, weren't you?' He was referring to a passage where I'd confessed that, upon first encountering Christie, I'd mistaken him for a passing vagabond who just happened to have a demon eye for

---

* A sure sign that my 'mind golf' had become 'losing my mind golf' was the moment when I'd dropped my book in the bath by mistake at my hotel near Mollington and begun to analyse how the error related to my on-course strategy. It is an inevitable part of golfing life to question yourself, but when that questioning extends to 'What does it say about me, as a golfer, that I knew the side of the bath was slippy, but I went ahead and rested my paperback on it regardless?' it is a sorry state of affairs.

hand action. In fact, when I met him at Edinburgh's Waverley station a couple of days after our phone call, he looked very dapper, and could easily have passed for a man twelve or thirteen years his junior. I asked him how he was keeping.

'Och, not good, Tom,' he said. 'I went to the doctor last week about my liver. I asked him what he could give me for it. He said, "How about some onions?"'

Jamie Daniel, who'd been with me at the range that day all those years ago, and who still sometimes saw Gavin for lessons, said he could 'listen to Gavin talk for hours', but had warned me about the jokes.*

On our way to the King's Acre golf course, six miles south of the city, Gavin talked passionately about British junior golf ('Once a kid gets selected for national amateur coaching, he has to change coaches – if he doesnae, he doesnae get picked!'), national selectors ('They're pointless! Get rid of them and replace them with an order of merit system!') and his three-decade relationship with the veteran British pro, BBC commentator and ex-Ryder Cup captain Mark James ('That's when coaching really works – when there's a continuity to it and a closeness, when you're learning off each other . . .').

We arrived at the club in the midst of a cloudburst. We sat in the car, the windows steamed up, and Gavin fumed a little more about the injustices of institutionalised junior coaching. He then explained that if I wrote about him for a magazine or newspaper, he would not, on any account, be photographed.

---

* Over the course of the next three hours, I would hear the liver story three more times.

'No way,' he said. 'I'm nae innnnterrested in all that bollocks.'

On the range, as I squirted a series of necky wedge shots into the drizzle, he looked bored and fiddled with his nails. I wondered if he was about to suggest we go into the clubhouse and have a cup of tea, with a view to discussing just why I should never pick a club up again.

'What's the lightest thing in the world?' he asked.

'Er, I don't know,' I said nervously, preparing for a lesson in the physics of the swing.

'Your cock,' he said. 'It's the only thing you can lift using just your imagination.'

A moment later he stepped forward and turned my right hand an inch to the right on the grip. It felt uncomfortable, but when I stepped forward and hit another shot, something magical happened. With this tiny movement, the entire line of my swing had been cleaned up; but it was more than that: the ball felt different on the club – softer, clingier, more whole.

Then the real alchemy began: a mixture of conjuror's arm movements, minute adjustments to my stance, expertly articulated feel triggers and abominable jokes straight out of Janet and Allan Ahlberg's *X-Rated Ha Ha Bonk Book*. I hadn't hit the ball this well since . . . well, never.

'Why have sex?' Christie asked me, as I made sumptuously gluey contact with another six-iron shot, and it bored 190 yards through a left-to-right crosswind, landing next to my target flag. I waited for the punchline, but there wasn't one. What he meant was: What's the point of intercourse, when you can get a better feeling from striking a golf ball?

Being given a lesson from Christie was like a golfing version of the classic Nice Cop–Nasty Cop police-room interrogation routine. Nice Guru stayed out of it most of the time, though his meagre input was crucial to the mix. 'But that's too simple, isn't it?' he would say, watching the ball admiringly. However, as soon as Nice Guru had told me that if I was an amateur and I stuck with him as my teacher, I could be 'playing off plus figures, easy', Nasty Guru stepped in. 'How old are you?' he asked me. I told him I'd just turned thirty-one. 'Och, no, you're finished,' he said. 'You may as well order your coffin.' He asked me if I was married, and I told him I was. 'Och, no, Tom. Och, dear,' he replied. When I confessed that I didn't play golf every day, his reaction – a single grave shake of the head – made me wonder if he'd misheard me, or perhaps thought that by 'play golf' I'd actually meant 'stay off crystal meth-amphetamine'.

He probably knew he couldn't dampen my spirits. With that turn of my right hand, my good mood had become irrepressible. I felt as if I could have walked out from under the range's roof through the deluge, umbrellaless, and arrived at the car park 300 yards away with not a drop of moisture on me. Here was a bright beam of confirmation that my instincts about the golf swing were correct after all. I had been right to abandon my lessons at Knightsbridge – I only wished I'd been to see Gavin sooner after doing so. Steve Gould's methods had worked wonders for other, more technically minded players, but I preferred Christie's reasoning. It seemed to go along with P.G. Wodehouse's Oldest Member's assertion that 'In every human being the germ of golf is implanted at birth.' A golf swing was an imprint of your soul. It wasn't something you built, nor was it something you styled, like a haircut; it was something pre-existing, that you just had to tap into. And that, in the end, was what was so great about Christie: what he told you didn't feel like a new idea to go haring after, it felt like something you'd known all along, that you might now be able to use to find peace.

'Donnae tell me anyone out there hits it better than that,' he said, as another six-iron was nonchalantly dispatched.

So why wasn't Christie better known? Because, as he continued to point out at approximate ten-minute intervals, he was 'nae innnnterrested in all that bollocks'. And also because, in his own words, he was 'a loose cannon. I've always done what I want, and I always will.' These days, your local dustman is Googleable, but the infallible Internet search engine only brought up three results for Gavin when I typed his name into it – all passing mentions, in connection with Mark James or his Euro Challenge Tour pupil Stuart Davies, with no biographical detail. He seemed to have exempted himself from the modern age – which was probably convenient, since he didn't appear too fond of it. He said he had never been on TV and never would be, no matter how much remuneration he was offered ('I'm nae innnnterrested' etc.), because he would see it as a betrayal of his pupils ('If I was on there and someone asked me how one of my players was putting and I said "Not well" then forever more he'd be seen as a bad putter, when that's not even what I'd said'). 'I'm nae giving away my secrets

in a golf magazine, either.'* To him, the answers to the
riddles of the golf swing were as sacred as the Magician's
Code: it was a point of honour not to reveal them.

After I'd finished hitting my basket of balls, we headed
into the King's Acre clubhouse. 'What's cheap?' Christie
asked the barmaid. I bought a panini for him and some
chips for myself ('Och, Tom, they'll nae do you any
good'), and he talked about the overcomplication of
modern golf. 'I would concede you have to eat well, but
all this physio and dietician stuff – it's all bullshit.'

'You need a degree in hieroglyphics to teach golf,' he
said. 'You can see what you're doing with all this video
technology they've brought in, but what you don't get is
a sense of how it feels. That's the important thing. It's
like if I say to you the word 'dough'. I could mean one
of three things,† and you wouldn't know which.'‡

So did he not think the standard of teaching, and of
golf in general, had improved in recent years?

'Och, Tom, you cannae compare it to the old days.
There's no one to match the guys from the past.'

'But surely the modern players hit it longer and
straighter?' I said.

'Don't tell me people hit the ball better nowadays than
they did before. It's all in the equipment. Answer me
this: What's easier? Hitting a four-iron into a par-four,

* He later confessed that he'd once almost considered writing for
Golf Monthly, but 'only if they paid me as much as David Leadbetter'.
† I supposed he meant a female deer, money, or the stuff you use
for baking.
‡ I refrained from telling him that, going on his reputation and nick-
name, I'd automatically think 'dough' in the financial sense.

or a nine-iron? My granny could hit a nine-iron onto the green of a par-four, and she's dead. But nobody has to hit a long iron any more, hardly ever. The R&A have made it too easy. They should at least have their own ball in The Open that doesn't go too far.'

Before our meeting, Gavin had told me that he would not go on the record with any negative comments about his fellow pros. Nonetheless, he had plenty to say about them. At one point, one of the employees at King's Acre mentioned an ageing former Ryder Cup player, to which Gavin responded simply by making a triangle over his crotch with his hands.* He seemed to have an opinion on pretty much everything, whether it was the demise of British boy wonders due to 'overloading their game', or the social and intellectual shortcomings of supposedly irreproachable British golfing figureheads. Did he ever upset people with his straight talking, I wondered.

'No doubt I do. I'm nae here to keep you happy, I'm here to get you right. If you're wanting a subtle bedside manner, donnae come to me. I'm nae fucking pussyfooting around. My players know that I'm on their side and I'm not down on them for the sake of it. You've got to be realistic in this game. I'm nae innnnterrested in working with bad players. There's nothing in it for me.'

---

* I hadn't seen this gesture before. I can't say I knew what it meant for sure, but I have my suspicions. What I am certain it didn't mean was: 'That ageing former Ryder Cup player that you mention has a triangle on his crotch, which he sometimes plays, when in need of musical relief.'

I took the plunge and asked him if he'd got pleasure out of the ninety minutes he'd spent watching me on the range. I had a feeling I was going to get an honest answer.

'Yeah, you see, because you got it, just like that.' He snapped his fingers. 'But let's see you playing at international level, then we'll see if you've got it.'

Gavin had taught some of the best of the previous generation of European pros – Howard Clark, Ian Woosnam, Mark James, Richard Boxall – but while he spoke highly of Luke Donald, he couldn't think of any of their modern descendants he was keen to work with. 'It's kids I'm interested in, but when you say that these days you're a paedophile.' Ideally, he said he'd like to take a junior under his wing from the age of ten and carry it all the way through, without them getting distracted by other coaches. 'But that's too pure, isn't it? You can only hope for it.'

This led him back to James, whom he'd first met when he'd been the pro at Burghley Park in the mid-sixties and the future Ryder Cup captain had been a promising junior. 'When you work with a player like that, you get feedback. He's teaching you.' For three and a half decades, Christie had not just followed James around the world from practice ground to practice ground, he'd also walked thousands of rounds with him – 'Some coaches think the work stops on the range, but it doesn't; you need to see how a player performs on the course, because what he thinks he's doing might not be what he's really doing' – but for the past six years they had not exchanged a word. Their rift had occurred when James had pulled out of the Seve Trophy in 2000. 'I was probably a bit rash getting mad at him,' he said, 'but it was Seve, for God's sake. You've got tae play for Seve!'*

Now, as we drove back into Edinburgh, he rhapsodised about James's formidable intellect and the uniquely symbiotic nature of their relationship, and I saw a watery redness materialise around his eyes.† We had almost arrived back at the train station now, and I felt I was starting to see that the soft underbelly of the Rhino had been bruised by a faddish golfing age. I wondered if, given a bit more time, Gavin might have admitted that he wished he'd had a bit more recognition. But perhaps he had just been lulling me into a false sense of security before mounting one last charge.

'So, Tom, what shall we call it?' he said, as he pulled the car to a halt. 'Two hundred and fifty?'

Two hundred and fifty what, I wondered. Balls? Shots? It took me a full twenty seconds to realise he was negotiating his fee.

'Now come on, Tom, this doesn't come for free.'

I had never paid more than £20 for a golf lesson in the past. Admittedly, that figure had been for a session a third of the length of the one I'd just received from Gavin,

---

* A couple of weeks after our meeting, Christie and James put their differences aside and began working together again.
† All year, I'd been developing a theory that the best golfers were either highly intelligent or a bit on the simple side. You either took a straightforward brain out onto the course, which meant you never had to overcomplicate matters, or you had an in-built acumen that allowed you to simplify your thought processes at will. When I told Christie this, he agreed, and became as animated as I'd seen him all day. 'That's right! The thing about the great ones who've got that intelligence, like Jack Nicklaus and Tom Watson, is that they can *condense* it.'

but I was stunned. The previous day I had arranged the second bank loan of my pro golf career and the trip to Edinburgh alone had cost me well over £100. It was yet another expense that had been easy to overlook, back when I'd been estimating the costs of my pro life. And I had seen Gavin just once. A committed pro was expected to see his teacher at least once a fortnight. It was outrageous! How was a Europro Tour player supposed to survive?

But there was another part of me that reasoned that today should not come cheap. In the none-more-materialistic sport of golf, £150 – the fee that I eventually settled on with Gavin – wouldn't even have bought me a top-of-the-range driver or a round at one of Britain's top courses. What Gavin had given me was more precious than either of those things. I had witnessed a glimpse of rare genius: not the kind of genius that popped up on Sky Sports in the spare time during an American network ad break and analysed David Toms' swing, but the kind that comes out of the mist on a winter's night in 1990, blows your mind, vanishes for sixteen years, only to return, just as obstinately as you had hoped, to blow your mind more extensively still, and turn powerless effort into effortless power. I might not see its like again.

Not only that, I got a little after-care service to boot. The afternoon after I arrived back from Edinburgh, I was burning some garden waste when Edie came out of the back door clutching my mobile phone. For much of the morning I'd been blasting balls up the driving range in freewheeling fashion. I'd tired myself out and made my thumb stream with blood again. My intention had been to come home and rest, but I'd found that I had nervous energy (and a dead tree) to burn.

'Someone's left you a message,' she said. 'It's quite a frightening one. They didn't say hello or goodbye or who they were, but whoever it is sounds a bit like that Scottish bloke from *Dad's Army*.'

I dialled my voicemail and listened to Gavin say, 'I'm just checking to see if you're praaactising.'

When you hear something like that, you don't ask questions or make excuses. Within twenty minutes, I was back at the range.

Nine

Shut that Door

One of the best things about deciding to be a pro golfer
is the inevitable moment, not long into your career, when
your friends offer to caddy for you. Back in January, I'd
received all kinds of unexpected offers from would-be
bagmen. My subsequent analysis of their potential for the
job had been enormous fun, and had prompted me to
think of the flaws and strengths of long-term acquaintances
in whole new ways.* But by August most of these offers
had dried up, as friends in regular nine-to-five employment realised the impracticality of travelling halfway across
the country to spend two or three unglamorous days helping
me look for my ball in heavy shrubbery, and friends out
of regular nine-to-five employment did the maths on a 10
per cent cut of nothing.

Casual slave-driving had always been a fundamental
part of my golf fantasy life. I liked picturing myself

---

* My entry for my rock musician friend Chris Sheehan, for example,
read thus: 'Strength: quick walker. Flaw: could get distracted by
worrying about hair in rainstorm.'

strolling the fairway, twirling my club, with some affable hunchback at my side eagerly humping the tools of my trade. A character of indeterminate age, he would have a nickname like 'Croaky Joe' or 'Ankles McGill', and would stare off wisely towards the flag and say things like, 'There's a lot of wind up there you can't see, sir.' After a remunerative week in a faraway place, I would send him off to explore the local nightlife with a wad of £20-notes in his fist, and he would not be seen until the following week's tournament, where he would be waiting for me faithfully on the range, a devilish flicker in his one remaining eye and a gnarly hand resting on a set of irons buffed to a face-reflecting shine.

It was painful to have to abandon this fantasy, but as a self-sufficient club carrier, I was far from alone on the Europro Tour. Only about a third of the players used caddies, and most of these were strictly part-timers: either elderly patrons from their home clubs, dads, or bored-looking girlfriends or wives. The remaining two thirds carried lightweight canvas bags or attached more formidable waterproof carrying devices to battery-powered trolleys.

There was a time when owning an electric golf trolley was tantamount to confessing that you liked nothing better of an evening than coming back from the allotment, popping your false teeth in the nearest drinking receptacle and putting your varicose veins up in front of an episode of *Last of the Summer Wine*. As I remember, during my time as a member, only three people at Cripsley Edge Golf Club had owned one. Two of them, it was rumoured, had artificial hips. The other was a man of at least 140 who had eerily jet-black hair and a way of walking with his arms stretched out in front of him that made him look like an extra from a George A. Romero film, and was known to the junior section by the affectionate nickname 'The Living Dead'. These days, though, it seemed that anyone over the age of sixteen with a quarter of an eye or more on a pro career owned a Powakaddy or Motocaddy or one of their cheaper rivals. This, I was ashamed to say, included me – although since I'd got my Powakaddy back in late spring I'd only taken it for a couple of tentative, quickly curtailed test runs.

By the time I set off for the Bovey Castle Championship in Devon, my sixth tournament of the year, my back pain had reached new heights. Barely a day would go by without at least a two-hour period when I was beset by the sensation of an invisible leather band crushing my internal organs. In view of this, and my stubborn reluctance to see a chiropractor, I probably shouldn't have been bashful about using an electric trolley, but I could still hear a little teenage voice in my head mocking me – the same voice that ordered me to ignore the supportive double-strap formation on my bag and choose to carry it in the old-school, low-slung single-strap style. I had also encountered a small technical problem: my bag was not big enough to fit comfortably within the trolley's holding compartment, and kept tumbling off – often with comically terrible timing. For the Bovey event, however, I had been blessed with a new, larger, snugger-fitting bag, courtesy of my well-connected ex-manager. It seemed only right to transport it in style.

A first glimpse of Bovey Castle served to validate my decision to use my trolley. On the whole, I'd been a little bit disappointed by the insights offered by the websites of Europro Tour venues. Looking at, say, Stonebridge Golf Club in the Forest of Arden, in the hope of getting a reserve spot in the Sweeneys Environmental Classic, I'd been left pretty much in the dark about the nature of the course, but had gleaned plenty of information about an upcoming Tina Turner Tribute Night. Bovey's site had been much more generously designed, and in the flesh it didn't disappoint. It was also the most undulating course I'd played all year. Set on the edge of Dartmoor National Park, it was cut through a steep valley, with two small rivers snaking in and out of play on the majority of its holes. You could have piled fifty versions of its manor-ish clubhouse hotel on top of each other and still not covered the airspace between the course's lowest and highest points.

As I traversed the first few holes, I was soothed by the buzz of my new battery-powered friend.* It was another of those moments that had become an increasingly-frequent feature of my golfing existence, when the words 'bolted', 'door', 'stable', 'horse' and 'shut' couldn't help but rattle around my mind. Why had I not done this earlier? What kind of hassle could I have saved myself? Had I not learned anything from the havoc vertebrae problems had wreaked on the careers of my heroes Seve Ballesteros and Fred Couples? My mum had always suffered from spine problems and she had been told that the cause had been the heavy schoolbooks she'd been made to carry in her rucksack as a child. I couldn't help but ponder the damage my generation of junior golfers had done to themselves by transporting much heavier objects. Was it any surprise that when I'd taken a fledgling-golfer friend to the 2005 London Golf Show, he remarked that he'd 'never seen so many people in one place with such bad posture'?

* Not a statement I recommend anyone to make in formal company.

At previous events I'd watched, with a doomed sense of underpreparation, as fellow players delved into bags big enough in which to grow cherry trees and unveiled obscure power drinks, energy bars, reserve baseball caps, towels, brand-new leather gloves and laser rangefinders. So at Bovey, with new golfing luggage and no compunction about overfilling it, I packed for peace of mind. As well as the usual balls and tees and pitchmark repairers and bottles of water and gloves* and crumpled local rules sheets and suntan lotion and permanent marker and pencil and car keys and mobile phone, I added a notebook, a packet of Nurofen, some plasters, a spare headcover, a bath towel, three bananas, a spare shirt, and my REO Speedwagon baseball cap (in case I tired of the straw boater). For the final touch, I included my secret weapon: a child-sized, circular-grooved, hickory-shafted seven-iron from the 1930s that I'd been given by a friend of my granddad's just before my first ever game of golf. With all this preparation, I was hoping to banish the feeling that my pro golf train had left without me. Bovey could be where everything finally came together: the place where the confidence that had been

---

* Well, two. Although I had replaced the blackened London Golf Show glove with a new leather Titleist model, the former had been experiencing a revival in recent weeks, owing to Karl Morris. Morris had given me a trigger in which I used green as my 'switch on' colour. I was supposed to rehearse my best shots whilst thinking of it, and look at it just before I started my pre-shot routine. I'd chosen green myself (Morris had told me to pick any colour I wanted) on the basis that on a golf course it would be everywhere. But I needed something more specific. The green label on the old glove seemed to do the trick. And besides, the Titleist glove had a hole in it now, in the exact place where my thumb was blistered.

planted at Karl Morris's house and grown in the presence of Gavin Christie started to bloom.

My confidence was further enhanced by the knowledge that, in contrast to Mollington, this week I would not be fighting for sleep on a hard hotel bed in a room without air conditioning or fully opening windows. I was lucky enough to have the use of my friend Emma's eighteenth-century farmhouse, a rambling idyll down a track on the edge of the moor with swifts darting out of its eaves and a stream trickling beneath its foundations. It seemed only logical that Edie should join me. Given the state of our bank account, it was going to be the nearest we got to a vacation in 2006.

If there was one drawback to my pre-tournament groundwork, it was that, for the second time in the season, I missed out on a practice round. The drive from Norfolk to Devon had taken an unprecedented, jam-blighted eight and a half hours, and we'd arrived just as the light was fading on Monday evening. On Tuesday, the course was closed for the pre-tournament pro-am* and some last-minute greenkeeping, so I had to make

---

* 'Featuring,' as I learned from the promotional literature on the website, 'tea, coffee and bacon rolls . . . followed by a Sportsman's Dinner hosted by snooker legend Steve Davies.' I assumed that, by 'Steve Davies', they were referring to the six-time world snooker champion who normally spelled his surname without the 'e', often with the unfortunate addition of 'Interesting' before it. Or maybe it was another Steve Davies altogether? Steve Davies from the Europro Pot Black Tour, perhaps? Whatever the case, it was doubtful that, in the minds of struggling Europro Tourers not selected for the pro-am, his presence compensated for the irritation of having to fork out an extra night of accommodation expenses in order to play a practice round.

do with walking the fairways and feeling the terrain out with my feet. But I couldn't complain. Here I was, in one of my favourite parts of the country, on a still, sunny day, feeling the peace that only a great golf course on a still, sunny day can provide – a peace that, for some bizarre reason, I'd once chosen to eliminate from my life.

Earlier, I'd marched boldly to the centre of the line on the practice ground – all fear of the dreaded shank gone. My sense of well-being had been buoyed further when a couple of players I vaguely recognised from Mollington said 'Hello, Tom' to me. I was even approached by a man in his sixties with a baseball cap who asked me if I was looking forward to tomorrow. I was dressed in cords, a long-sleeved collarless T-shirt and trainers, my hair wild and scruffy, and I was without golfing paraphernalia, yet there seemed to be no doubt in this stranger's mind that I was a competitor.

'I come here every year with my family,' he said. 'When I found out this event was on as well, I thought, "All the better!" I think you boys are amazing. I can't see any difference between the way you hit the ball and the way Phil Mickelson and wassisname, that old Ernie Els, do.'

For much of the year I'd been forced to see myself through the pro golf world's eyes as an out-of-place, outdated anomaly. It wasn't just the way that Jamie had looked at my swing at Hollinwell and evaluated it so curiously – like an antique dealer appraising a novelty lamp – or the similarly toned admission from Paul Creasey, John Ronson's caddy, that his first impressions of me were 'torn between hacker and one-off talent'.

When Gavin Christie had got onto the obligatory topic of Michelle Wie, he'd asked me not what I felt about her taking the place of me or one of my pro colleagues in a men's tournament, but what I would have felt if I'd had a 'son' who was a pro golfer and she had stolen his place in a tournament.

But now, suddenly, I was one of 'the boys'? I suppose I should have been happy. But I wasn't sure if I was entirely comfortable with the concept. What I was sure of was that the prospect of teeing off was not accompanied by the sensations of dread and incongruity that had followed me all year. There was still dread, but it wasn't the kind that sucker-punched you in the kidneys and rendered you a human blancmange. It was a different kind, that kept its distance but gave you a nasty little pinch from time to time. It was the dread of wasting a good thing.

In the other sports I've enjoyed – badminton, table tennis, tennis, football – I've had the occasional day when a feeling of rightness has rushed through me. In those cases, the results have rarely varied: I have played to the best of my ability, immersed in the fast-spin cycle of competition. In the more ponderous sport of golf, though, days like these are no guarantee of success. There is always time to talk yourself out of something, no matter how good your biorhythms, no matter how good the conditions.

My first round at Bovey Castle started, however, with one of the greatest shots I have ever hit.

The first hole at Bovey – which is actually the eleventh during non-tournament play – is a long par-four of 460 yards. The tee shot is not as narrow as some on the course, but executing it well is vital. With a steep slope in front of the green leading down into a pond, any second shot that doesn't fly all the way to the putting surface is a terrible mistake, and not just because it will almost certainly prompt someone in the vicinity to make some clichéd crack about 'getting your wetsuit on'. The important thing is to drive powerfully, rendering the second shot as short as possible so it can be easily controlled, missing the water and stopping quickly enough to avoid the thick, goading foliage a few feet beyond the green.

I'd pondered this second shot for several moments the previous day, and I didn't particularly relish pondering it any more, so I'd tried – overambitiously, as it turned out – to time the long walk from the practice putting green to the tee to leave just enough time for a few practice swings, the ritual of swapping cards with my playing partners, and the standard local rules briefing from the starter. Not only did I arrive to find the official frantically calling out my name and radioing through to the tournament office to find out where I was, I also found that the threeball directly in front of mine had barely left the tee. There was going to be a wait of ten minutes or so, and it would be all I could do not to think about that pond.

It's at periods like this that it's the starter at a golf tournament's unofficial job to break the tension by making banter with the players. In this regard, today's volunteer – a silver-haired man with a Moretonhampstead Golf Club jumper and an air just a little too patrician for him to fall into the Ron or Roy category – was a little more garrulous than most.

'We've had some humorous moments here on the tee already,' he explained, with a slight guffaw. 'Just a little while ago a bevy of beauties went by in a golf buggy. And – this really was very funny – there were six pros on the tee at the time and they all simultaneously said, "Sod this! I'm off!" and threw their drivers into that bush.' He pointed over to some foliage just to the left of the tee.

His anecdote-telling skills obviously needed a little sprucing up, and it was possibly a bit of a shock for all concerned to realise that there was still someone alive in Britain who used the phrase 'bevy of beauties' in a non-ironic context, but the result was successful. A couple of minutes previously, my playing partners, Paul Coburn and Adam Hawkins, and I had all made tight-lipped, perfunctory introductions, then immediately retreated into our cocoons of concentration, but now we began to quiz each other merrily about our golfing fortunes over the previous eight months. And if this was only out of fear that if we let up for a moment we might be subjected to another recollection of a 'humorous moment' – possibly involving 'lithe lovelies' or some other would-be caption from a 1975 *Sun* newspaper pictorial – it at least passed the time. The moment to tee off was upon me quickly, and when it was, I felt loose and focused. This was the happy kind of being caught off-guard: finding yourself wholly in the present, with no time for negative hypothesising.

What Gavin Christie preached was sometimes referred to as 'the flail'. It was all about spring and twang: the golfing equivalent of skimming a stone. I'd managed to keep this springiness for more than a week now, but I sometimes yearned for Gavin's gruff tones in my ear, spurring me on, reminding me of the movement's true texture. Now, however, as I took my backswing, I could almost hear him: a granite Obi Wan Kenobi telling me to 'use the force' of my hands (but obviously without *too* much force, and with an ultimate sense of effortless power). The ball took off straight and true, just like those of Paul and Adam, but when we arrived in the fairway five minutes later, there was an unexpected ego boost: I had outdriven both of them by around twenty paces. At 340 yards from the tee, I was left with only an easy pitching wedge to the green. Devilish pond? What devilish pond?

For the next few holes that same confidence always seemed within reach, but I wasn't quite able to touch it again. The Brain Worm did its bit, but this time its wiggle was a subtle one. My ball-striking, and my luck, were just a fraction off. Putts would eye up the hole, but fail to drop. A well-struck iron would catch an untimely draught and fall just short of the green into the maws of a deep bunker. A wayward drive would find an adjacent fairway subject to a freakish out-of-bounds rule of which I'd been unaware.* The outcome was that, as I stood over my ball in the wiry rough to the right of the sixteenth fairway, surveying the miserable result of a tee shot that, two minutes earlier, I'd been sure had been on the short grass, I was certain

---

* Just to compound the misery, a day later I found out that the fairway wasn't out of bounds, and the scorer on the fourth tee had given me incorrect information.

that my seven-over-par aggregate represented the worst I could possibly have scored. It was a naïve conclusion at which to arrive – one that paid no heed whatsoever to what I'd learned at Hollinwell about golf's infinite capacity for disaster – and the smothered six-iron that followed, finding a water hazard to the left of the fairway, probably served as punishment. It was just then that I saw the camera.

I'd watched a considerable chunk of Sky Sports' Europro Tour coverage before, though it was easy enough to overlook. Presented in edited highlights form, it was usually broadcast at least a week after the tournament in question, squeezed in between a minor-league darts match or a crucial heat of intervillage amateur league curling. And by 'highlights', what I really mean is 'mediumlights'. Although the leaderboard gave evidence of plentiful birdies and eagles – it was not uncommon for Europro Tour events to be won with scores of ten or more under par – the camerawork rarely backed it up, instead lingering on unremarkable lag putting and caddieless players indifferently shoving irons back into their bags, whilst commentators outlined the 'action' like bored CCTV operatives, seemingly permanently on the verge of a yawn. The one obvious attempt to pep things up had been the addition of presenter Ruth Frances, a blonde model with a look of the golf-wife-in-waiting about her who was best known for her work on late-night viewer-participation quiz shows, but even she had disappeared from more recent programmes (much to the disappointment of some of the more chivalrous players on the Tour). One could only deduce that she'd died of boredom.

I'd long since found out that the Europro Tour, with its two-men-and-a-dog galleries and conspicuous lack of autograph-hunters, was not a place oozing with glamour, but it wasn't half as unglamorous as the TV coverage made it look. Now I had the chance to witness the problem first-hand. Maybe there had been more than one camera on the course, but if so, I hadn't seen the others. And now it was trained on me. Not Kevin Harper or Sean Whiffin, the joint leaders at four under par; not Phil Rowe, who was putting together a very nice round of 67; but Tom Cox – currently at seven over par, and poised to make a dramatic move further in the wrong direction. Quite frankly, the Evil Brain Worm found this outrageous. In view of the fact that he was facing a chip – his friend the Panic Squid's least favourite kind of shot – he made an informed decision. If this camera crew was going to waste so much time on his pathetic servant, he would at least make an effort to put on a show for them.

Over the years, much has been made of the putting yips, the dreaded affliction where a player – through nerves or a mental block – is liable to jerk putts of six feet and under far wide of the hole. Few golfers are unaware of the cautionary tale of Germany's Bernhard Langer, the disease's most notorious repeat sufferer, who was once struck down so extremely that he took five putts on one green in The Open. Less has been said about the putting yips' even more malevolent brother, the chipping yips – or chyips. If, to borrow one of my favourite non-PC Tiger Woods phrases, you 'yip-spazz' a three-foot putt, it does not skitter thirty yards through the green into a water hazard. It rolls past the hole.

Then, once it has, and you have apprehensively dollied the five-foot return putt to the holeside, you safely tap in. A chyip, by contrast, has almost unlimited capacity for destruction.

The chyipping of the ex-European Tour player-turned-Sky Sports pundit Ross McFarlane became so terrifying during the later days of his playing career that he would aim to mishit the ball into the flagstick to stop it. Sometimes, in desperation, McFarlane would hit chip shots one-handed from as much as sixty yards from the flag. Then there was Dan 'Jellylegs' Davies, my fellow Cabbage Patch Masters organiser, who had been known to emerge from playing a perfunctory twenty-yard lob shot with matching grass stains on his knees.

There were remedies for chyipping out there, but nobody seemed agreed on their reliability. Back at the beginning of summer, I'd watched an outsider called Chris Coake overcome his chyipping demons by placing his left hand awkwardly below his right on the club, and go on to win the PGA Tour's Zurich Classic of New Orleans. But the purist in me didn't much like the look of the technique. I wasn't exactly encouraged, either, by a search of Internet golf sites, which informed me that yipping your chips is: a) 'an official medical condition', b) 'an affliction that has nothing to do with nerves and pressure' and c) 'an affliction that is all about nerves and pressure'. I'd been struggling with my wedge game all year, but I had enough other golfing ailments to worry about, and it always seemed easier to shove my chyips into a cupboard and deal with them later. I could find temporary ways to ignore them, using a putter from further and further off the green,* but I probably should have anticipated that, with the pressure on, the cupboard doors would burst open and my denial would rear up and bite me.

Now, with the camera trained in my direction, I looked desperately for something to draw on – a good chip from the recent past, perhaps – but I found nothing. I searched for that 1930s seven-iron, but it had slipped so far down into my bag that I couldn't get it out. My fingers might as well have been made out of sponge. It was an effort even to drop the club limply down into the grass two feet behind the ball and advance it onto a grassy knoll, six yards short of the green. It was an even bigger effort to subsequently skim the bastard thing ninety feet past the hole. This could have gone on indefinitely. The resulting quadruple-bogey eight shouldn't have felt like an achievement, but it did.

Half an hour and another dropped shot later, standing on the tee of the par-five eighteenth with a driver in my hand, my small sense of achievement from earlier had turned to unadulterated self-disgust. In 2006 I'd already had embarrassing rounds, scrappy rounds, and desperate rounds, but this was different. It was a *squandered* round. As such, it was probably my most painful to date. My golfing objectives now boiled down to a simple need: I wanted to hit the ball, hard, and when I had, I wanted

---

* Even the redoubtable Jamie, once a man who could nonchalantly nip a sand wedge off a bare lie and stop it on a sixpence, admitted that an attack of the chyips had taken its toll on his game. He now preferred to use the straighter-faced, less risky seven-iron when around the green.

to run after it, and hit it again, even harder. A delay on the tee amped my frustration. All thoughts of yardage charts were gone now. Who cared where the ball went, as long as the little white fuckpig was out of my sight? When the fairway finally cleared, the threeball behind us were waiting with us on the tee, and the group behind them were tramping noisily up the gravel path from the seventeenth green. I should have waited for the noise to stop. I didn't. I also realised belatedly that I hadn't put my glove back on after taking it off to putt on the previous green, but what help would a glove be? Could a glove take me back to the first hole? No. My drive, on the other hand, could. And that – possibly out of a subconscious need to rewind the recent past – was precisely where I put it, hooking it so far to the left that it carried past trees, boulders and rough and found the middle of the adjacent fairway.

As a reminder of what I'd frittered away, it was too cruel. I'd stood on this fairway five hours earlier, in almost the same spot, facing in the opposite direction, as a sportsman. Now I was no better than a flailing caveman with a stick. I thrashed and watched, surprised, as my ball soared towards the spot where I thought – or rather, haphazardly hoped – the green was. Later, looking at my yardage chart, I would realise the implausibility of what I'd attempted: a 290-yard carry over a copse and rough that probably hadn't seen a lawnmower since Harry Carpenter was the face of BBC golf. What was amazing was how close I came to pulling it off, how late in the ball's flight it crashed against an overhanging branch.

Earlier that day on the practice ground, I'd heard a

pro – possibly one who'd recently spent some time in the company of Gavin Christie – ask his friend, 'If a man says something wrong in the woods and there's no woman around to hear him say it, does he still make a sound?' As jokes went, it wasn't quite the worst I'd heard in the last two weeks. But I preferred my own, new version. It went like this: 'If a ball falls in the woods and there's nobody around to see it drop and those woods happen to have two-foot grass and leaf mulch within them and there are two groups waiting behind to play their shots, and it's the last hole, and the ball's owner is more tired than he has ever been in his adult life, and he doesn't open his mouth, does he still make a sound? Yes. He makes the sodding sound of his fucking soul slowly dying.'

I would have to remember to use it – possibly some other time, when my soul wasn't slowly dying.

For five minutes, Adam and Paul and I – helped first by a couple of spectators and then, finally, also by a rules official – searched frantically. For five minutes, we found every long-forgotten sunken, misshapen ball imaginable. Mine, though, had vanished. I was long beyond caring about my score now. All I could think about was that ever-growing queue on the tee behind as.

The rules official was speaking into his walkie-talkie by this point, just out of earshot. They did that a lot, these Europro Tour officials, and I sometimes wondered if they quite liked it, and how many of their discussions involved anything more vital than that night's dinner. But now paranoia struck. What could the official possibly be saying?

'It's that Cox again, holding play up. Yes, that's right,

the one with the REO Speedwagon hat. What's he want to advertise his love for REO Speedwagon for anyway? They were shit. Although I suppose "Keep on Lovin' You" is all right to sing along to, if you've had enough to drink. Over.'

'Yes, I know. He's a pain, that one. I already had to come away from my sudoku to give him a ruling on the fifteenth when he put that ball in the stream, then make him retake his drop because his hand was in the wrong place. Bit of a puffy swing, too, I noticed. Over.'

He turned back in my direction.

'I think your five-minute time limit is up,' he said. 'Come on. I'll buggy you back.'

In a professional golf tournament, players are prohibited from using buggies,* but in 'special circumstances' – for example now, when play needed speeding up – a member of the tournament staff may be permitted to give them a lift. It is impossible to say quite how grateful I was for this ruling, as we zipped back through the rough, and I think I can safely say that Paul and Adam, who were now putting up on the green, felt the same.

I stood, once again, in the fairway of the first hole, just a few feet from the divot mark my wedge had made at the beginning of the round. I was now playing my

---

* Probably a good thing. In my experience, where a golf buggy goes, trouble follows not far behind it. The last time I took the wheel of a buggy, I got a little overzealous and crashed it into a ball-washer pod. And while I was slightly jealous of the members at my last club but one who drove around the course, I was slightly less jealous of the fact that, every time they got close to the road that ran parallel to the course, a Subaru Impreza driver would inevitably materialise, wind down his window, and shout 'Wanker!' at them.

fourth shot on the eighteenth. After another drop – for which I tried to strike a balance between 'raising my hand high enough to stay within the rules' and 'not raising my hand so high that it looked as if I was taking the piss' – I selected a four-iron. As I waggled, I told myself, 'Just a safe shot, back into the fairway, then let's wedge up onto the green.' Maybe I could still salvage a bogey six out of this.

I knew the shot was going to be sweet, six inches into the downswing. I looked up, confidently . . .

To see the ball heading into the exact same deadly copse where I had hit my previous shot.

As I hauled my clanking joints back into the buggy, I probably shouldn't have allowed myself a sneaky peek back to the tee. We'd called one group through, but now three more were congregating there, watching all this unfold – fatigued, frustrated men, desperate to get back to their hotels and B&Bs to rest, eat and re-gel their hair. Even the stern demeanour of my rules official friend had cracked now, and as he looked across at me he pressed his lips together in sympathy. I wondered what was the worst that could be happen if I bailed out of the buggy and began to run, not stopping until I reached the summit of Dartmoor, then, using sticks, animal excrement and sheep's wool, built myself a shack where I could hide from the rest of the professional golf community for the next decade or two. Obviously I'd miss Edie terribly, and I'd take time to adjust to the new diet and the lack of satellite TV, but it couldn't be that bad, could it?

This time, after another frenetic search, we located the ball, but it was a close-run thing. Four hurried slashes of my wedge later, I stepped over a thirty-foot putt, and confidently curled it in for a nine, and a sixteen-over-par round of 86.

To their credit, Adam and Paul still seemed to be on speaking terms with me. I imagine, even in the creakingly slow environment of tournament pro golf, neither of them had ever spent fifty-seven minutes on one hole before.

'Well done for finishing,' said Paul, patting me on the back. 'A lot of people would have just given up.'

It was a nice thing to say. But I wondered if I could detect a silent 'sensible' before the 'people' bit.

And, just like that, it was all gone: the free-flowing limbs, the confidence, the temporary hint of a competitive edge.

In the middle of that night, an exterior door in Emma's farmhouse that had been locked on the inside flew inexplicably open. It unsettled me, but probably not as much as the events of the final hole. In my fitful dreams, I played a par-five eighteenth which felt as if it would never end, then, when I finally reached the green, a big, gothic door swung violently open, leading me back to the tee. By the following day, my swing had once again become an ungainly mystery. That 'It's not how, it's how many' mantra was annoyingly apposite once again, and not in a good way. My score – 88 – was in the same gruesome-verging-on-humiliating ballpark as its predecessor, but that was where the similarities ended. Yesterday, I'd built a nice boat that had unaccountably sprung a steady leak that had turned into a flood. Today, I was in the water before I even began, clinging to whatever driftwood I could find. My standards had never been lower. Once, my hope had been to match my best ever amateur score of 67 in a pro tournament, possibly even better it. That had been modified to 'I hope I break 80.' Now, I quite simply didn't want to come last.

I was not the only one struggling as the wind got up, and the two-round cut came at six over par. Paul, one of the easiest-going men I'd met on Tour, who'd seemed so unflappable throughout the woes of a 77 yesterday, began well, but finally cracked after a misjudged iron on the par-four fifteenth, his scream of 'FUUUUCC-CKKKING CUNTTTTT!' causing a crow to fly out of a nearby tree in terror in a way that might have been comic under less painful circumstances. Adam, who had a touch of Woody Harrelson in *Natural Born Killers* about him, bemoaned the lack of prize funding from the Europro Tour. 'I'm OK, because I own my house outright and I know I can make twenty-five grand a year playing in pro-ams,' he said. 'But not everyone's in that posi-tion. We're coming out here every week and paying nearly three hundred quid, before expenses. If we're breaking even, we're doing well.' He rested his foot on a slightly shabby tee marker bedecked with the Europro Tour logo, as if to illustrate his point. 'It sometimes seems a bit of a con. The Tour doesn't pay for the courses that host the tournaments, the courses pay them for the publicity. And they've got all this sponsorship, and 160 or more players giving them 275 quid every week. If they're not going to raise the prize fund from £40,000, they could at least make the money stretch further back into the field.'

Adam did not quite fit in with the inexpressive, wet-look image I'd come to associate with the up-and-coming pro ranks. He had a piledriver swing, a background in the navy, and a haircut and manner to match. I liked him immediately. He had travelled to the tournament with a friend in a camper van, and this morning had given a young boy-racer pro a talking to for cutting him up on the club driveway. When a fellow pro annoyed him – like David Fisher, the 1993 English Amateur Champion, who Adam claimed had blanked him recently when he'd said good morning to him – he had no reservations about talking about it. 'You can tell he's a twat, just by the way he dresses,' he said of Fisher, who had a reputation for wearing the most outrageous outfits on Tour.*

I'd seen Fisher on the practice ground earlier that day. He'd stuck in my memory partly because he had the longest hair and only proper beard I'd seen on a golfer all year, and partly because, when a cow had let out a moo in a nearby pasture, he'd called over to a fellow pro, 'Oi! Jezza! Listen! It's that bird you pulled last night!' A week later I saw him again, this time on Sky Sports, as the main subject of a report on snappy dressing on the Europro Tour, forming part of the Bovey Castle Championship programme.

I'd just about started to rationalise my Bovey disaster by that point. I took some comfort from the fact that I had not only achieved my goal of not coming last, but

---

* The word 'outrageous' is used here in a strictly relative sense. Most of the outfits I saw Fisher in – thick-rimmed performance sunglasses, Farah-style slacks, liberally buttoned polo shirts with a crucifix necklace dangling underneath – brought to mind nothing quite so much as the casual wear of a somewhat reserved, retired disco dancer.

had beaten the former Arsenal footballer-turned-pro golfer Lee Dixon (84–94) into thirteenth-from-last place by four shots. Nonetheless, that sixteenth-hole cock-up in the first round in front of the cameras was proving hard to erase from my memory, and it had been with a slight sense of trepidation that I'd switched on the Sky Plus to watch the Bovey show.

The coverage unfolded at its usual drowsy pace, not particularly enhanced by an interview with the England cricket international Andrew Flintoff, who was holidaying at Bovey Castle, and explained that he 'didn't know a great deal about the Europe [sic] Tour'. I was beginning to think I'd made a lucky escape as the first two rounds drew to a close and the presenter, Matt Dawson, began to address the more important business of the final day's play. But as Fisher – whose clothes were clearly a lot snappier than Sky's editing skills – spoke repetitively of the joys of 'jazzing up his gear' I looked up from my cup of tea and noticed a flash of something familiar and hairy. I hit rewind, and watched, for all of two seconds, as my dejected form appeared on the screen, squeezed in between footage of a serious-looking man in a diamond sweater and bright-blue trousers and what appeared to be a random shot of one of the greenkeepers. On the voiceover, Fisher talked about the number of pros who were 'trying something different' with their clothing. The only thing I'd been trying to do differently at the time was not to shank my chip shot. But if the producers at Sky wanted to categorise some cheap H&M trousers, a French Connection polo shirt that had shrunk slightly in the wash and an REO Speedwagon trucker cap as part of the vanguard of golfing fashion, that was fine by me – particularly if it meant Sky viewers didn't get to see my chyips at their worst. I was pleased to note, also, that if you looked at the screen quickly, you might not even have noticed the stain from the milk that I'd splashed down my front that morning while rushing my cornflakes.

Ten

Mighty Mouse

Ben Witter wanted to show me a new trick. Its execution was not as complex as that of many of his others, such as the one where he hit drives while kneeling on a giant inflatable fitness ball, or the one where he used a special club twice as long as his body. Its charm was all in the element of surprise. Most importantly, it was original. 'You've got to keep on your toes here,' he said, gesturing at the rest of the World Golf Trick-Shot Championship competitors warming up a few yards to our left. 'Everyone's always looking for a new idea.' The trick involved placing a tiny firecracker behind his ball when he teed it up. As his driver made contact with it, there would be a small bang and a puff of smoke, leaving the spectator momentarily unsure where to look: at the explosion, or at the ball, drilling into the distant sky.

There were some, however, who might have said that in Witter's case such firepower was superfluous.

Witter was long off the tee. Not Stephen Lewton long, either: a whole different kind of long that seemed to hint at a childhood plunge into a cauldron of magic potion. A moment before he showed me the firecracker trick I'd watched, eyes goggling, as he smashed three wind-hampered drives over a lake and three of Hanbury Manor's fairways and into a hedge. At least, I thought it was a hedge. Who knows? It could have been the tree-line a few miles down the road, bordering the M25. I'm a touch short-sighted, but to follow Witter's shots you would have needed not just laser surgery, but laser vision too.

'You should have seen me before I got ill,' he said. 'I'm only operating on about 80 per cent of my old power these days.'

A Giant Redwood of a man from Pennsylvania, Witter had an almost Schwarzenegger-esque, superhero-ish bearing, and a backstory begging for a biopic. As a promising young pro, he'd been diagnosed with a rare form of salivary gland cancer – a large portion of his jaw had been removed. Despite this, he had recovered sufficiently to twice win his country's National Long Drive Championship. More health problems arrived in 2000 – a car crash left him with a detached retina. Only last November he'd been diagnosed with cancer for a second time, and had two thirds of his left lung removed. This made turning his body incredibly difficult, although you would never have known it from watching him swing.

'That never gets old!' he said, turning to me with an enormous grin after another gargantuan hit.

How far did that one go?

'Oh I'd guess about 340,' he said. 'Not massive. My personal best in competition is 409.'

I chuckled internally, thinking back to those times when I'd hit drives at Thetford and Diss and my playing partners had called my hitting 'monstrous'. My drive on the first hole at Bovey Castle had been a long hit, but I'd had an assisting breeze, and it had been a bit of a one-off. Most of my driving seemed pathetic now. I felt like an Action Man doll coming face-to-face with a full-sized member of the SAS.

I'd come to the World Trick-Shot Championships after receiving an invite from its organiser, Jeremy Dale. At one time Dale had been a playing pro, but over the last twelve years he had found more success on the trick-shot circuit, perfecting such routines as 'Edward Scissorhands' (a trick of patted-head-stroked-tummy co-ordinative complexity that involved walking forward and hitting a row of balls at high speed by swinging two clubs, one-handed, in opposite directions) and 'Magic Chair' (which involved Dale hitting 200-yard drives while sitting on some patio furniture). The World Trick-Shot Championship was a relatively new project of his – an attempt to bring together golf-trick mavericks from around the globe. Featuring all manner of golfing paraphernalia, from club shafts made of garden hoses to six-foot-high tees to clubs whose faces were bigger than those of the men wielding them, its jovial, experimental atmosphere could not have been more different from that of the tournaments in which I'd been competing. For me, it was a chance to see where a failed pro might go, if he wanted to continue to hit balls for a living.

I had another, possibly more pressing, reason for

coming to Hanbury Manor. Since Bovey Castle, two weeks before, something worrying had happened to me: I'd lost all desire to hit a golf ball. I'd waited for the buzzing sensation in my hands, the irresistible mental pictures of wedge shots landing on slick, well-watered greens and spinning back, the sudden urge to form my fingers into a Vardon grip around the vacuum cleaner tube – classic symptoms of golf fever that had been present even on my darkest amateur days – but they had not arrived. I had reached a curious state of acceptance about my game, a state that, ironically, was as phlegmatic as the one I had tried and failed to achieve on the course. I knew that the low-level, introverted misery I had witnessed at Bovey Castle and Mollington and Hollinwell and Stoke-by-Nayland was just the everyday stuff of a tough sportsman's life, but it was a million miles away from what *my* everyday life had been until 2006, and I had let it get to me. There had been low points on golf courses when I'd been a kid, too, but at least they had been offset by the promise of larking around in the club snooker room or burying your mate's sun visor in a bunker afterwards. It was not just that I had realised I was not made to compete in this environment. I was having doubts, too, about continuing to watch others compete in it. 'The thing you'll notice out here is that every single person can hit it,' I'd been told on numerous occasions by people on and surrounding the Europro Tour, Challenge Tour and Open Qualifying. And there was something heartbreaking about seeing people do exactly that – hit it, in a way almost identical to the players at the very top of the game – yet, unfathomably, fail to live up to their potential. There was such an inherent injustice to this that hot-headed outsiders might have wondered how the players of the Europro Tour confined themselves to a miniature kick at a tee marker or a quick profanity – why weren't they running amok across the greens with their sand wedges? But a good player could not allow his anger to triumph; he had to let it out in short, sharp, controlled bursts, as if opening the valve on a tyre.

One could say that the Trick-Shot Championship was another part of the same sad enigma – another illustration of the difference between scoring and striking. How could someone be able to curve the ball at will whilst using a club that was only nine inches long, or send a ball 250 yards from his knees, yet have failed to succeed at the comparatively straightforward business of hitting fairways and greens and holing a few putts? But the trick-shot ghetto also provided a much-needed reminder of a more playful side to my favourite game, that it wasn't always about sombre, teeth-grinding endurance, that it could be whooped over and laughed at. Essentially, the World Trick-Shot Championship was a grown-up, controlled version of the kind of larking around that I'd done with my Cripsley Edge mates in shiftless moments as a teenager. Had I decided to extend my golf gimmick repertoire beyond sand wedge keepie-uppies and putter wanging, I might have been here as a competitor too.

All the action at Hanbury was a welcome relief – particularly the bits involving fitting protective jockstraps to members of the crowd, then hitting balls off their crotches – but I found myself gravitating, again and again, towards the competitors who had made power-hitting their trick-shot *forte*. Of all the things that had changed about golf since the late nineties, nothing had changed quite so drastically as the tee shot, and nothing had impressed me more. In 1993, when John Daly led the PGA Tour's driving statistics, he averaged 288.9 yards. By contrast, the leader at the close of 2006, Bubba Watson, averaged 332.0. Even the most curmudgeonly nineteenth-hole bore could no longer make the claim 'Distance isn't an advantage' with eight of the top ten spots in golf's world rankings occupied by men who, in windless conditions, had no problem carrying a golf ball 295 yards or more. Golf was troubled by this. With every major championship that arrived, the debate about how the power game was humiliating the world's best courses raged that bit more fiercely. Gavin Christie wouldn't have liked to hear me say it, but I couldn't see anything wrong with the new muscularity. In my experience, golf has always been a much more macho sport than it has been given credit for, and the fact that its missiles go further than those of any other ball game is one of its obvious plus points.

Driving technology had come on so much in the last decade that even its lingo had become more hi-tech. Pros no longer talked about 'lashing' or 'nailing' their tee shots; they were 'bombing' or 'nuking' them. As of 2006, the World Long Drive Championship carried a total purse of $500,000, in contrast to the £100,000 up for grabs in the Europro Tour's most lucrative event, the Azores Tour Championship. It was not surprising that the likes of Witter, and fellow Hanbury big-hitters Paul Barrington and Ron Lampman, had started to eschew conventional eighteen-hole play for full-time monster hitting.* 'The nickname helps,' said Barrington, pointing to a badge on his arm which said 'The Striker'. 'I'm doing an event almost every week in the summer now.' He admitted, though, that at thirty-six he was 'getting on a bit' and couldn't 'get anywhere near some of the guys out there' – guys like Jason Zuback, who once hit a ball 511 yards.

What quickly became apparent, upon speaking to long-hitting experts, is that there is no one failsafe way to biff a ball over 320 yards. Barrington and Lampman both had surprisingly short swings, and to a casual connoisseur of golfing physics, Lampman's in particular seemed too shallow in its angle of attack to send the ball any great distance. Witter's, by contrast, was a thing of great fluidity and twang, which rubbished the old 'left arm straight at the top for maximum power' rule. Working on the basis that the lower the loft, the further the club hit, I was surprised to see that both Witter and Lampman had 10-degree lofts on their drivers: John Daly was well known to have 6.5 on his. But then, in their universe, John Daly was no longer the grip-it-and-rip-it benchmark.

'In 2002, the sponsors of the World Long Drive Championship offered a $100,000 prize for any player who could outdrive Daly,' explained Witter. 'Nine out of the twelve guys who tried pulled it off.'

'I think I'm probably comfortably past John,' Lampman told me. 'But most of the guys are, these days. There was a big balloon towards the 400-yard

---

* Barrington joked that one of his problems in tournament play was that 'My putts sometimes go as far as my drives'.

mark at the World Championships the other year, and a lot of the guys were hitting it. The drive was downwind, though.'

I tried to picture exactly how far 400 yards was. What immediately sprang to mind was the second hole at Cripsley Edge. I remembered the day I'd first managed to hit the green with only a nine-iron for my second shot, and how I'd boasted about my feat to Jamie and our friend Mousey. Even back then, I'd been obsessed with distance. This year, despite being twenty yards behind most of my playing partners off the tee for much of the year, the obsession had reignited. When I made a list in my golf diary of the ten shots that had given me most pleasure, eight of them were drives – and this was in a year when my driving had been ailing as much as the rest of my game. Even in my despairing state on the journey back from Bovey Castle, I'd taken an irrational amount of satisfaction in the fact that my performance had been bookended by two of the finest 300-and-something-yarders I'd ever hit.

'It's weird,' I remembered a mid-handicap playing partner saying to me, looking at a score of mine in the high seventies shortly after my long golfing lay-off. 'You seemed to play a lot better than that.'

'I suppose so,' I'd replied. 'I try not to let my score bother me. I hit a few good long drives, and that's what really hits the spot for me these days.'

What had happened to that relaxed weekend player who was happy just to 'hit a few good long drives'? How had he been gradually sucked back into golf's competitive vortex, with its illusion of life-or-death importance?

He'd been lost for a while, but now I could sense him re-emerging from his thirty-something crisis.

On the surface, I'd been very realistic when I'd decided to turn pro. I'd known I'd be an outsider, I'd known my age and lack of play would put me at a disadvantage, and I'd known it would be extremely tiring. But I'd also been quite naïve. When I'd imagined professional life, I'd imagined, at least partially, an extension of my junior golfing life: a life of calling 'How you scoring?' to friends on adjacent fairways, of analysing one another's rounds over a drink afterwards. I'd underestimated the seriousness of a profession where only the most devoted of the devoted survive. I'd also, quite preposterously, thought that I could splice 1992 to 2006, putting the excess years to one side for possible later use. In the summer of 1992, golf had been the summation of my aims in life. I may have reached my full physical height, but that aside, I was barely grown. I may have thought I was an unlikely golfer, but I was just another golf kid who had substituted a fairway life for a life.

These days, however, I had a life and a career outside of golf that I loved, and I must have been insane to have believed that the cultural and personal components of it would not affect my sporting brain. Stephen King once pointed out that 'A writer is someone who has taught his mind to misbehave.' A golfer, by contrast, was someone who worked his hardest to teach his mind not to. I liked my unruly psyche, and wasn't sure if I wanted to change it. I'd given it a go at Mollington in those first few holes of my first round, and I'd (very briefly) seen that it could bring results. It had made me think, 'Gosh

– I'm really staying focused here and playing solid golf!' but it had simultaneously made me think, 'This is sort of boring, isn't it?' For all the trouble the Evil Brain Worm gave me, I could not bring myself to be mad at it. If I had been able to, I'm sure I would have scored better. Despite what Ken Brown had told me about the evenness of temperament needed to play great golf, you needed a certain fire in the belly as well, and I had discovered I did not have it. Certainly, I called myself a crapweasel sometimes and growled a bit under my breath, but when my frustration valve opened, it did not hiss violently; what came out was no more urgent than the gust of air from a half-inflated party-balloon. And while I could have pretended that my reluctance to flip my lid in the throes of golfing misfortune was a mark of my maturity, it was probably just a mark of the fact that I could always rationalise any situation with the words, 'It's only golf, isn't it?'

In the end, those three words – 'It's only golf' – were the difference between me and every other pro I met. They were words that, before he walked off the course at the Beau Desert Stag in 1992, my teenage self would rather have snapped his five-iron than uttered. They were words that marked me out as an impostor who, when all was said and done, had realised he was happy to 'just go out and hit a few long drives'.

By September 2006, my golfing travels had put more than 20,000 miles on my car. During my journeys I would frequently tire of my iPod, and turn to audio-books for amusement. One of my favourites was a collection of the golf-loving journalist Alistair Cooke's

Letter from America broadcasts from the 1960s and seventies. There was a gentle, ghostly pull to Cooke's moist-throated mid-Atlantic delivery that transported me far away from traffic jams and roundabouts into pre-Watergate America, but not so far that I stopped watching the road altogether. An added bonus was that Cooke often talked about golf. He had some great stories about the unusual practice routines of the eight-year-old Jack Nicklaus,* and of being invited to the San Francisco Golf Club to discuss plans for the Soviet Union's first ever golf course with the Russian Consul General and Bobby Jones's son ('like being invited by a rabbi to lunch with the Pope to discuss stud poker').†

Away from the topic of golf, Cooke said something else that hit home: 'I have nothing against clichés. Most of them are true, though you have to live through the denial of them to know it.' The previous summer, I'd written off all the hoopla that friends had associated with turning thirty, then promptly succumbed. I was now reappraising another cliché: the one about 'never being able to go back'. When I'd heard that saying in the past, I'd always shut my ears, taking it for so much hot air;

---

* In order to achieve the stillness of head required to swing well, Nicklaus had his head gripped by an assistant pro during practice for an hour every day for a whole year.

† 'The great game is not only a major exercise in military strategy and tactics,' wrote Cooke, 'but also a minor rehearsal of the Ten Commandments.' I could see what he was getting at, but I hadn't spotted any oxen on the Europro Tour. And if I had, I doubt I would have had time to covet them. That said, some cud-chewing skills might have come in useful after my second shot on the eighteenth at Bovey Castle.

now it was starting to take on a new resonance. Golf still mattered. But I could never go back to a time when it mattered more than anything.

You can never go back in friendships, either, although sometimes you find that both parties have moved forward to places that, though distant from one another, have surprisingly good lines of communication. I'd enjoyed reuniting with Jamie at Hollinwell and I was looking forward to my next round with him, at Cripsley Edge. But what excited me even more was that the trip to Nottingham would also give me the opportunity to catch up with Mousey, who back in the early nineties had been the telltale heart and mischievous soul of the Cripsley Junior Section, and had probably spent even more time hanging out in the club's unofficial pro-shop common room than us.

I'd been hearing some intriguing rumours about Mousey over the past two or three years. He was always the smallest and squeakiest of the Cripsley boys, and his position as our resident tearaway had been pre-ordained by his size and by the flak the rest of us gave him for his short hitting. Traces of a new, more muscular Mousey had already been evident back in 1993, when I'd last seen him, but now, when Pete Boffinger and Jamie updated me on his fortunes, they used words like 'monster' and 'animal'. Reports of his long-hitting feats had even got as far as the Europro Tour. 'Oh, you used to be a member at Cripsley Edge?' a pro had said to me at Mollington. 'I guess you know RJ?* Man, can that guy *tonk* it.' Despite playing off scratch and having the power

* Mousey's real name is Ross Jones.

to turn all but the longest par-fives into elementary par-fours, Mousey had never even considered turning pro as an adult, yet as a kid he'd talked about the prospect every day.

'You never really know with Mousey,' said Jamie, as we waited on the first tee for our friend. 'Sometimes he can be bothered to play, sometimes he can't. Sometimes he turns up, sometimes he doesn't. But when he does, something interesting usually happens.'

We'd been joined for the round by Jamie's dad, George – never a golfer when we were kids, but now an astute single-figure handicapper who had put his engineer's brain to use on the kind of military on-course strategies Alistair Cooke had talked about on my CD. To make the reunion even sweeter, between his duties at two important Midlands junior matches, Bob Boffinger had also come to watch us tee off. A flair for timekeeping – he was still the only person I'd ever met who talked in half-minutes when giving ETAs – a strong constitution and his newly retired status meant that Bob had no problem flitting between under-eighteen events. At seventy-four, he still had Richard Widmark good looks and walked somewhere in the region of forty miles a week in the cause of his duties with the English Golf Union and the Nottinghamshire Boys' Team. He'd seen better, more dedicated golfers since Jamie, Mousey and I had passed through the junior ranks. But I got the impression that he still regarded us as a schoolteacher would regard a favourite, unruly set of pupils from his past. 'I better be off now,' he said, looking at his watch.

'I've got to be on the other side of Nottingham in twelve minutes, and it can sometimes take up to thirteen and a quarter minutes to cover it when the lights are against me. Be good!'

It was now half an hour after our supposed tee time, and there was still no sign of Mousey. We killed some time in the shop, speaking to the veteran pro, Steve Kimbolton. I'd been a bit worried about seeing Steve, since I'd once compared him to a squirrel in print. However, he wasn't visibly concerned, and obviously had more pressing matters to worry about, like a garbled message from his assistant that had cost him a free round at the sumptuous Loch Lomond course (the assistant had got the Scottish Open venue mixed up with Trent Lock, a rudimentary municipal course six miles to the west of Nottingham). Mousey wasn't answering his mobile phone, so we decided to tee off without him.

Our friend finally joined us on the sixth tee. Or rather, some enormous bloke who had eaten him joined us. It takes a special kind of ingenuity to make a rock-and-roll entrance on a golf course, but this came close. After a quick shake of my hand and an 'All right, chief?' the longest hitter of a golf ball in south Nottinghamshire flicked his cigarette onto the grass beside him, tossed a headcover over his shoulder and, without so much as half a practice swing, cannoned a tee shot somewhere roughly in the region of Ashby de la Zouch. If an amateur dramatics society had been asked to reinterpret a two-fingered punk-rock up yours through the medium of golf, they would have been hard pushed to come up with something better than this.

'Bit past Seve Wood, that one, chief,' he said. 'How you been keeping?'

Despite the fact that he was approximately twice as big as he had been when I last saw him in every part of his body apart from his hands,* there was a lot about Mousey that hadn't changed. Although his voice had deepened significantly, it still had a hint of squeak about it. He still called his clubs 'me spanners' and his two-iron 'me jack-knife' and talked about forgotten Cripsley junior concepts like 'Seve Wood' – the nickname we'd once given to the small copse 220 yards from the sixth tee, from which we would often play extraordinary escape shots – as if it had only been a week or two ago that he'd holed the winning putt in the Nottinghamshire Junior Team Matchplay Trophy. He still had the body language of the rebel, and talked about practice in the way the cool kids at school talked about homework. He had always been fascinated by power golf, and I wondered how much of his prodigious strength and size was down to sheer force of will.

As we progressed to the back nine, his swing became roomier, his drives even longer. On the twelfth, all four of us struck beautiful tee shots, and our balls finished in the middle of the fairway, directly in line with each other but spanning a full hundred yards in length. We could have been looking at a diagram intended to illustrate the many guises of the long hit. There was the long hit of the mid-handicapper who knows he can hit it a bit further than most people of his ability (George's);

---

* These were, by contrast, three times as big as they had been when I last saw him.

the long hit of the bloke who once thought he was a long-hitter until he woke up and smelt the burning rubber* of his professional betters (mine), there was the long hit of the bloke who knows he's a long-hitter and doesn't think it's anything remarkable (Jamie's); and there was the long hit of the out-and-out extra-terrestrial (Mousey's).

Since I was now thinking outside the box regarding my working life in golf, I began to plan a little career guidance talk with him. He said he was happy in his job as a builder, and he undoubtedly had the hands for it, but I wondered if he had ever considered the long-driving circuit. I could see it all now in Technicolor: the 'Mighty Mouse' logo on the baseball cap and tour van, the theme tune, the nonchalant swagger as he emerged onto the floodlit range. With his brawn and my map-reading skills, it could just work.

'Sounds like a laugh, chief,' he said noncommittally when I told him about Ben Witter, Paul Barrington and Ron Lampman, and asked him if he would consider doing the same thing.

We talked some more, telling stories of our former junior cohorts. Most unfathomable among these was Ben Wolfe, Cripsley's resident entrepreneur and 'energy waves' enthusiast, whose twin obsessions of hubcap-collecting and befriending clothing designers had led him away from the fairway into the world of fashion, and who had, for mysterious reasons, changed his first name to Ricardo by deed poll. But Mousey had his own unusual story – one that may

---

* Well, burning Urethane Elastomer, to be exact.

have gone some way to explaining his newfound insouciance.

In the mid-nineties, not long after I lost touch with him, he'd started a new job in the stockroom of a department store, and had been having a bad time, not getting on with his co-workers. One night he went out to the Black Orchid, a nightclub in a retail park just outside Nottingham, and began seeing shadows in front of his face. 'The next morning, I lost it,' he said. 'I started thinking all sorts of weird stuff, like that my dad was going to kill me and shit. I was telling strangers that I'd won the lottery.' Jamie remembered taking nonsensical calls from Mousey from the hospital, asking 'When are you picking me up? You were supposed to be here ages ago!' Mousey was put on several kinds of medication, and spent the next few months in hospital. On his birthday, he received a card signed by several of the members at Cripsley. 'I don't remember any of it now, but I punched this nurse and escaped and came up here and ordered some food from the bar. Steve Kimbolton had to phone my dad and get him to take me back to the hospital.'

This all rang only the slightest bell in my head: an encounter with my friend Robin when I'd learned, without specifics, that Mousey 'hadn't been well recently'. I felt terribly guilty, suddenly aware of how completely and impetuously I'd removed myself from golf back then. Certainly, I'd needed a break, but had I really had to lose touch with my friends so drastically that when one of them had a major life crisis it completely passed me by? I said I was sorry that I hadn't been around at the time to visit him in hospital.

'Don't worry about it, chief. I don't know why it all happened. I think I just used to let things get to me. It's a long time ago now. These days I don't let anything bother me.' The six-iron second shot that he launched onto the (once virtually unreachable) par-five fifteenth green appeared to confirm this.

Had he not thought about turning pro at all, in the years since he'd been feeling better?

'No. Too much fucking hard work, yoof.'

He was right, of course. The difference between him and me, perhaps, was that he had never kidded himself it could be any other way.

As much as I told myself I was having fun, I *had* worked hard this year. Maybe it wasn't the kind of graft I'd experienced when I'd worked in a supermarket and a restaurant aged seventeen, or on a factory floor aged nineteen, but it had taken more out of me than any of those things. I'd lost three quarters of a stone in weight, hit around 50,000 balls, stared at thousands of miles of motorway, given my body some worrying wear and tear, and brought the office home with me like never before.*
But even that wasn't the work of the real pro; it was the work of the guy who thinks he can find a shortcut, who thinks he can busk through on maverick spirit alone. I'd tried being fire, I'd tried being ice, I'd even tried being lukewarm water. None of it had worked – at least not for long. Every sensational golfing doctrine was a contradiction of another that could be equally revelatory, if you saw it in the right light, and had got bored enough

* Which was saying something, since my writing office was at home in the first place.

271

experimenting with its antithesis. In the end, being a great golfer at the highest level wasn't primarily about attitude or methodology, it was about making a long, arduous sacrifice to your green god and doing all you could to mould yourself in his image. Chevy Chase was right: you really did have to 'be the ball'.

I was sure other sports took plenty of dedication, but it was hard to believe that any could be quite as consuming and insular as golf, or could have so many people willing to call it a career while earning next to no money. 'If you go for a trial at Manchester United or Everton and Alex Ferguson says you're shit, you give up and go and do something else,' Karl Morris had said to me. 'In golf, though, there's nobody to tell you you're not good enough.* There's no cut-off point. No matter how bad it gets, there's always the belief that there's something great around the corner.'

Even now, based on the high points from Bovey Castle and Mollington, I could see a future for myself on the Europro Tour. It would involve even harder graft, more practice, more money, going to a chiropractor, getting fit,† and then, one day, in a year or so, when my biorhythms were good and there was no wind and there was no farmhouse ghost keeping me up the night before and I genuinely focused on my awareness of the shaft and didn't modify that and focus on the ball instead and I got out of my own way but didn't swing as if I was

* As of July 2006, Karl Morris remained unfamiliar with the working methods of Gavin Christie.
† That clicking in my hip told me that my dozen or so swimming sessions and two aborted attempts at yoga just weren't cutting it.

trying to get myself out of *the* way and didn't dwell on what I had to lose and I kept my hands light on the club, I might, just, if I was lucky, shoot a couple of rounds of one or two under par and make the cut in a tournament. *And I would still not even be verging on the kind of dedication that it takes to compete at the top level of the game.*

Today was so much simpler: three old friends having a laugh, occasionally taking the piss out of one another (yes, I did remember the time I tried to get in that sauna with all my clothes on; yes, Mousey did remember when he'd claimed the definition of a links course was 'woodland or fir'), driving the odd par-four (well, three of them, in Mousey's case) and exorcising the odd demon (my eagle on the sixteenth, a hole that had once seen what I was certain was the most unfortunate ricochet in the history of the Cripsley Club Championship: a collision with a sprinkler head that had sent my ball from greenside safety into the back garden of a minor committee member). Maybe this was what Ben Hogan, that most professional of professional golfers, had derisively termed 'jolly golf', but it was also golf that didn't leave you gibbering on the floor, golf that brought out the best in me. Maybe this wasn't what the three of us had hoped for when we'd lain flat on the ground behind the range at Wentworth, studying every inch of Seve Ballesteros's swing through the crowd's legs, but this was adulthood. And part of adulthood was realising that getting close to perfection did not necessarily make you the happiest person, or the best person; it just made you close to perfection.

And who said golf was a game of perfect, anyway?

In the bar afterwards, over a pint of Guinness, George reminisced about one time that his wife, Maggie, had arrived here to pick Jamie up and been reprimanded by a stuffy member who explained that she had crossed the boundary into the gentlemen-only bar ('That's funny,' responded Maggie, without missing a beat, 'because I don't see any in here!'). We contemplated the wall of past captains' photographs, stretching back to the 1920s: waste-management executives and foremen and landlords in suits and ties, peering proudly at the camera like noble border collies on the front of old-fashioned boys' birthday cards. For all the nicknames we gave them, these men had once seemed like prime ministers to us. Back then, we'd been sure that we wanted to be pros, but how could we have been trusted to know what to do with our lives, when our world was this insular?

George talked about the moment when he realised that Jamie might not have what it takes to be a top pro. 'It was at the British Amateur Championship, and he was five up on the kid he was playing, and he turned round to me and said, "I feel sorry for him." You can't afford to feel sorry for anyone in this game.'

I looked across the table at Jamie, half-expecting him to bristle at this, but he had an even, accepting smile on his face. I'd never seen him more relaxed. Knowing nobody else could do it for him, he'd been brave enough to decide on his cut-off point a couple of years ago, and was happier for it. Now he could afford to feel *genuinely* sorry for his former opponents, many of whom were still in the thick of it, juggling their credit cards and trying to get out of their own way. It was up to me to decide on my cut-off point too, and now seemed as good a time as any, at the course where I'd started playing, a course it was highly likely I would never play again, in good company, with an eagle fresh in my mind, and my insides suffused with the warm glow that only a good inconsequential round of golf, an empty stomach and a pint of Guinness can create. The dream was almost over, but I was going to allow myself just a couple of final pit stops on the journey back to my senses.

Eleven

Streets Ahead

'Right,' said Liam White, producing a fistful of £20 notes from his pocket and licking a finger, 'let's see how we did, Tom, cos I haven't got a flippin' clue.'

A little baffled about where 'we' came into this, I watched as he counted the money and looked around the clubhouse of Wollaton Park Golf Club in Nottingham, wondering what he intended to do with it. There appeared to be quite a lot of it, and with the exception of a fruit machine and a menu offering some teacakes and a small selection of hot beverages, very little potential in the nearby vicinity for disposing of it.

'Not bad,' he said, with a nod. 'I'll get this.' He gestured to the pot of coffee on the table in front of us.

By his own admission, Liam was a little hungover this morning. In the five minutes we'd been sitting in the lounge of Wollaton, three people had approached him and said the same thing: 'Hello, Liam. You look . . . *well*!' In truth, he looked a little grey-green around the gills. As he poured a second cup of coffee, and then, quickly, a third, his hand shook. He had been to the casino last night, he said, and it had 'turned into a heavy one'.

I'd last seen Liam fifteen years previously, when he'd been Nottinghamshire's best golfer. Back then I'd watched with my friend Ollie as he'd flashed and lashed his way around Coxmoor Golf Club in an important county match, one of his last games as an amateur. He'd seemed oddly outgoing for a good player, and had taken time out from his tussle with Lincolnshire's Jim Payne – another soon-to-be-pro, but an altogether more serene golfing being – to chat with us and ask us about our handicaps. Watching his quick, wristy swing and his chirpy manner with the crowds, Ollie and I had been convinced we were seeing a future star: a kind of blond Seve on permanent fast-forward, or maybe more appropriately, with the benefit of hindsight, a British council-estate Sergio Garcia.

That autumn, he'd been selected for the Great Britain and Ireland Walker Cup team to play against America at Portmarnock, and alongside Ireland's Paul McGinley had defeated Bob May and the mighty Phil Mickelson in the foursomes. Chubby Chandler from International Sports Management had been waiting on the final green, contract in hand, and Liam had immediately turned pro, going on to win the 1994 Dutch Open with an astonishing final round of 63. Rumours followed about his sleeping on the beach the night after the tournament and spending a vast chunk of his prize money on a handbag for his girlfriend. But then . . . nothing. His name vanished from the money list. When I asked, 'What happened to Liam White?' most of my Nottingham friends just shrugged. There was talk of a very public disagreement with a veteran European Tour player, and a subsequent social blackballing. When I'd brought Liam's name up with fellow pros this year, I'd drawn a blank. After much research and a lot of help from Bob Boffinger, I'd finally tracked him down to the Chesterfield branch of JJB Sports, where he was the manager of the Bike, Golf and Fitness department.

'Is this a wind-up?' he asked, when I told him I wanted to talk to him.

He'd suggested we meet at Wollaton, a gently captivating parkland course three miles from the city centre, where I'd once narrowly missed decapitating a deer with a skulled seven-iron, and where Liam had been playing the majority of his golf since his mid-teens (Liam had been a late starter, as well as an early finisher). That had surprised me slightly. One of the Liam rumours I'd heard involved him being banned from Wollaton's clubhouse for putting his cigar out in a committee member's drink. 'Oh yeah,' he said, 'I've been barred twice. Once was for fighting at the men's Christmas dinner. I can't remember what the other was for. The worst thing about it was that I weren't allowed to come in and see me cabinet. That hurt. One day I played with three committee members and I couldn't even come in and look at my stuff.'

Liam's cabinet, which he also referred to as 'The Shrine', still stood intact in Wollaton's foyer. Packed with clubs, trophies, newspaper and magazine articles and other memorabilia from Liam's glory years, it must have served as a constant reminder of how much he had lost. It was also evidence that Liam had once been on a fast track to the big time: not just another former scratch player scraping a living, but a player so promising that *GQ* magazine had awarded him with a five-page profile ('They must have taken 2,000 photographs of me, but they only used three').

Liam had been late for our meeting, and while I waited for him my brain had gone into overdrive hypothesising about what he might look like. My image of him was a little fuzzy, and it always gives you cause for fertile thought when someone says, 'I'll meet you outside the pro shop – I'll be the one with the Mohican.' By the time I saw a bright yellow souped-up Fiat Punto hurtle into the car park, I'd got a bit carried away and was starting to picture an ageing version of the synth-pop star Howard Jones in an Argyle sweater.

The Punto scouted around for a space then, seeing none free, pulled flamboyantly into a no-parking area in front of the clubhouse delineated with orange stripes.* The figure that emerged from the driver's seat was instantly familiar, but that owed more to his John Wayne walk than his frightened-cat's spike of hair. He did not look a bit like Howard Jones.

In their 1992 profile, *GQ* had said that Liam looked more like a rugby player than a golfer. Now he looked more like an ex-rugby player with a job in retail management. He had an old-fashioned way with slang and a smoky, cardigany scent that reminded me of a bygone working-class Nottingham: the Nottingham of my granddad, the Nottingham of Alan Sillitoe's *Saturday Night and Sunday Morning*. His upside down traffic cone of a body seemed kind of old-fashioned too. It was too

---

* 'I've just got me licence back,' Liam explained later.

short and stout to be a modern golfer's physique. Going down from his huge, jutting shoulders, everything tapered. His forearms were enormous, but his wrists were, as he pointed out, 'tiny'.

'That was what finished me, really,' he explained. 'I got tendonitis in my wrist. I kept going to tournaments, and I'd just end up in agony, hitting these 150-yard shots to the right off the tee. Even when I play now, it throbs for a couple of days afterwards.' At the end of 1994 he applied for a medical exemption from the European Tour, but his application arrived too late. For a few months, he'd continued to receive invites and to practise hard. 'Then,' he said, ' all of a sudden a year had passed and I'd only played a bit of golf, and I didn't miss it. Easy as that.'

Liam's last round of golf before speaking to me, which had taken place the previous Friday, had been only his ninth in two years. 'It's still so easy. Even now, people say to me, How can you just pitch up and shoot the scores that you do? The thing is, I've never thought about the game. I'm lucky, you see. It's easy to me. There are very few people who are pros – Lee included – who can't play without having some kind of thought.'

It was his first mention of Lee – and I guessed he meant Westwood. Did he ever watch his Nottinghamshire peer and find himself thinking, 'That could have been me!'?

'Loads of people ask that,' he said. 'I tell you what, I've lost more money on that silly prat than anything, and that's the only time I get pissed off with him. I just love seeing him do well. People don't realise – outsiders, especially – that there's no bitchiness or jealousy, because when you're at a certain level, you know your day's gonna come. You're always pleased for other people, and when your day does come, they're always pleased for you.'

Had Westwood usurped White's place at the top of the pecking order in east Midlands golf? It seemed that way. But the truth was that, aside from the fact that they had both been paid for hitting a ball, shared the same management team, initials and home county, the pair had very little in common. Their swings alone were as different as fire and ice. Where Lee appeared to talk to people through the layers of a protective shell, Liam had no such psychic protection, and it was hard to imagine he ever had done. Wollaton's clubhouse was scantly populated this morning, but every person who entered it made a beeline for Liam, and he had time for all of them. There was nothing guarded about him as he talked of his friends, all of whom seemed to have nicknames like 'Village' or 'Trigger'* and were either gravely ill or a 'brilliant laugh' or permanently drunk or mucking up their life by going out with an 'ugly bird'.

He had plenty of brilliant memories from his life as a contender. There was the time in the Walker Cup that he watched Phil Mickelson split a wooden tee-peg down the middle with his fingers ('I don't know if you've ever tried that, but it's really hard'), then, standing several yards from his bag, flip his driver dispassionately in the air by its butt and land it in the precise compartment where it belonged ('I was shaking like a leaf!'). And the time when Ian Woosnam was playing in front of him in the Irish Open and picked up one of the fake Guinness

---

* 'Mine's "Voltage",' said Liam. 'Because of my hair.'

glass tee-markers and pretended to drink out of it ('I was thinking, "I wish I was that cool"!'). Liam obviously enjoyed recounting these incidents, and while he did not do so without the odd hint of longing and regret, I got the impression that he was still somewhat overawed that he'd ever got the chance to compete on the European Tour in the first place. If I had not had to leave for lunch at my nan's house, I sensed he might have happily continued for several more hours. I couldn't help but wonder aloud if he had been too gregarious for the life of the touring pro.

'Well, yeah, I am, aren't I? I always have been. You know that, Tom. When I first went out there I was a bit cocksure, but you need that cockiness, and when I had it, that was when I seemed to do well. Pros are quite shy people, loners really. I did get lonely out there, and that was a big part of the problem. I'd get up at four on a Tuesday, drive down to Heathrow and fly out wherever. Then I'd get home at anywhere between eleven and one in the morning, Sunday night, get up Monday, and come down here, and then obviously every man and his dog would be asking, over and over again, "What happened on sixteen?" or whatever.* But I'd go out and

---

* Fielding these questions is an occupational hazard for every former Golden Boy going through hard times. A few days before I met up with Liam, I'd spoken to Michael Welch, the former England Boys' Champion (the one who'd laughed at my hat at Mollington). After several years struggling on the Europro Tour and the Challenge Tour, he had decided to quit tournament golf. 'Sometimes it felt like every time I came back to the clubhouse after a tournament there would be someone asking me what had gone wrong with my game,' he said. 'If I knew the answer, I would have fixed it.'

have a game with the lads, and that was like my release. Sometimes a lot of the players would stay out in Spain for three weeks on the bounce and stuff, but I could never do it. Coming home was harder, but just being here for that one day made me feel so much better. Even though I could have saved myself a lot of money, bearing in mind it was costing me twelve hundred quid a week to play.'

Liam called Monday 'wash day', and I wasn't quite sure if this was a reference to Monday being the day when you cleansed yourself of the psychological dirt of the previous week's tournament, or simply another old-fashioned Nottinghamism (my paternal grandparents had called Monday 'wash day' too). Whatever, he did not strike me as the kind of person who would just wash and go. Obviously it must have been irritating to repeatedly field questions from his fellow members at Wollaton regarding exactly why he wasn't following his Dutch Open victory up with more rounds of 63, but if he *had* shot 63, or even 68, he probably would have gleefully talked you through every nuance of it – in much the same way I'd been warned against by James and numerous others.

Had Liam ever had that essential cold-minded, determined belief in his right to be on Tour? Perhaps not. Perhaps, in the days when professional tournament golf been less crowded – both inside and outside the ropes – and lucrative, it had not been quite such a vital part of the golfer's psychological make-up. He had been cocky for a while, as he said, but I wondered if that cockiness had manifested itself in a different way to the way it has in Westwood:

a less controlled, noisier, more vulnerable, lovable way.

'You can't turn it on and off.' If I had received a pound for every time I had dwelled on that comment this year, I'd probably have at least one less bank loan than I did. But why *couldn't* you turn it on and off? Why couldn't you stand over the ball and be frosty and calculating and convinced of your own brilliance, then walk away and be a self-deprecating, jocular, lovable human? It was because when the pressure was on, you could not let it become apparent to you that there were an infinite number of bad permutations, and only one good one, to the shot you were about to play. And to do that, you had to be solid and leave no room for cracks. Such solidity didn't just mean standing over the ball and being unswerving about your goal. It also meant not going into the clubhouse and making jokes about your Panicked Squid swing, or how you couldn't close the deal on a downhill six-footer even if the hole was twice the size and had an 'Enter! Good will to all comers!' sign above it. You could not afford to give a millimetre's thought to the dark places.

I'd seen a good example of that solidity at Bovey Castle. It had occurred in the second round, on the sixteenth, a hole that, after my televised chip fiasco of the previous day, I'd already begun to think of as my *bête noire*. With Adam Hawkins, Paul Coburn and me all destined to miss the cut, a perfunctory, desultory fug had settled over us, and we couldn't have displayed more eagerness to get home if we'd been tossing our car keys nervously from hand to hand. And things didn't get any better when it became obvious that James* Ruebotham, a player in the group ahead of us, had lost a ball, preventing us from teeing off.

Having waited several minutes – me assuming that the group in front would call us through – we watched as Ruebotham, the travelling companion of Coburn and a winner on the Tour two weeks ago at Mollington, trudged back towards us to play the dreaded 'three off the tee'. Then we watched – me still assuming that Ruebotham would call us through, or allow us to play our shots up with him, or at least acknowledge Coburn with a smile or a 'How you doing?' – as Ruebotham silently teed up, then strolled, in no particular rush, back up the fairway. I felt almost certain at this point that Coburn or Hawkins would comment on Ruebotham's rudeness (or obliviousness, as it may have been), but both remained silent, apart from a brief appraisal of his tee shot ('When he shanks it, he shanks it straight').[†]

Ruebotham's attitude to our threeball brought to mind a scene from *The Bogeyman*, George Plimpton's book about competing in 1960s PGA pro-ams, where

* Memo to British PGA HQ: Something must be done about this James business. Would it not be more logical simply to change the name of British professional golf's governing body to the JGA? Obviously the ensuing dialogue might sound a little odd – 'I've been really practising hard since I turned James'; 'There are a lot of misconceptions out there about the life of a James' – but I'm sure everyone would soon get used to it, and it would help separate us from our American counterparts.

† It was in situations like this that one realised that pro tournament golf and amateur golf are games not just of vastly different standards, but of vastly different styles of etiquette, too.

Plimpton, playing in the group ahead of Arnold Palmer's, is caught in the rough within range of Palmer's tee shot. Plimpton describes Palmer as looking 'like a man sitting at his desk who has just noticed something moving in his wastepaper basket'.

After my round, I thought a lot about the ironclad lengths one would have had to go to – on and off the course – to get into Ruebotham's state of mind, and I speculated about what I would have done in his situation. I find that, on the whole, when I lose a ball on the golf course, I tend to have an instinct to sink into a deep depression or drink myself into a mild coma, but this is always overridden by a stronger instinct to sweep myself up out of the way of better-faring players. Seeing Ruebotham deal with his crisis was not just like watching a different attitude in action, it was like watching a whole different species. And this is a player in the dress-rehearsal environment of the Europro Tour we're talking about – a man whose 2006 winnings, at the time, stood at just over £12,000. If he needed to be so tight-lipped and robotic, what did it take to be a US Open winner?

I'd already made some decisions pertaining to my unsuitability for the pro life by the time of the Ruebotham incident, but it served to firmly underline them. By the time I'd come away from my encounter with Liam White, I'd moved still further away from my ideals about playing high-level competitive golf. Liam's story – and his talent – further confirmed that I'd done the right thing by qutting when I had. Undoubtedly, I was sad that I'd failed so comprehensively to make an impact on the Europro Tour and The Open, but I was glad that I had found out what I'd been missing for all these years.

I was also starting to see another future for myself as a golfer. It needn't have to be as intense as a typical playing-pro existence, but neither did it have to be an admission of defeat.

When I'd asked Liam White what was the most valuable thing he'd learned about being a pro, he passed on some advice that the former Portuguese Open champion Peter Mitchell had given him. 'Whatever you do at home, Liam, replicate it here,' Mitchell said. 'Some people come out here and say, "I've got to drink orange juice," "I've got to eat salads," "I've got to go to bed early," and that's fine, but only if that's what you did before. You shouldn't change your routine. If you go out and have a few pints and a greasy kebab when you're at home, do it here as well.'

The advice might have been dated – in this new, more athletic age, it was doubtful that anyone on the Europro Tour had two pints the night before a tournament, never mind 'a few' – but I could hear some wisdom at the core of it, and I could apply it to myself, too. In turning pro, I'd not had the confidence to move forward with the game I already had. Instead, I had spent a year reaching for something extra. I'd been convinced that I needed to hit more balls, alter my swing, find a magic thought. The irony was that if I'd stuck to the game that had given me my pro delusions in the first place – haphazard as that game was – I would have scored better. Maybe not well enough to win any money, or make a cut, but better.

Now I knew all this, I was keen to begin the rest of my golfing life. I wanted to reacquaint myself with the player who'd had that hole-in-one all those months ago, the player who did things his own ramshackle way, the player who stepped onto the tee with his puffy swing and couldn't predict whether his tee shot was going to go 240 yards or 340 yards. He would be wiser and happier within himself now, I felt, and – who could tell? – perhaps all that sporting excellence and the wisdom of Gavin Christie and Karl Morris had been absorbed, somewhere in his unsporty mind.

In the weeks following my trip to Nottingham, I began what I thought of as a belated Phase Two to my pro career. I made a tentative foray into teaching, preaching my own rudimentary version of 'the Christie Flail' to my golf virgin brothers-in-law, Jack and Sam, with surprisingly powerful results. I made a guest appearance at the British Pitch-and-Putt Championship, playing alongside a lady in her sixties called Doreen with a golf bag made of guttering, and against numerous rowdy men from Dagenham in tracksuit bottoms, all of whom were determined to beat the pro who had made the mistake of thinking he could waltz, willy-nilly, into their breakaway faction from the 'long golf' world.* Simon, Scott and I staged the inaugural Pneumonia Invitational over a windy, rainy couple of days at the delightful Thorpeness and Aldeburgh courses on the Suffolk coast, losing an unprecedented total of twenty-seven balls between us. I felt like a car that had thought it was for the scrap heap, only to realise it just needed its oil changing. On the other hand, my back still ached, and – despite what I told myself about my terminal wetness as a competitive

* Several of them did, comprehensively.

being – I was surprised to find myself niggled by my lack of results for the 2006 season. Surely I could find more to show for all my effort than that thirteenth-from-last-place finish at Bovey Castle?

With winter fast approaching, I had one last chance to shine.

It is doubtful that anyone who has ever had a casual kick-around in a cul-de-sac has believed that, by doing so, they are spearheading a revolutionary sporting movement. Similarly, when, on a quiet day in 1986, in our home street in suburban Nottingham, my friend Ben and I began to re-enact the previous year's Ashes using a lamppost for a wicket, we did not think for a moment that we were doing anything that would surprise or offend Richie Benaud or David Gower. But it is a testament to golf's uniquely non-urban, and non-urbane, nature – or possibly to its unique capacity to offend and be offended – that when an architect called Jeremy Feakes started whacking a few golf balls through the streets surrounding his east London office in the early noughties, people sat up and took notice. In the two years since he'd founded it, Feakes's Shoreditch Urban Open had acquired a subversive reputation that had done much to confuse the golfing establishment.

The argument regarding how far back you could trace the roots of urban golf – or street golf, or cross golf, as it was also called – was a fuzzy one. Feakes, along with an enormous dreadlocked friend of his known only as 'Chewie', had been playing it illegally in the two or three square miles surrounding Old Street tube station since the turn of the decade, but the game's historians claimed that it went back as far as 1992, when a German office worker called Torsten Schilling got a little overzealous during a golfing house party. I could even see a rudimentary form of street golf in some of the more experimental late-eighties rounds Jamie, Mousey and I had played, when we'd agreed to temporarily waive the out-of-bounds rule regarding the greenkeeper's sheds and clubhouse car park.

Like its indoor namesake, urban golf was proof that golf had come to the city. But unlike James Day's soothing, simulator-filled havens, this was an altogether more anarchic kind of metropolitan hacking. Taking part felt as much like involving oneself in an elaborate bit of street theatre as helping forge the ground rules for a new mini-sport. Like the conventional game, traditional clubs were used, and a par system remained in place, but the unruliness of the crowd, the unpredictability of the balls – which were stuffed with feathers, covered with leather, and had seams that could lead to some unpredictable bounces – and the severity of the course meant it represented an entirely foreign test of skill for the more pastorally inclined competitor.

Astroturf greens were laid down in the middle of the road, and players were permitted to carry a mat on which they could place their ball in order to keep from scuffing their clubs on the tarmac, but buildings, kerbs and lamp posts all counted as integral parts of the course. Where players were used to avoiding bunkers, now they had to avoid Audi TTs and Chelsea tractors. When they finally stroked their glorified hacky-sack into the hole – and by hole I mean 'an opened up fire hydrant in the middle of the street' – they could breathe a sigh of relief that they hadn't been run over by a motorcycle courier, lost their ball in an underground car park or been berated by a local wino or Shoreditch poser. However, even then there was always the chance, were the fire hydrant a particularly deep one, that their ball might vanish in the hole itself, making its way down to the mysterious subterranean London of rats, disused tube stations and that bloke in the horror film who keeps foetuses in jars. It was advised, at times like that, not to reach your arm down too far into the abyss, for fear of what might bite into it. Far better to move on to the next tee and ask a nearby marshal for a replacement.*

So far, the pro fraternity was yet to make its mark on the Shoreditch Urban Open. In the inaugural 2004 event, a rather bewildered-looking Ronan Rafferty – winner of the 1989 European Tour order of merit – had teed it up near Old Street only to finish in a disappointing fourth place, behind a total unknown called Tuna. Choosing your own golfing nickname was an important part of Urban Open culture, and it was my hope that the Panicked Squid (career highlight: 2003 Thetford Golf Club Scratch Cup; current world ranking: unspecified) could improve on Rafferty's performance, not to mention his own showing as an amateur two years previously when, lying in third place, at eight over par after nine holes, he'd been forced to abandon his round in order to file a news report about the event for the *Daily Telegraph*.

As I signed in at the clubhouse (i.e. a local pub called

---

* These were, after all, free, which, when you'd spent the last nine months shelling out £4 a piece on Titleist Pro-Vs, could be counted as an unusual luxury – even if they did bounce with all the consistency of a bruised pomegranate.

the Tarbernacle) and began my practice routine (i.e. blasting a ball at the wall of a nearby solicitor's office), I scouted the area for my peers from the Tour. James Conteh, perhaps, who'd kicked the tee marker over at Mollington? Michael Freake, the smooth swinger who'd commiserated so generously with me at Stoke-by-Nayland? I recognised nobody. To my left, a man in plus fours and a cloth cap furiously tried to flatten down a bit of the kerb outside the Tabernacle (on closer inspection, I realised he was just having a practice swing). It was one of the contradictions of the SUO that, although it had been set up as an alternative to the diamond-patterned exclusivity of most golf clubs, most of its participants delighted in playing up to the game's most ceremonial sartorial image. The majority of the people around me had the clothes of golfers, but that was as far as their play-acting went. Some swigged from tumblers of whisky, others chatted amiably with one another or shouted 'You da man!' as their friends ricocheted warm-up shots off BMWs, others gyrated to the sound of the PA system installed outside the Tabernacle. And what were these fair, lush-haired creatures I saw amongst them? It seemed, if my eyes did not deceive me quite as much as they had when trying to line up my three-wood shot on the eighteenth at Bovey Castle, that they were . . . *women*. And while some of these women were employed by a firm called Eye Candy Caddies (slogan: 'Golf Made Gorgeous')* which had some kind of corporate deal with the event's sponsors, it was

---

* Sample promotional soundbite: 'With an Eye Candy Caddy by your side, other golfers will be green with envy.'

clear that others were here of their own volition. Not as wives or girlfriends, but as spectators and – surely it couldn't be true – *competitors*. Perhaps more bizarrely still, not one of them was Michelle Wie.

I had walked back into 2006.

Just as I was reeling from this realisation, I felt a tap on my shoulder. I spun round, and stood face to face with Paul Creasey, the former pro who had caddied for my explosive playing partner at Hollinwell, John Ronson.

'I had a feeling I'd see you here,' he said. He was wearing a T-shirt upon which was emblazoned the logo for 'Autogenic Golf'. I asked him what it was.

'Oh, that's my website,' he said. 'It's sort of for people who think of golf more as an art form, and it's based around urban golf. Me and my mates have been playing it at night in Spalding, where we live. For me, it puts the creativity back into golf. We have to be careful, though, cos we've been given a couple of warnings by the police. Of course, we play with real balls, not these softer leather ones.'

Back at Hollinwell, Paul had murmured something about being interested in 'this urban golf craze', and about his disillusionment with life as a tournament pro, but I hadn't realised how serious he was. After playing on the Europro Tour and getting quickly disillusioned – 'Everyone looks at each other in a way that says, "I'm better than you are"' – he'd abandoned his playing ambitions, and started working in a whole new area. 'Shotmaking is fun. Acting like a Tour player isn't fun. This right here is so much more creative,' he said, gesturing towards a bloke in a fedora chipping over a Nissan Micra. 'As a teaching platform, it's untapped ground.'

I had reckoned on being the only pro at Shoreditch, but now it was plain that I would have some serious competition from Paul – or 'Lucky Hands', as he would be known for today's purposes. The intimidation factor went up dramatically when I realised he had brought along not only his own caddy, but his own cameraman, in the form of two of his junior pupils from Spalding Golf Club. Once again, I had found myself without a bagman in an important tournament. A string of pleading last-minute text messages to friends had yielded only one offer, from my folk songwriter friend Chris Sheehan. But Chris, who like most musicians saw it as against his religion to get up before eleven o'clock on a Sunday, said he would only be able to join me for the back nine.

I had brought just a small portion of my golfing weaponry to Shoreditch – partly because of my aching back, partly because Shoreditch Urban balls tended to nullify the intricacies of lofts and shafts, and partly because the previous day The Bear had unleashed another virulent jet of steaming urine onto my new Taylor Made golf bag. But that wasn't the point. A pro needed a caddy. Inspired by the guttering bag of Doreen from the British Pitch and Putt Association, Edie and I had fashioned a temporary carrying apparatus out of a large cardboard tube, sealing one end shut and taping to its outside the strap from an ageing holdall. I couldn't have looked a very appealing prospect as I wandered awkwardly around outside the Tabernacle with my *Blue Peter*-style DIY Tour bag banging against my back, but, with less than a minute to go before I was due to tee off, I managed to find a man called Thom who, despite having 'only come for the free whisky' and knowing 'sod all about golf', seemed happy to step into the breach. I soon learned that his day job was as a postman, which probably explains the instant ease with which he handled the packaging.

While not delivering letters, Thom played in an alternative folk band called the Outdoor Types (I was sure Chris would not, in principle, be heartbroken that I had found another man for the job, but that this man was another folk musician seemed like a slight betrayal). He had a fluffy, droopy moustache which was reminiscent of that sported by David Crosby from the Byrds and Crosby, Stills, Nash and Young, but I liked to think of it as having more in common with the model showcased by 'Fluff' Cowan, Tiger Woods's old caddy. 'Who?' said Thom when I told him this. My question about wind strength and pin position on the second hole drew a similarly blank response. He would obviously need a briefing on golf history, strategy and etiquette, but I sensed he was a quick learner, and by the time my ball had got itself stymied between an empty beer bottle and a lamp post on the third hole,* I was pleased to see that he was adopting the recognisable obsequious posture and wise, wizened tone of the true golfing underclass.

'It's definitely a tough shot to read,' he said, crouching behind the ball and surveying the tarmac ahead. 'Knock it over to the left, and let the slope bring

---

* The urban balls might not have travelled very long distances, but it seemed that when you shanked them, they still went a long way off-target.

it round. Either that, or smack it at that BMW and see what happens.'

There were good reasons not to use a normal golf ball in urban golf – not just the insurance issues, but the fact that, as Jeremy Feakes pointed out, 'proper golf balls roll forever on tarmac' – but that didn't mean I didn't miss using one. As I lashed into my tee shots ever more fiercely, Thom, my playing partners the Baron, Malcolm and Andy yelped and cheered in an impressed manner, but there is only so far a hacky-sack can travel, even if it's being hit with a swing that incorporates a Happy Gilmore-style run-up. There were other frustrations, too. A few of the rules seemed a little vague. On numerous holes, not everyone appeared to be quite sure which fairway was which, especially since some of them cut back on themselves at 180 degrees. And if you hit the lid of the open fire hydrant that served as the hole, did it still count as having gone 'in'? When my six-iron shot on the seventh fairway flew full-toss into a passing website designer, damaging his carefully coiffed ironic hairstyle and ending up in the gutter, should I have been able to replay the shot? Nobody could quite decide. 'Not knowing the rules is sort of the point,' Feakes had told me before my round. 'Otherwise it just gets too anal, and the fun goes out of it.'

To be fair, street golf was in its infancy, and could be permitted a few teething troubles. When Dutchmen began to fashion curved sticks and first play the ancient game of goff in the fourteenth century, it must have taken much drawn-out negotiation for them to decide on their definitive set of rules as well. I suppose the main difference was that those Dutchmen didn't have to decide where exactly was the correct place to take a free drop from beneath the wheels of a Renault Espace.

There were plans for other Urban Opens in the future, as far afield as Johannesburg and New York. Feakes talked of a special new ball being designed for next year's event that would go considerably further. The Shoreditch Open was now a regimented event, attended by several dozen marshals and police, with its terrain closed off to (all but the most vital) traffic for its duration. It was clear, though, that not everyone in the area had been put in the picture. On the eleventh, a motorcycle courier blatantly rode across the line of one of Andy's putts. A couple of holes later, a nasty scene almost arose when an Audi-driving local opened his door and got hit on the knee by my six-iron shot (he thought twice about protesting after the Baron – real name Paul – shot him a 'Yeah, and what of it?' look). Scott, who'd played in the event in 2004, recalled a heated argument developing after one of his playing partners shanked his ball onto a nearby pub table, knocking over three full pints of lager. And I got a bit nervous when a passing wino muttered something about 'golf twats' to Malcolm's bagman – a high-spirited hip-hop-loving American who called himself the Mack Daddy Caddy and claimed to be writing four books about his club-carrying experiences on the PGA Tour.

Even in the most raucous, drunken moments of my youth, I had never played golf in such chaotic circumstances. If I wasn't trying to maintain my concentration as the Mack Daddy Caddy shouted 'The Squid!' at me, I was climbing over a wall to retrieve my ball from a car park, or turning around to get a club off Thom, only to find he had disappeared into a nearby pub. All year, I'd played the most distracted golf of my life. But now, in what were truly distracting circumstances, I found that the external chaos drowned out its more insidious internal equivalent. With only the extremely severe par system and the travails of my playing partners to go on, it was hard to work out what constituted playing well, but by the final few holes my scoring had improved dramatically. Realising that I could get the best results on the green by forsaking my putter for my six-iron, I racked up four birdies on the homeward nine. To add to the excitement, a group of eighty or so spectators had built up around my fourball, beating my previous biggest gallery (at Hollinwell) by at least sixty heads. After a birdie chip-in from the kerbside, I acknowledged the cheers, thanked Thom and, as five or six complete strangers patted me on the back, threw my ball triumphantly into a nearby car park.

I walked over to the large blackboard leaderboard next to the Tabernacle and searched for my name. 'Panicked Squid,' it said. '14.'

Fourteen what? I wondered.

A conversation with two men with walkie-talkies standing next to the leaderboard elicited the information that fourteen, in this case, meant 'over par'. It didn't sound good, by normal golfing standards, but par here was what Peter Alliss would call 'a tough mistress' – particularly on the hole where you had to carry a twelve-storey apartment block in order to reach the green in two. A further scan of the board told me that most other players who had finished had not fared any better than me.* Of those still out on the course, only two players seemed to be anywhere near my score: Lucky Hands, at plus twelve, and Mike Denardo, at plus fourteen.

'So you're in second place,' said Thom, appearing beside me. 'Fucking hell! We're going to win!' I was touched that he was so excited, and also that, in the six hours we had been together, his caddyspeak had come on so far that he now used the word 'we' when referring to his player's good fortunes – I like to think that, in true caddy fashion, this would have reverted to 'he' during my next bad round. It seemed the least I could do was to buy him a whisky and a baguette for his pains.

'I wouldn't worry about the whisky. I've got these,' he said, producing eight or nine balls from his pockets. 'They're special ones with stickers on. I picked them up earlier. You hand them in and you get a free drink.' He gave me three, which I thought was very magnanimous for a man who'd been forced to spend the last several hours sporting a bag with the phrase 'PANICKED SQUID' on it. I gave him two back.

As I supped on what would regrettably be my second and last drink of the day, I began to rue bringing the car with me. I was so used to fleeing golf tournaments in disgust at my bad play, it hadn't occurred to me that I might want to bask in the aftermath of this one. Twenty minutes later, Paul 'Lucky Hands' Creasey arrived in the doorway. He looked annoyingly cheerful.

---

* Who exactly was 'Cheeky Pete', and how precisely had he got to 114 over par?

299

'That is probably the most free I've felt playing golf,' he said.

I told him that I knew what he meant, but my eyes asked him a question all of their own.

'Oh, don't worry,' he said. 'You beat me. I finished twenty over.'

Ten minutes later, the news came in: the final result was a tie between Denardo and me at fourteen over par. I asked a few people for information about my new sporting nemesis, but mainly elicited shrugs. All I could glean was that he was Canadian, that he had played golf before, and that he looked not unlike the TV mind-control expert Derren Brown. None of this information filled me with hope for a sudden-death play-off. That is, if there was going to be a sudden-death play-off.

'No, we don't usually bother,' said Feakes, when I quizzed him on the outcome. 'We'll probably toss a coin or something. You can share the trophy. Or you could, if the trophy was here – we're still having it designed, actually. Anyway, we've got to hurry, cos it's getting dark and we have to get rid of the winner's podium before they open the streets up again.'

As we waited nervously in the Tabernacle, Thom and I watched footage of the final stages of the Ryder Cup on the TV behind the bar. The closing ceremony – which included a tearful, gluey-haired Darren Clarke, a lady compère with a flesh-coloured mike, and the appearance of two little girls who looked like the dead twins from *The Shining* – would probably have been bizarre with the sound on. With the sound off, it seemed even more so. What was odder still was that normally I watched every minute of the event religiously, but this week I'd completely forgotten about it. The only time it crossed my mind was when I received a text message from Simon, who was over in Ireland at the K Club, watching the action live, to say that his dad had been hit on the leg by an errant Sergio Garcia drive. I had to admit that my chances of ever getting that head-to-head battle with Sergio were looking slim now. He was four hundred miles away, his usual mercurial, frustrating self (the deflection from Simon's dad's leg had sent the ball back out into the fairway, enabling him to make a birdie), helping his European teammates to another victory over the Americans. And where was I? Sitting with a drunk postman, after my one good round of the year, at a novelty golf event played with balls that went no further than I could kick an apple. I was no closer to Garcia than I had been at the beginning of the year, but I could honestly say that, at that moment, there was nowhere in the golfing universe I would rather have been.

It seemed to me that the Garcias, the John Dalys, the Seve Ballesteroses were the freak cases. They were the men – and this, perhaps, was where their real conjuring talent lay – who could make the robotic discipline required to play pro golf appear charismatic and explosive. On the whole, though, the people in pro golf who seemed to get the most out of it were the people who beat their own path, just off to the side of the well-trodden one: the Paul Creaseys, the Jeremy Dales, the Ben Witters, the James Days, the Gavin Christies.

But who was to say what golfing happiness was, anyway? Golf is a lonely game, and a player has to find his own fulfilment. For me, that fulfilment was not going to come from conventional tournament play. I might reapply for my amateur status, or I might not, and decide to give The Open qualifying one more shot for the hell of it. I might decide to play a bit of golf over the winter, or I might spend it writing instead. I might develop my trick shots, or work on my long driving, or I might just carry on playing in make-believe tournaments against Simon and Scott. My joint victory in the Shoreditch Urban Open might lead to a whole new subsidiary career, or it might not. The point was, I had options, and now felt relaxed enough to explore them without a big question mark chopping away at my brain like a sickle. Not far from where, only a couple of months previously, I'd seen a big door closing on my golfing life, other little ones were opening. And – this was the most surprising thing of all – *it was OK.*

It was more than OK. It was exhilarating.

Thom and I had moved towards the podium now. As Jason Bradbury, the event's compère, thanked everyone for their participation, an old golfing worry kicked in like a reflex: the worry of 'What am I going to say in my speech?', the worry of 'What am I doing here anyway?' It did not take long to squish it. By the time Bradbury had handed out some auxiliary awards for Most Unusual Shot and Biggest Ladies' Man (winner: the Mack Daddy Caddy) and announced the scores, I felt calm, in my element. Asked to call, I chose heads. 'Heads it is!' shouted Bradbury. Balls pelted the stage, and Bradbury helped me into the winner's jacket. It was hard to see it in the dark, but I don't imagine that the one that you get for winning the US Masters is anything like as comfortable.

Camera bulbs flashed from all angles. Balls pelted the

stage. A lady from Sky Sports News asked me if I'd like to say a few words about my day. How many times had I let the prospect of moments like this – moments, let's be honest, like this but far more pedestrian and dull – loom heavy and crush a good round of golf? Now, however, I surprised myself. Confidently, I took the microphone and thanked my playing partners for their good cheer, Thom for his patience and his instinctive understanding of my game, Edie for her help in the construction of my golf bag, and the weather for holding off and not turning it into papier mâché. I had half handed the mike back when one last crucial point occurred to me. I wondered, in the end, how I could have been so stupid as to have almost forgotten it.

'I'd like to thank the greenstaff,' I said. 'for the condition of the course.'

Acknowledgements

A special thanks goes out to my excellent editor Tristan Jones, and to Edie Mullen, James Day, Simon Farnaby and Scott Murray, all of whom helped keep me going when the going got tough. I'd also like to thank the following for their help on the journey: Karl Morris, Daniel Bursztyn, Simon Trewin, Ariella Feiner, Gavin Christie, Steve Gould, Dave Musgrove, Paul Creasey, John Ronson, Emma Hope, Jeremy Dale, Ben Witter, Ron Lampman, Paul Barrington, Charandeep Thethy, Steve Lewton, Mike Lewton, Peter Gorse, Peter Crone, Chris Wellstead, Dave Wilkinson, Pete Benson, Alan Benson, David Elliott, Ken Brown, Doreen Powell, Lee Westwood, Liam White, Andrew Seibert, David Brooks, Keith Perry, Thom Gordon, Jeremy Feakes (RIP), Eddie Hearn, Dave Allen, Mark Harrowell, all the players on the Europro Tour, and all the gang at Urban Golf.